ISBN: 9781407680170

Published by:
HardPress Publishing
8345 NW 66TH ST #2561
MIAMI FL 33166-2626

Email: info@hardpress.net
Web: http://www.hardpress.net

THE DOCTRINE OF THE ATONEMENT

VOL. I.

Nihil obstat

F. G. HOLWECK
Censor theol.

Sᴛ. Lᴏᴜɪs, *17th November* 1908

Imprimatur

O. J. S. HOOG, V.G.

Sᴛ. Lᴏᴜɪs, *17th November* 1908

THE DOCTRINE OF
THE ATONEMENT

A HISTORICAL ESSAY

BY

J. RIVIÈRE, D.D.

PROFESSOR AT THE THEOLOGICAL SEMINARY OF ALBI

AUTHORISED TRANSLATION

BY

LUIGI CAPPADELTA

VOLUME I

"Non æqualiter mente percipitur etiam quod in fide pariter ab utrisque recipitur."
AUGUSTINE, *In Joan.* tract xcviii. 2.

1909
KEGAN PAUL, TRENCH, TRÜBNER & CO. LTD.
LONDON
B. HERDER
17 SOUTH BROADWAY, ST. LOUIS, MO.

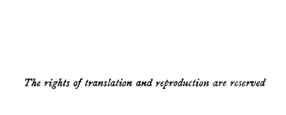

Letter of Approval from Card. Merry del Val.

Rev. P. Rivière,
Direttore del Seminario Maggiore
di Albi.

No. 16,864.

Illustrissimo Signore,

Dal Santo Padre ricevo il gradito e venerato incarico di rendere grazie alla S. V. Illmã per il cortese e filiale omaggio, che Ella Gli ha fatto coll' umiliare ai piedi del Trono Pontificio il Suo libro portante il titolo: "Le Dogme de la Rédemption." Sua Santità si compiace della nobile e dotta 'opera spesa da lei ad illustrazione e sopratutto a difesa di tale dogma, e le tributa la meritata lode per avere Ella non soltanto messo in rilievo ed in luce la storia della verità cattolica della Redenzione, ma ancora fatto comprendere e sentire piu profondamente la grandezza del mistero della Croce. La Santità Sua la esorta poi a proseguire con sempre crescente alacrità nel nobile arringo degli studi storici, ed a dedicare ogni più bel frutto del suo ingegno al patrocinio della dottrina cattolica, oggi più che mai insidiata da speciosi argomenti di incomplete ricerche e di infondate ricostruzioni.

A testimonianza di benevolenza e ad incoraggiamento nella tutela dei sacri dommi, l'Augusto Pontifice le imparte di cuore l'Apostolica benedizione: del che mentre la rendo intesa, godo dichiararmi con sensi di ben distinta stima,

Di V. S. Illmã,

Affmõ per servirla,

R. Card. Merry del Val.

Roma, 6 Aprile 1906.

v

CONTENTS

OF THE FIRST VOLUME

TRANSLATOR'S NOTE

WHILST all the Author's quotations from the Greek Fathers have been verified in the original works, we have not thought it necessary to do so in the case of mere references, nor for quotations given in Latin, the Author's scrupulous exactitude being a sufficient guarantee for their accuracy.

We have altered the scope and enlarged the contents of the Alphabetical Index of the original, adding a list of the recurrences of certain Greek terms which may be of interest to the student, and a Scripture-Index, which we give, not merely for convenience of reference, but because it is practically a list—though by no means an exhaustive one—of the texts on which the doctrine of the Atonement is based.

Another addition to this translation is the *Conspectus Patrum*, showing the position in the ages of all the ancient writers whose names occur in the course of this work. In most instances the dates are those given by Funk in his *Lehrbuch der Kirchengeschichte* (1907 edition).

AUTHOR'S FOREWORD

MUCH has been said of late about Professor Harnack's work "Das Wesen des Christentums,"[1] and finally not a few have come to the conclusion that, properly speaking, Christianity has no essence whatever. This conclusion has not, however, prevented each writer from insisting on that particular side of Christianity which he assumes to be most essential.

Without being suspected of holding similar views, we think we may plead that, of the articles of our faith, all of which are equally essential, one of the most important, both by reason of the elements it contains, and of the consequences with which it is pregnant, is the mystery of the Atonement. Whatever may be said of the scope of the Incarnation in a world different from ours—which of necessity must be more or less unintelligible to us—in our present fallen state, which alone is and remains real, the Incarnation has no other end in view than the restoration of sinful humanity, or, to speak more accurately, than the expiation of the sins of mankind by means of the death of Christ. This is why, from the Christian's point of view, the trend of Christ's whole mission was towards the cross, whilst it is on the cross that the sacraments, grace, and, in a word, all supernatural life depends. Thus it seems that the doctrine of the Atonement is on the one hand the very centre of God's providential plan, and, on the other, the deepest foundation, the very bed-rock, of our own salvation

---

[1] [English translation by T. Bailey Saunders, "What is Christianity?" London, 1901.]

xi

and the most practical outcome of Christianity—that
is, if it be true that the pardon of our sins is our most
pressing need.

For this reason the study of this mystery long
occupied, and continues to occupy, a first place in
Christian thought.   Theologians have pointed out
its causes and results ; sacred orators have devoted
their eloquence to depicting its wonders ; mystics owe
to it the sweetest outpourings of their inner selves ;
in a word, every believing soul finds in it food for
pious reflection.

Nevertheless, like other mysteries, this one has
been made the butt of criticism.   Rationalists of
every epoch have not failed to discover in it all kinds
of absurdities, and quite recently they have found
the means of attacking it in its very source.   At the
present day a tendency is making itself felt among
students of the history of dogma to describe the
Christian doctrine of the Atonement as utterly devoid
of traditional basis ; many scholars significantly point
to the variations of Christian thought on the subject
which are manifest as we pass from the Gospel
to St. Paul, and from the Fathers to the Middle
Ages ; texts in hand, they never tire of asserting the
wholly human and provisional character of our dogma.
Under these circumstances it will be useful, and even
necessary, to defend this essential element of our faith,
by confuting the new objections which have been
arrayed against it.

But it seems that no theory can be effectually
refuted unless we are prepared to substitute a better
one in its room, and thus we have been led by the
logic of things to construct in our turn a historical
synthesis.   Hence, after having laid down the Catholic
doctrine, which so often has been incorrectly rendered,

we have endeavoured to sketch the main lines
of its history, from its origin in St. Paul and the
Gospel, down to what we may consider as its final
development in the Middle Ages under St. Thomas.
It will thus become apparent whether anywhere the
continuity of its growth has been broken, or whether,
as a matter of fact, there is not from end to end
perfect agreement and oneness, not indeed the static
oneness and sameness of a lifeless fossil, but the oneness of the seed, which grows and becomes perfect
without losing its identity.

The task of thus showing the evolution of so
complex a doctrine was in itself formidable enough,
but in addition to this we had at every moment to
combat opponents who had already entrenched themselves in positions from which they could level their
arguments at our devoted head.   Like the Jews in
the time of Esdras, we had to defend our city walls
even whilst building them, holding in one hand the
trowel and in the other the sword ; a single one of
these tasks would have been amply sufficient for our
feeble strength ; God grant that the unavoidable
dispersal of our forces may not have spoilt the total
effect, and neutralised all our efforts, but that our
building be well established, and our battle well
fought.

Albi, December, 1904.

.   .   .   .

When penning the above lines we had not dared
to believe that our double work had been successfully
achieved, and that this, the labour of our youth,
would ever be worthy of seeing the light.   Yet so
it appeared to the learned body which constitutes
the theological faculty at the Catholic University of
Toulouse, for, after having accepted this work as a

dissertation for the Doctorate, they were pleased to encourage us to publish it. Their wish is the only excuse we can offer for our rashness, and their protection will form for the present essay the best possible recommendation. This book belongs largely to them. Here and there they will find direct evidences of their teaching, and we also hope that they will notice throughout the work the unswerving application of their methods, and the abiding influence of their spirit. If there be any merit in our work, it is to them that we are happy to ascribe it, only wishing that it had been more worthy of their teaching and example.

At least our work stands as a witness to our earnest endeavour. May it also be, in spite of its shortcomings, a contribution to that historical study of our beliefs of the need of which the best minds are now so conscious, and may it also render some modest service to the great cause of Catholic Truth.

Albi, April, 1905.

THE DOCTRINE OF THE ATONEMENT

CHAPTER I

SUMMARY OF THE CATHOLIC TEACHING

" AFTER more than a century of controversy with gentlemen of the Church commonly styled Reformed, it is now high time to cease discussing the subject-matters on which they based their rupture of relations with us, and to turn our attention to disposing their minds to conceive the sentiments of the Catholic Church. Thus it seems that we cannot do better than expose in all simplicity what our doctrines really are, whilst carefully distinguishing them from those which have been wrongly ascribed to us. Indeed I have frequently had occasion to notice that the horror which certain of the aforesaid gentlemen profess for most of our opinions is a result of the erroneous pictures they have conceived of them, and sometimes of certain expressions which seem to them so shocking that they never dare enter into their inner meaning."[1] These words are as appropriate to-day as when they were penned by Bossuet. Disputes with " gentlemen of the Church commonly styled Reformed " have never ceased, and the leaders of Protestant thought have not only not accepted

---

[1] Bossuet, *Exposition de la Doctrine de l'Église catholique sur les matières de controverse,* c. i.—*Œuvres complètes* (Besançon, 1836), viii. p. 614.

our dogmas, but they still appear to be unable even to grasp their very meaning. To-day we still find them clinging to erroneous conceptions of our doctrines and to certain expressions which play the part of bogeys to their easily frightened minds ; in fine, as a general rule when they wish to combat Catholic dogma they commence operations by disfiguring it.

The doctrine of the Atonement has not escaped such misunderstandings, and this is the reason why, before broaching its history, we have the intention to sketch the outlines of the Catholic view and separate it from all false alloy. By so doing we shall be able to define beforehand the object of our research and clear a piece of ground which, as we shall see hereafter, is much encumbered with ambiguities. For this two-fold reason some such preliminary explanation has seemed to us necessary ; to solve a problem satisfactorily we must first state it correctly.

I

"The Atonement" is a general term used to designate the complexus of divine workings, which have for their object the raising up of mankind fallen through sin. God in creating man did not confine Himself to imparting to mankind the perfection essential to human nature. Being full of generosity for the creature of His love, He had overwhelmed him with extraordinary or preternatural gifts ; He had moreover elevated man by His grace to a state of divine or supernatural life. The first man was to have benefited by these gifts and after a fitting trial to have transmitted them to his posterity ; for on the first man, in virtue of a certain solidarity established by God Himself, there depended, not only the natural, but also the supernatural future of mankind. Adam fell under the temptation, and thereby he also fell from his high estate, and we in him, " in whom all have sinned " (*Rom.* v. 12).

The evil did not stop there ; the first fault was a nefarious spring whence was to emerge a whole torrent of iniquities. Once man had deviated from the path of godliness, he lost no time in forgetting even the elements of natural truth, and soon sin set up its empire in the world, of which the most manifest sign was the universal idolatry. Out of this corrupt mass of humanity God then chose a nation which He made the depositary of His promises. But the Jews, even after countless punishments had rid them of their inborn love of idols, fell as a people into habits of narrow formalism in which the spirit was crushed by the soul-destroying yoke of sterile externalities. Man having thus become the slave of sin, and being without hope of restoration by dint of his own efforts, looked forward, more or less consciously, to a deliverance which should be effected by God.

At last God remembered His mercy and, when there came "the fulness of time " (*Gal.* iv. 4) marked by Providence, He sent the Saviour whom, on the occasion of its first fall, He had promised to mankind. This Saviour was not an ordinary prophet ; He was the very Son of God, become flesh for our Salvation ; He preached justice and love, Himself setting an example in every virtue ; He educated disciples to continue His work; and lastly, He died on the cross ; this life and death of the God-Man were our Salvation. Thereby man has found anew the way of truth and virtue, has learnt to know and love the Father who is in heaven, and to serve Him " in spirit and truth "

(Jn. iv. 23) ; in a word, has recovered his title to Divine adoption.   Thus by a wondrous work was God's plan readjusted and humanity lifted up from its degradation and restored to its primitive destiny. Such is the general outline of the Divine plan of the Atonement, that focal mystery which, as it were, summarises all the designs of the Divine mercy for our salvation, and constitutes the very basis of our faith.

II

But we are still at the surface of the mystery. Theology allows us to enter into it more deeply, when, after having taught us the general fact of the Atonement, it proceeds to instruct us concerning the reason and manner of its effects.   We are now trenching on one of the highest questions of Christian metaphysics.

Between God and man, ever since Adam's fall, there was the obstacle of sin.   Now sin does not merely hurt our soul, it has a far deeper grievousness, which, in traditional language, is expressed by saying that sin is an offence against—*i.e.* an insult to—God, not of course meaning thereby that God is injured in His own nature, but, as God and as Creator, He expects from His creatures complete submission to His Will, this complete submission being what we call God's honour ; now whereas the lower, material creation follows its accustomed course according to its laws, whereas God can ever predicate of it that goodness which is already ascribed to it in *Genesis* (i. 31), the rational creature—that creature from which He had the right to expect just that spontaneous homage which alone is to Him of any account—

frequently utilises its paltry freedom for refusing obedience to its Creator. This is sin. It is offensive to God because it is a disorder,[1] because it is a violation of that moral law of which God is at once the Author and the Guardian. Accordingly, no matter what some may think, what we ascribe to God is not the mere exasperation of a slighted prince; for God's honour is not a personal prerogative of His, or, as it were, a haughty assertion of His superiority; in reality it is the same thing as the law of the subordination of beings, as what we sometimes—making use of a vague but nevertheless profoundly true expression—call the " order of things." Of course we are not unaware that the Gospels depict God in the guise of a Father, but we also know that the Gospel did not wipe out from the list of God's attributes His Justice and His Sanctity.

Hence man had sinned, and sinning had grievously offended God; now every offence demands reparation, injured honour awaits satisfaction; justice moreover demands that the offender, to secure his pardon, should offer the injured some proportionate satisfaction—*i.e.* some act of submission out of the common and also free, which, constituting an unusual and extra honour, shall compensate for the injury done.[2] But if it be true that the measure of the offence is the dignity of the person offended, and that the measure of the reparation is the dignity of the offender who offers satisfaction—and according to law and to public opinion this is really the case in human matters—is it not evident that between offended God and offending man there is an irremediable

---

[1] " Peccatum proprie nominat actum inordinatum," says St. Thomas, *Sum. Th.* i^a ii^ae, q. 71, art. 1.

[2] *Cp. ibid.* q. 87, art. 6.

disproportion ? In effect, as sin is in some sense an
offence against God, it has a grievousness which surpasses everything finite and may in a sense be called
infinite,[1] whereas the act of the repentant sinner—
even supposing that God bestows on him the grace to
repent—has but a human value, falling infinitely short
of the greatness of the fault. Man,—having committed sin, was thus powerless to remedy the offence.

III

God might have left man in this state of misery
in which there was no escape from everlasting
punishment. The Atonement, however congruous,
was in no sense necessary, and if God willed to
save us, this was out of His goodness alone. Moreover, granting that He elected to forgive us, there
were open to Him manifold ways of so doing,
amongst them being the alternative of granting to
all sinners a free pardon. He could, without His
Justice thereby suffering in the least, have made the
sacrifice of His honour and been content with a
partial reparation, or He might even have dispensed
man from any reparation whatsoever. Hence there
can be no manner of doubt that His design of atoning
for the world by the death and Passion of His Son is
one wholly dependent on the Divine will. If He
chose this means rather than any other, it was because
He deemed it the most apt to manifest at once His
Justice and His Mercy, and also the most likely to
excite in us the love of God and the fear of sin.[2] For
in that labour of love, the Atonement, God made less

---

[1] St. Thomas, *Sum. Th.* iii[a], q. 1, art. 2, ad ii[um]. " Peccatum
contra Deum commissum *quamdam infinitatem habet.*"

[2] *Cp. ibid.* iii[a] q. 1, art. 2, and q. 46, art. 1-3.

account of His own rights than of our needs. It was by love that He willed to atone for our sins and it was by love that He chose not to grant us a free and gratuitous pardon, but to exact for our sins that complete satisfaction which He had the right to expect.

As we have already seen, such a satisfaction being beyond man's power, God offered him a substitute in the person of the Incarnate Word. He planned the Incarnation not merely that His Son might become our Master and our example, but principally that He might be the scapegoat for our sins. This mission was undertaken by Christ knowingly and willingly, through obedience to His Father and through love for us.[1] It was thus of His own will that He embarked on His tragic enterprise, encountered the prejudices of the common people, the hatred of the Pharisees and the vulgarity of His disciples. Soon His foes began to plot His death ; He foresaw this and yet did nothing to prevent it ; on the contrary He seemed to seek it, and when the fatal hour came, He accepted it without a murmur and offered to His Father this last act of love as a reparation for our sins. To satisfy Divine Justice, which man was incapable of appeasing, a God condescended to put Himself in the place of the guilty and die for them. The Passion and death of the God-Man, having an infinite value, furnished God a satisfaction, not merely sufficient, but superabundant, for all the crimes of mankind. Such, in its outline, is the common doctrine of vicarious satisfaction.

But theology itself suggests another and better view of the matter, a view which is too often neglected. It is clear that the least suffering, or indeed the least action of the God-Man—because in

---

[1] *Cp.* St. Thomas, *Sum. Th.* q. 47, art. 2, ad iii[ium].

virtue of the hypostatic union its value was infinite—
formed in God's eyes a full and perfect satisfaction.
Yet Christ did not rest content with this, among
other reasons for that given by St. Thomas : " *Christus
voluit genus humanum a peccatis liberare non sola
potestate, sed etiam iustitia. Et ideo non solum
attendit quantam virtutem dolor eius haberet ex
divinitate unita, sed etiam quantum dolor eius
sufficeret secundum humanam naturam ad tantam
satisfactionem.*" [1]   Thus, strictly speaking, the Passion
was a kind of divine surplus, a piling over and
pressing down of the measure.   Jesus, to show us
the abundance of His love, so to speak, divested
Himself of His Divine honour and drew out of His
humanity all the moral worth of which it was capable.
In such wise His Divine dignity, far from cancelling,
rather makes more evident the human price of His
sacrifice.   In such wise did the love of the Son
fulfil the plan conceived by the love of the Father.

As is evident, we take our stand in the category
of things moral ; we do not, as some have done,
put into the scales on one side Christ's Passion and
on the other the grievousness of sin, endeavouring
as it were to find in one the material equivalent of
the other ; sin is a moral disorder and requires a
moral act as its reparation.   It was not so much
the death or Passion of Christ which paid the price
of our sin, as the love with which He endured it.[2]

But Christ was innocent and as such He had not

[1] St. Thomas, *Sum. Th.* iii[a], q. 46, art. 6, ad 6[um].   On this point see
Janssens' recent commentary : " In ipso Homine-Deo, Homo tot in
se assumeret pœnas solvendas, *quasi non ex divina dignitate sed ex
humana expiatione reparatio exspectaretur.*" *Sum. Theol.* (Freiburg,
1901, v. p. 677).

[2] *Cp.* St. Thomas, iii[a], q. 48, art. 1, ad i[um], and Franzelin, *De
Verbo incarnato* (3rd ed., Rome, 1881), p. 504.

to suffer for Himself; hence, if He suffered, it was for us alone, literally for us—*i.e.* in our stead ; thus we come to say that Christ took on Him the penalty due to our sins. This idea of a substitution is the very soul of Christian piety and of Christian preaching, and rightly so, for this idea does represent the outer and as it were tangible side of the mystery ; and if it has its shortcomings, if it does not represent the Atonement in its fulness, nevertheless from what we have said it is evident that, deficient though it be, it has a foundation in reality ; it is the necessary explanation of the unmerited sufferings of God-made-Man.

But here we must put ourselves on our guard against exaggeration. God the Father has not seldom been depicted inculpating and as it were loading His Son with the burden of our faults; this done the Father sees in the Son naught but sin, and treats Him accordingly, as guilty of all the sins of mankind, striking Him without mercy until His righteous wrath has cooled. Not without justice have our preachers been accused of such faulty expressions, and, to quote but the greatest among them, it is difficult to let pass without censure, even in such an orator as Bossuet, words like the following :— 'Divine Justice looks at His Son with flaming eyes, with a glance darting fire. . . . He looks on Him as a sinner and *strides against Him with all the adjuncts of Justice divine.*'[1] Or again a passage such

---

[1] Bossuet, *Œuvres oratoires*, ed. Lebarq, iii. p. 382. *Cp.* the passage: 'He had to hurl all His thunderbolts against His Son; as He had imputed to Him all our sins He had also to wreak on Him His just revenge,' *ibid.* p. 380. And again, *ibid.* p. 416: 'I see a vengeful God who exacts from His Son the whole debt that is due.'

as the following :—' It is an unheard of thing that a God should persecute a God, that a God should abandon a God, and that the abandoner should turn a deaf ear to the plaints of the abandoned ; yet this is what we behold on the cross. The blessed soul of our Saviour trembles with the fear of God's wrath, and when it would fain seek refuge in the arms of its Father, it sees His face averted and itself abandoned and delivered over bound hand and foot *as a prey to the fury of outraged Divine Justice.*' [1] A few lines farther on, Bossuet speaks of ' the open war waged by a vengeful God against His Son,' and again, in a passage which is otherwise of remarkable beauty, he compares Divine Justice to a storm ' bursting over the Son of God and gradually dying down, as the pent-up energy is dispersed in the flood.' [2]

Bourdaloue is even worse. To begin with, he presupposes between God's Justice and His mercy ' a kind of contest ; one was ready to strike but the threatening sword was held back by the other.' Christ having taken on Himself our sins, it is on Him that Justice will take its course : ' Clothed in the leprosy of sin *God's Justice looks on Him as an object worthy of every punishment,* wherefore it takes up arms against Him, and sword in hand pursues Him, and pronounces on Him the sentence of death.' On Calvary, ' Sovereign Justice itself is present and all-invisibly presides at the scene of the fearful execution.' Christ is already sated with suffering ; ' but what does this matter ? Justice is not yet assured, and the hand will not cease to strike until its victim has

---

[1] BOSSUET, *Œuvres oratoires,* iv. p. 286 *f.* Cp. v. p. 206.

[2] The simile is hinted at in iii. p. 383, it is more fully worked out in iv. p. 287, and is repeated in v. p. 217.

been destroyed.'[1] In another sermon we read : ' The Eternal Father, whose conduct in all its rigour is adorable, forgetful of His Fatherhood *looked on the Son as His foe* (pardon me such expressions) and declared Himself His persecutor, or rather the chief of His persecutors.' Farther on, when commenting upon Christ's being forsaken on the cross, Bourdaloue goes so far as to say that ' this rejection by God is in a sense the pain of loss (*pœna damni*), which it behoved Christ to experience for us all.'[2]

However much allowance we may feel disposed to make in these passages for rhetorical exaggeration, we are bound to admit that they rest on a completely false idea. This sanguinary, cruel God is not the God of reason, still less is it the God of the Gospel. Catholic doctrine cannot be made responsible for such statements as those to which we have just listened. " God," says Aquinas, " delivered Christ in three ways ; by decreeing in His eternal plans that Christ should suffer that the human race might be freed, by imbuing Christ with the will to suffer and die for us, and by not protecting Him from His enemies."[3] It seems to us that this view of a sane theology is quite as touching from the standpoint of the heart and much more satisfactory from the point of view of the mind ; it does not perhaps explain the mystery but neither does it fall into the absurd.

We must beware of allowing ourselves to be dragged away by metaphors in weighing the effects of the Atonement. It is often said that, by our Saviour's death, divine anger was soothed, that thereby God was re-

[1] BOURDALOUE, *Exhortation sur le crucifiement et la mort de J.-C.—Œuvres complètes* (Besançon, 1823), ix. pp. 161, 165-169. Cp. p. 175

[2] *Mystères. Ier sermon sur la passion. Ibid.* x. pp. 157-160.

[3] *Sum. Th.* iii^{a}, q. 47, art. 3.

conciled with man, and man again restored to His love.
This is true, but we must not forget that God never
ceased loving man, even sinful man, and this before
the Passion as well as after ; otherwise how came He
to will to redeem him ?   God's love is the reason, not
the result, of the Atonement.   Nevertheless our
Saviour's death was really efficacious and was truly
the effective cause of our salvation, because God willed
to make His pardon subordinate to the merits of
Christ Jesus.   These merits apply to us because God
has made us one with Christ, just as He had made us
one with Adam ; and thus we were saved by one,
just as we had been lost by one (*Rom.* v. 15).   This
does not exclude our own co-operation ; on the contrary
God demands it, and our trivial actions gain in God's
sight an infinite value from the merits of Christ.   The
initiative of our salvation is indeed God's, but its
working out needs our loyal co-operation.

Thus was the fault of our first father atoned for and
thus did mankind again find the way to heavenly
bliss, because it pleased the Divine mercy to " restore
all things " in Christ Jesus (*Eph.* i. 10).

Such is, in reality, the Catholic doctrine on the
Atonement through the satisfaction rendered by
Jesus Christ, though it has never been defined as
such.   The Council of Trent did no more than allude
to it,[1] and the Canon of the Vatican Council which
was to have decided the matter unfortunately never
got further than the agenda papers.[2]   But, though it

[1] *Conc. Trident.* Sessio VI. c. vii.   " Iesus Christus . . . sua sanctis-
sima passione in ligno crucis nobis iustificationem meruit *et pro nobis
Deo Patri satisfecit.*"

[2] " *Si quis non confiteatur ipsum Deum Verbum in assumpta carne patiendo
et moriendo pro peccatis nostris potuisse satisfacere vel vere et proprie
satisfecisse . . . A. S.*"   *Cp.* HURTER (10th ed.), ii. p. 531.

has not been formally defined, there can be no doubt that it is the doctrine universally held in the Church.[1] Even more so than in the creeds, it is writ in every Christian heart as the most touching and vital truth of our religion. Possibly it is because it lives so firmly in the practical faith of her members, that the Church has never yet seen the need of formulating it in an official definition.

IV

Though our summary has failed to render the Catholic doctrine in its fulness, yet we hope that it may serve to show both its depth and its simplicity, in which heart and mind alike can find satisfaction. Nevertheless certain modern Protestant theologians cannot sufficiently express their contempt for this outworn doctrine, though, when we come to study their objections, we soon perceive that they are far from understanding the view against which they inveigh ; that which they attack as the Catholic doctrine is the merest travesty, and, as often as not, we find that the principles and the doctrine urged against us are our very own.

See for instance how Auguste Sabatier summarises the Catholic doctrine in order to show that it was unknown to St. Paul.

[1] For which reason we find it difficult to understand how certain Catholic theologians pass it by in silence, for instance GRATRY in the *Compendium Fidei* with which his *Connaissance de Dieu* closes (Paris, 1903, ii. p. 376 *ff*). We also sought it in vain in *la Philosophie du Credo*, even in the chapter which deals with the Atonement, p. 131 *ff*. [See however LABERTHONNIÈRE, *Le dogme de la rédemption, Annales de Phil. Chrét.* February, 1906. 4th series, vol. i. p. 516. The author's reply and his opponent's rejoinder appeared in the issue for May. *Trans.*]

" The Church's theory of expiation, far from trans-lating the Apostle's thought, actually contradicts it. The idea of an external satisfaction offered to God to wring from Him the pardon of sinners is foreign to all the epistles. Paul nowhere says that God must be appeased, in fact he starts from a contrary supposition ; the forgiveness of sins is ever a free act of God's love ; it was His sovereign grace which took, and retains even now, the initiative in the work of the Atone-ment. Christ's sacrifice, far from being the cause, is the result of the Father's love. The great sacrifice did not take place outside the sphere of grace and, as it were, independently of God, and thus determine the Divine will ; ' God was in Christ reconciling the world to himself' (2 *Cor.* v. 19). Paul has nothing to do with the traditional dualism between love and justice." [1]

This programme is drawn out more elaborately by M. Sabatier in his special work on the Doctrine of Expiation [2]; from this work we shall now quote a few striking passages.

" The gravest consequence of the old legal, juridical point of view was the introduction of a sort of dualism into the Christian idea of God. . . . There was conjured up a kind of conflict between His Justice and His mercy, with the result that one could not act without detriment to the other. Christ instead of being conceived of as the Saviour of men became a mediator between two aspects of God Himself, having for His mission to reconcile the two hostile attributes and to make peace within the Deity "

[1] *L'Apôtre Paul* (Paris, 3rd ed., 1896), p. 323.

[2] *La doctrine de l'expiation et son évolution historique* (Paris, 1903). [English trans. by LEULIETTE, *The Doctrine of the Atonement.* London, 1904.]

(pp. 99-100). "Anselm was the first to oppose God's Justice to His clemency" (p. 53). "His doctrine has now taken deep root in the tradition of the Catholic Church" (p. 63). But nothing of the sort is found in Scripture. "With Paul there is no question of reconciling God's justice and mercy, God has not even any need to be reconciled to men" (p. 29). Above all "had Jesus Himself the slightest notion that He was to die in order to furnish His Father with a penal satisfaction, short of which the Father would no longer be as a Father?" (p. 23). For we must not forget "that to punish even the contrite belonged indeed to the harshness of Roman and Jewish law, but that the preaching of the Gospel is to forgive everyone who heartily repents. What makes the Christian idea of God's Fatherhood seem so noble is precisely the fact that by means of it we get away from the idea of vengeance and penal retribution; that in it what is sought after is not the death, but the conversion and life of the sinner" (p. 95). Hence it is "a very low conception of justice which demands punishment for punishment's sake and for the mere pleasure of causing suffering" (p. 100).— Quite so, but was any theologian ever guilty of such statements, or is there any theologian who would not willingly consent to make his own the very propositions urged against us by M. Sabatier?

"The Father is perfect and His perfection consists in that His Goodness is Justice and in that His Justice is also His Goodness. . . . True Divine Justice strives after the victory of good over evil, and hence is necessarily one with love, for, having a like end, it gives and communicates itself like the latter. Again, Divine love is Holy, for its ultimate aim is to deliver us from evil" (pp. 100-101). "Hence it would be ridiculous to speak of God mediating with Himself, or of any outward Satisfaction furnished Him independently of His own free Will. . . . The sending of Christ into the world and His death were not the cause but the effect and the showing forth of God's mercy" (p. 102). "To work out the salvation of sinners Christ had not to act upon the Father whose own love had taken and still retained the initiative of pardon" (p. 105). "Christ's death ever remains the means and not the cause of the Atonement, the cause being solely God's love. Far from Christ's death being the determining motive of God's love, it was this love which delivered to the world His Son" (p. 39).

Likewise the part played by the Son must be wholly explained by His love. "What is it that gives Christ's death its moral and religious worth? Is it not the love of which His soul was full, His perfect obedience to His Father's will, His yielding His life for the sake of the Gospel which He had preached, for the sake of the Kingdom of God and of the new covenant which He had established?" (p. 96). "Christ's death is essentially a moral act of which the meaning and worth is derived from the very intensity of the spiritual life and of the love to which it testifies" (p. 93). Were we to add lastly that, Christ having carried His cross, "those who follow Him have to imitate Him and likewise to carry a cross for the world's salvation" (p. 112), and that "He desires to live again in each of His disciples, continuing in them to suffer and to sacrifice Himself, and to effect by them and through them the Atonement of mankind" (p. 113), then we should have, in the very words of M. Sabatier, the main elements of the Catholic doctrine.

At the very outset of his work M. Sabatier had stated the question in its right terms. " In the Christian consciousness the forgiveness of sins and the death of Christ are brought into close relation with each other. . . . This relation may be conceived of in two opposite ways ; we may conceive of Christ's death as the cause of the remission of our sins, or else we may reverse the hypothesis and consider it as the means and result. In the former case we should say that the death of the Innocent One, by satisfying God's justice, determined God to pardon the guilty. . . . In the second case on the contrary the sinner owes the pardon granted, simply and solely to God's sovereign pleasure. It was because God willed to pardon, and because God is love, that He sent His Son into the world, and consequently the Coming, and the work, and the death of Christ are simply the means adopted by the plans of Providence for accomplishing its great enterprise of mercy and salvation " (pp. 1-2).

M. Sabatier is quite right, he only goes astray in insinuating that the second system does not represent the doctrine of the Church.

B

CHAPTER II

A GLANCE AT THE NEO-PROTESTANT SYSTEMS

IF we have succeeded in dissipating some of the misunderstandings which prevail respecting the Church's teaching, we have already done much towards gaining our end, and without of course having thereby silenced our opponents, we shall have at least deprived them of one of their principal weapons. We must now consider the real differences of view which separate them from us.

I

The doctrine which we have sketched is opposed by a whole host of systems having this one point in common that they do not admit in Christ's death anything more than the moral value of an example. Of the olden heresies, none explicitly controverted the dogma of the Atonement, though several contested it indirectly by denying either the real humanity or the real divinity of the Saviour. At any rate this doctrine was never directly called into question, and, as we shall see, the Fathers based on the fact of Christ's Atonement, as on a universally acknowledged principle, the arguments by which they sought to establish the real character of His person. In the sixteenth century the Reformers, far from denying, were prone to exaggerate the doctrine of Satisfaction, in fact it was they who were guilty of the excesses which their modern disciples are now so anxious to ascribe to us. " From the time of the *Interim* and all through the seventeenth century—it is one of theirs who is speaking—the doctrine of juridical satisfaction was steadily acquiring new elements, the absurdity of which vied with their outrageousness, contributing to utterly discredit it among moderns." [1] It will be sufficient to allude to one point of their doctrine ; in their desire to find a real quantitative proportion between Christ's expiation and the penalty due to our sins, Protestant Schoolmen opined that Jesus must have suffered the pains of Hell, that He was during His last hours, and in fact during His life, really the object of God's curse and the butt of His anger.[2] M. Grétillat, though he does not adopt this extravagant opinion, can only censure it with the mild words which follow : " It is a theory, of the mistake and danger of which we are not unaware, but which, when preached by pious lips, probably did less harm to the cause of truth than the jocose refutations of which it became the object." [3]

The doctrine of Christ's satisfaction first met with opposition from the Socinians. These heretics, pushing to the very end the principle of private interpretation which Protestant orthodoxy, all too late, sought to restrain within arbitrary limits, denied the Atonement in common with the other mysteries ; probably the very exaggeration of the Protestant schools had not a little to do with this rejection. At any rate the Socinians rejected the doctrine be-

---

[1] A. GRÉTILLAT, *Essai de théologie systématique* (Neuchâtel, 1890), iv. pp. 291-292. *Cp.* pp. 332 and 333.

[2] See the texts in GRÉTILLAT, *op. cit.* p. 293. *Cp.* LICHTENBERGER, *Encyclopédie des sciences religieuses.* Art. *Rédemption,* t. xi. pp. 143-144. SABATIER, *op. cit.* pp. 66-67.

[3] *Op. cit.* p. 336.

cause they considered it unreasonable ; they were also
the first to level against it the objections which have
since become famous.[1] According to them Christ's
Atonement means nothing more than the example
which He set us, by His life and death, of faithfulness to His mission. It is true that the Socinians
still speak of a Sacrifice, but it is one which takes
place in heaven, where Christ offers to God on our
behalf His powerful intercession.

M. Sabatier admits that Socinus was " less fortunate " in his constructive efforts ; but he certainly
can claim the honour of having criticised the older
system—*i.e.* of having completely denied the traditional doctrine. As, however, the Socinian heresy
was a product of the extremist party among the
Reformers, it confined its attention to Protestant
orthodoxy, for which reason it was never much
noticed by Catholic theology and never received the
honour of a formal anathema. Our theologians
are now usually satisfied with summarily executing
the Socinians in the list of objections which forms
the appendix to their chapter on Satisfaction[2] ; in
a word, they deal with them just as they still, by
force of habit, deal with the objections of the ancient
Arians and Monothelites ; the Socinians appear to
them to have merely an historical—we were almost
saying archæological—interest.

II

Nevertheless the Socinians found successors if not
disciples among the philosophers of the eighteenth

---

[1] See these objections in SABATIER, *op. cit.* pp. 68 73. *Cp.*
LICHTENBERGER, *loc. cit.* p. 144.

[2] As an instance of the administration of such form of justice see
BILLUART, *De incarnatione*, diss. xix. art 4.

century ; according to these too, the life and death
of Christ were only those of a hero whose deeds are
valuable for the sake of their example. But as many
pious souls found this theory too dry and simple to
satisfy their religious cravings, there arose the many
other systems which, more or less clearly, endeavour
to explain our Saviour's work of salvation. The
pietists of course remained obstinately faithful to
the older theory, but among more thoughtful Protestants the dogma of the Atonement has been the
sport of every new current of ideas. "The oneness
of the theory," says Lichtenberger, "has been definitely shattered, and every interpretation is now
freely mooted, though the effort to reconcile traditional formulæ with modern ideas, and to satisfy at
once the moral feelings and the religious consciousness, frequently leads to regrettable ambiguities and
misunderstandings."[1] In a word, each one interprets
the Atonement in the fashion most convenient to
his pet system. Kant considers it as the equivalent
of his austere moralism ; Schleiermacher touches it
up with his sentimentalism ; all of them are fond
of losing themselves in hazy abstractions ;[2] finally we
find all these theories issuing in that "faith without
belief," or "undogmatic Christianity," which just now
has captivated the minds of the best thinkers of the
Protestant body.

Of this ultimate form of liberal Protestantism,
which had all along seemed to be the necessary result
of Protestant individualism, Albert Ritschl, the re-
nowned Göttingen professor, was the prophet and
high priest. In 1870 he published three huge

[1] *Op. cit.* p. 147.

[2] To test the truth of our statement see LICHTENBERGER, pp.
146-152, or SABATIER, *op. cit.* p. 78 *f.*

volumes, the result, as he says, of twenty years' reflections, on the Christian teaching of Justification and
Reconciliation[1]; in reality this work is an attempt
to reconstruct theology in its entirety on the basis of
a new doctrine of the Atonement.

Ritschl's Theology rests wholly on the idea of
God's Fatherhood.   God is love ; this is all that
Scripture tells us of Him, and in fact all that our
soul is capable of feeling about Him.   As Ritschl
holds in abhorrence anything smacking of metaphysical speculation, he takes care to keep to the bed-
rock of religious experience.   " Love is *the* Divine
attribute . . . which comprises, and from which flow,
all the other excellences of God's person."[2]   Ritschl
then proceeds to show, by subtly inquiring into the
logical meaning of the words "justice," "anger," and
others, and by examining the Scripture texts in which
they are mentioned, that what we call God's "attributes" are really only different manifestations of love.
This love is constant and unchanging; it presides
over all God's plans, directing them towards the one
great end, which is the establishment of the Kingdom
—*i.e.* of a "community of moral beings . . . comprising all those whose acts are inspired by love."[3]   This
is the leading idea of Ritschl's theology, in which

---

[1] Published by Marcus at Bonn.   We shall hereinafter quote it
from the 3rd ed. (1889).   The main points of the Ritschlian theology
have been treated by various French Protestant writers, in particular
his doctrine of the Atonement was criticised in a long thesis by M.
Ernest Bertrand, whom we shall have frequent occasion to quote.
On the outlines of Ritschl's theological system see the excellent
summary in M. Goyau's *l'Allemagne religieuse* (Paris, 4th ed., 1901,
pp. 93-103).

[2] Quoted by Bertrand, *Une conception nouvelle de la Rédemption*
(Paris, 1891), p. 89.

[3] *Ibid.* pp. 44-45.   *Cp.* pp. 49-51 and p. 180.

M. Bertrand is pleased to see a " certain practical
and moral taste reminding us of the parables of
Jesus."[1]

Jesus by His perfect consciousness of God the
Father became the revealer of Divine love and the
founder upon earth of the Kingdom. Of real pre-
existence He had none ; Ritschl indeed allows to
Christ an ideal eternity in the plans of God, "but as
a pre-existent being He is unknown to us"[2]; or as
he puts it in another passage, "Pre-existence is a
matter of utter indifference to the spiritual life ; to
him who believes in it, it is of no direct value and of
no practical use."[3] Opposed to the Kingdom of God
stands the kingdom of sin. Sin at all times consists
in a lack of trust in God and in a want of love for
man ; it originates partly in our inborn ignorance
and partly in our natural craving for boundless
freedom ; sin is deepened by heredity until finally it
assumes a social character, when its power over man
becomes almost irresistible.

But as sin is but a weakness, and as God is good,
good and kind in spite of all, there can be no question
of any Divine anger against sin. Man deceives himself when he fancies that he has become the object
of God's wrath. Neither physical evil nor death are
punishments of sin ; both one and the other are
necessary results of the organisation of the world, or
at the very most they are God's fatherly corrections
and a means by which man can perfect himself
morally.[4] Hence it is not God who stands in need
of being reconciled to man, rather it is man who

---

[1] BERTRAND, *Une conception nouvelle de la Rédemption* (Paris, 1891),
p. 184.

[2] *Ibid.* p. 61.   [3] *Ibid.* p. 207.

[4] *Ibid.* pp. 71-74.   *Cp.* pp. 260-263.

must needs be reconciled to God; this was the purport of the message, of the good tidings brought into the world by Christ; He was the first to reveal to man that Divine love which pardons and justifies, and for this reason we call him our Saviour. "As it is the consciousness of guilt which makes man live apart from God, the remission of sins consists essentially in delivering man from the feeling of sin and in giving him free access to heaven"[1]; Christ's death has no other meaning; it saves us by showing through His example that earthly sufferings are not penalties, but so many helps sown on our way by Providence. In the midst of His sufferings Christ was in full and perfect communion with His Father, nay more His sufferings enabled Him to show forth His patience and His submissiveness; His death was the summing up of His life of obedience, and this is the reason why we ascribe the benefit of the Atonement principally to His death.[2] We thus learn not to fear death and to live in union with God even in the midst of the sorest trials. In a word, Christ's work of Atonement was a wholly human work, which M. Bertrand thus sums up: "He came to reconcile us with our destiny and invite us bravely to bear our share of the miseries and labours inseparable from human life."[3] According to Ritschl, however, the saving grace of Christ is not directly meted out to each individual Christian, but is only to be obtained through the ministry of the Church, which alone has received power to forgive sins.[4] Consequently Ritschl requires not merely faith but also works, a

---

[1] BERTRAND, *Une conception nouvelle de la Rédemption* (Paris, 1891), p. 112.

[2] *Ibid.* p. 127. *Cp.* pp. 381-398.

[3] *Ibid.* p. 400.   [4] *Ibid.* p. 130 *ff.* *Cp.* p. 139.

condition which has led to his being accused of
Catholicism by the more old-fashioned Protestants.[1]

"A species of rational scepticism with a touch of
Pelagian moralism, vainly endeavouring to clothe
itself with the principles of the Reformation and the
outworn mantle of Lutheranism." Such is Zahn's
sarcastic description of Ritschlianism,[2] and doubtless
its crudity is the "most manifest sign of the senile
debility of Protestantism," but this very crudeness,
united as it often is with a genuine sort of moralism,
explains the prodigious success of the theory. Moreover it was opportune and answered to a need felt on
all sides, for, as it has been well shown, with all its
lack of originality, it is the synthesis of that move-
ment of ideas of which Kant was the promoter.[3]
Hence it was useless for the old rationalist school of
Tübingen to attack Ritschl with its weapons of
exegetical criticism, and for the orthodox old-pattern
schools of Protestantism to invoke worn-out categories
and hint at anathemas ; the new master, in spite of
all, sees the number of his adherents steadily growing.
Already in 1882 Lipsius had occasion to speak of the
"great influence exercised by Ritschl in many spheres
of contemporary theological thought,"[4] and the
following year he pointed out that it was influencing
"a large number of young professors and ecclesi-
astics."[5] There can be no question about it now ;
a new school has arisen to succeed the older one, a
school which proclaims itself the true heir of Luther

[1] BERTRAND, *Une conception nouvelle de la Rédemption* (Paris, 1891),
p. 414. *Cp.* GOYAU, *op. cit.* pp. 113-114.

[2] Quoted in WURM, *Kirchenlexicon*, art. *Protestantismus*, x. p. 510.

[3] HENRI SCHŒN, *Les origines historiques de la théologie de Ritschl*
(Paris, 1893).

[4] B. PUENJER, *Theologischer Jahresbericht*, 1882, p. 285.

[5] *Ibid.* 1883, p. 272.

and his methods. Everywhere the praises of Ritschl's " wonderful new theology " are dinned into our ears ; he is greeted as an up-to-date " Albertus Magnus," and all are advised to undertake " a pilgrimage to the sacred mountain of Göttingen." [1] A member of the new school, Julius Thikötter, writes a lyrical defence of the new system which is immediately translated and circulated in France by Pastor Aguiléra, under the significant title " The Theology of the Future."

Matters have passed beyond the bounds of mere admiration, Ritschl has become the object of a positive worship ; such at least was the opinion ventured on by the level-headed Lipsius, whilst Lemme does not hesitate to state bluntly that "Ritschlianism does not signify so much a new theology, as a new religion." [2]

Ritschl's theology had other results besides provoking enthusiasm among the young ; it also led to many earnest scholars applying in other directions the methods of the master. The name of the theologians who have been influenced by Ritschl is legion,[3] and among his disciples are to be numbered the most brilliant professors in the German universities ; Lobstein, Herrmann, Kaftan, and, the best known of all, Harnack.

In France Auguste Sabatier became, though not always openly, the populariser of the new ideas from beyond the Rhine. Others have been before us in showing that we have in his *Esquisse* a but slightly veiled adaptation of the German theology and more particularly of that of Ritschl. The question of the

---

[1] B. Puenjer, *Theologischer Jahresbericht*, 1884, p. 304.

[2] Quoted by Goyau, *op. cit.* p. 103, note 2.

[3] *Cp.* Prat, *Études*, 5th Nov. 1903, p. 320, note 1, and A. Garvie, *The Ritschlian Theology* (Edinburgh, 1899), p. 32 *f.*

Atonement was treated by Sabatier in a special work of which we have already spoken; fundamentally it explains Christ's sufferings by the principle of solidarity. "No one can make himself independent of the organism to which he belongs, so that the whole body suffers through the faults, and benefits through the virtues, of the members which compose it" (p. 20). "There is no longer any reason to speak of a supernatural or particular condemnation of which Jesus bore the results on the cross; Jesus indeed suffered more and better, but He did not suffer otherwise than Socrates, the martyrs, or the wise men of old, or in a word than all the just who through their very life in the world became entangled in the trammels woven here below by the crimes of the wicked" (p. 87). Elsewhere he compares Christ's sacrifice to that of Leonidas, of Winkelried, and of the knight d'Assas (pp. 97-98). He concludes by sounding the true keynote of his system. "When once we reduce the drama of Calvary to its real proportions, it becomes what it originally was, *a human, historical drama,* though the greatest and most tragic one of history" (p. 110). This drama excites us by the love which it reveals; Christ's death urges us to love and repentance, as would the sacrifice of a mother who exposes herself to every outrage to gain the heart of her guilty son. "In the cross is the forgiveness of sins only because the cross is the cause of that repentance by which remission may be gained" (p. 107). Evidently, the explanation of the Atonement has changed very little from Socinus to Ritschl, and from Ritschl to Sabatier; it has not ceased to consist in a somewhat crude sentimentalism containing a very large element of the old Socinian rationalism.

This system, however, will serve us the better to express by contrast the essence of the Catholic doctrine. We scarcely need state that we too see in Christ's death the most sublime of examples and the most fruitful source of love ; to prove this would be labouring to establish a truism[1] ; it is for this reason that in the course of our work we shall have but little to say about this matter ; but to the excellences of Christ's example we give a real foundation by making of His death the providentially designed expiation of our sins. Neo-protestants consider that the whole influence of Christ's death is in the subjective emotion it arouses ; we believe it to have an objective efficacy ; for a mere fact of human solidarity we substitute a mystery of supernatural solidarity.

III

As the mainstay of their system our opponents have always sought to undermine the Catholic teaching ; for many years they endeavoured to effect their purpose by merely logical weapons, and, as we said, even some of the most modern among them do not disdain occasionally to furbish the old arguments of Socinian dialectics. If they all confined themselves to this sort of warfare, our work would not be so very difficult ; we should only have to determine the true ground of debate and clear it from the ambiguities and misapprehensions which encumber it ; the few rationalist objections which really touch our teaching are perhaps not so very formidable, and they are moreover sufficiently dealt with by the hand-books

---

[1] *Cp.* St. Thomas, iii³, q. 46, art. 3. "Multa concurrerunt ad salutem pertinentia præter liberationem a peccato."

of theology in everyday use. But at the present day we are faced by new difficulties. It is contended now that in history there can be found arguments which suffice to deprive the Catholic teaching of that claim to prescriptive rights which is for us theologians the strongest evidence in our favour, and, as it were, our excuse for the mysteries which we teach. The earliest Socinians freely admitted that they had tradition against them, whereas according to modern Protestant historians, tradition, if only it be rightly examined, really bears witness against the Church.

As early as 1838 Christian Baur wrote a history of the doctrine of the Atonement. With this work Ritschl finds fault for not making sufficiently clear the general trend of each period, in other words for not being sufficiently systematic. Ritschl accordingly devotes the first volume of his own work to the consideration of the historical problem. This part of his work can certainly not be accused of the same fault as the work of his predecessor. In the course of a few pages he boldly sums up what he considers the leading ideas of each individual Father, concluding with a synthesis of startling simplicity. "Roughly speaking" the ideas of Justification and of Reconciliation were unknown to the Greek Fathers. Their idea of Christ's work, though similar in appearance, is in reality totally different; they deemed it to consist in the Redemption and perfecting (*Erlösung und Vollendung*) of fallen man.[1] Christ as God restored to men the immortality ($\dot{\alpha}\phi\theta\alpha\rho\sigma i\alpha$) they had lost through sin, and, as immortality is God's essential attribute relatively to creatures, this

---

[1] *Rechtfertigung und Versöhnung*, i. pp. 3-4. [English trans., *Justification and Reconciliation*. London, 1870. *Trans.*]

great benefit is termed a deification of man (θεοποίησις).
Hence it was not the Saviour's death, but the Incarnation itself which saved us. If in any sense
Christ's death was claimed by God's Justice this was
only by way of ransom to the Devil for destroying
his right over men.[1] Restoring mankind to Divine
life and paying its righteous debt to the Devil, such
are, we are told, the two fundamental ideas which
sum up all the Greek Fathers' theology on the
Atonement. Moreover the Latin Fathers followed
the Greeks; only in the Middle Ages, in the works
of St. Anselm, who took his idea from Germanic law,
do we meet for the first time the doctrine of Satisfaction. This is sufficient to show that in Ritschl's
view history is a very simple matter.

Ritschl's thesis, being embodied in a manual of
theology manifestly written to prove a theory, might
be suspected of not being an impartial statement of
the question. Hence the professional historians
among his disciples deemed it well to apply the same
ideas in the fields of objective science. In his *History
of Dogma* Harnack follows, occasionally even down
to the minutest details, the historical views of Ritschl.
So far as Greek orthodoxy is concerned, he states :
" Salvation in Christianity consists in that the human
race was redeemed—*i.e.* bought back—for Divine life
from the state of perdition in which it had been
and from the sin connected with it. . . . This redemption was accomplished by Christ's Incarnation
. . . their leading thought is that of a deification of
man."[2] In the West, " under the twofold action of
the penitentiary discipline . . . and of the legal spirit

---

[1] *Rechtfertigung und Versöhnung*, i. pp. 16-18.
[2] *Lehrbuch der Dogmengeschichte*, French trans. by CHOISY, *Précis
de l'histoire des dogmes* (Paris, 1893), pp. 144-145. [English trans.

which peculiarly distinguished all Western theological speculations, Christ's work of atoning for sin began to come to the forefront. But here it is no longer the Incarnation—though of course it is presupposed—but rather Christ's death which takes the first place."[1] The value of this death was stated in legal form, but "to tell the truth, the West was not yet in possession of any settled theory; it still accepted those Gnostic ideas of the East, according to which a ransom had been paid to the Devil."[2]

French Protestant writers soon adopted these views and exaggerated them till they bordered closely on paradox. For instance Lichtenberger is not far from reducing the whole history of the Atonement down to the Middle Ages to the "mythical" opinion of the Devil's rights. M. Sabatier goes even further and without more ado states that "this long history may be easily summed up; it falls into three periods," of which "the first, that of the Fathers of the Church, was wholly inspired by the mythological notion that God had paid a ransom to Satan. Though this theory professed to be based on the biblical metaphors of Redemption and ransom, the conception is none the less a product of mythological habits of thinking which survived paganism and obtained a footing in the imagination of the early Christians" (p. 90). The second period, characterised by the conception of a legal satisfaction, in due time made room for a moral conception which in reality is the only reasonable and Christian one possible. Thus has Ritschl's opinion become, to-day, a commonplace in the history of

by MITCHELL, *Outlines of the History of Dogma*. New York and London, 1893.]

[1] *Dogmengeschichte* (3rd ed.), iii. pp. 50-52.
[2] *Ibid.* pp. 174-175.

dogma, showing incidentally that reputedly independent searchers sometimes know how to bend to
the yoke of a pet tradition their own private judgment. At any rate we can see how serious the
objections really are, and—especially when they are
backed up by well-known names and enforced with
well-chosen texts—how apt they are to make an impression more particularly on modern readers who,
with the progress of criticism, are now ready to expect
any change, no matter how fundamental, in ideas and
things. " After having considered the Christian faith
for centuries, now in the light of mythology, now in
that of Catholicism, has not the time come at last for
us to think evangelically of the Gospel realities ?"[1]

Against all these arguments and insinuations traditional theology so far has had nothing to set. The
invaluable compilations of Petavius and Thomassinus
do not cover the more recent objections, and no
modern Catholic work that we know of even touches
the subject.[2] Even Döerholt's book,[3] well written and
learned though it is, is in one respect too like some
theological text-books where all the Fathers repeat
each other *ad nauseam*. No doubt it was laudable
enough to string together some sixty pagefuls of
Patristic dicta,[4] but history requires something more.
At any rate the last-mentioned writer seems quite
unaware of any historical difficulties and confines
himself to refuting the rationalist objections of the
Socinians and of Hartmann, their modern representative.[5]

[1] SABATIER, *op. cit.* p. 99.

[2] [By an oversight our author has missed H. N. OXENHAM's work.
Trans.]

[3] BERNARD DÖERHOLT, *Die Lehre von der Genugthuung Christi*
(Paderborn, 1891).

[4] *Ibid.* pp. 65-124.   [5] *Ibid.* pp. 152-170.

Hence the history of the important doctrine of the Atonement yet remains to be written. Such a history would at any time have been of interest, but to-day it is absolutely necessary in order to defend a belief of which our opponents profess to have destroyed the basis. This is sufficient to justify our endeavour, though no one feels more deeply than ourselves that the work should have been taken in hand by one better qualified.

PART THE FIRST

THE ATONEMENT IN SCRIPTURE

CHAPTER III

THE SUFFERINGS OF THE MESSIAS, ACCORDING TO THE OLD TESTAMENT, AND ACCORDING TO JEWISH OPINION

IT has been said that the history of the Atonement begins with the history of mankind. In the very earliest pages of the Bible, side by side with the account of the Fall, we find the promise of a Restorer ; for God did not will to leave fallen humanity without hope, and no sooner had sin entered into the world than we find God revealing the outline of the plan which His mercy had evolved for reconciling the world to Himself. Ever since, the prophets had never ceased reminding the nation of the promised Saviour, and one after the other under the guidance of the spirit of God they drew His portrait, each adding his stroke till the whole was finished. Of the characteristics of the coming Saviour, suffering was to be one of the principal. We find this suffering described in detail in the Psalms and by the Prophets, we find it also foreshadowed in the offering of Isaac and in the ancient sacrifices, more especially in the paschal lamb and in the scapegoat. All these victims seem to be but halting figures of the great Victim, whose death alone could purify and reconcile mankind. Above all in *Isaias* liii., which has been called the *Passio secundum Isaiam*, we find depicted under the figure of

34

the Servant of the Lord, suffering and dying for his people, a man of sorrows who can be no other than Jesus who died for the sins of men. Thus do theologians, exegetists, and apologists interpret the Old Testament according to their fancy. All of them do not go as far as the well-known preacher who opined that " every pious Jew learned in the Law could perform his Stations of the Cross long before the Cross itself had been reared to bear on its blessed branches the fruit of our salvation,"[1] but with scarcely an exception they delight in collecting the scattered texts which recount the suffering story of the Messias. Döerholt, following in the footsteps of his many predecessors, also narrates the story, and goes so far as to head his section : *The Doctrine of Christ's Satisfaction in the Old Testament.*[2] He, at least, makes no attempt to conceal the anachronism.

I

Of course we have not heard the last of this matter. History still acknowledges the universality of bloody sacrifice, and though it is no longer satisfied with the explanations of Joseph de Maistre,[3] yet it is far from having discovered the meaning and the origin of this rite. So far as the Mosaic sacrifices are concerned, A. Sabatier finds a facile explanation in a few " very simple primitive ideas " ; that of a homage paid to the Almighty, that of being united with God by partaking of the same blood, or still worse in the idea that the

---

[1] MONSABRÉ, *Introduction au dogme catholique,* 17th Conf. (Paris, 1882), ii. pp. 208-209.

[2] *Op. cit.* p. 39.

[3] *Soirées de St-Pétersbourg* (9th et 10th Entretien) and *Eclaircissement sur les sacrifices.* Oddly enough we find similar views in HARNACK, *Das Wesen des Christentums* (Leipzig, 1900), pp. 98-101.

beast sacrificed serves God as food. "What propitiates God is the giving of something which is agreeable to Him ; the pandering to His tastes."[1] Serious exegetists are by no means so sure of their ground. Smend, for instance, believes that in the Levitical ritual we have traces of the moral feeling of sin and of expiation,[2] whilst Holtzmann[3] finds in it the very "ideas of substitution and of penal satisfaction," which Sabatier declares to be "totally absent."

On the prediction of Isaias there was much to be written and writers have not failed in their duty. We shall first of all give the text of this famous prophecy. Quite apart from its beauty, which struck even Renan, we shall have so frequently occasion to allude to it that it is only right to put it at once before the reader.

"Behold my servant shall understand ; he shall be exalted, and extolled, and shall be exceeding high. Even as many have feared him, for that his image was inglorious among men, and forasmuch as his spirit hath been other than that of the sons of men, so shall he be a cause of joy unto many nations. Kings shall shut their mouths before him ; for they shall see that which was not told to them, and they shall learn things they had not heard. Who hath believed our report ? and to whom is the arm of Yahweh revealed ? And he shall grow up as a tender plant before him, and as a root out of a thirsty ground. There is no beauty in him, nor comeliness ; and we have seen him, and there was no sightliness that we should desire him ; despised, and the most abject of men, a man of sorrows, and acquainted with suffering, like him from whom men turn away their faces, we despised him, and we esteemed him not. Surely he hath borne our infirmities and carried our sorrows ; and we have thought him, as it were, chastised, and as one struck by God and afflicted. But he was wounded for our iniquities, he was bruised for our sins, the chastisement which gives us peace has fallen upon him, and by his wounds we are

---

[1] SABATIER, *op. cit.* p. 12. *Cp.* pp. 9-16.
[2] *Alttestamentliche Religionsgeschichte* (2nd edit., 1899), pp. 326-332.
[3] *N.T. Theologie,* i. p. 68.

healed.   All we like sheep had gone astray, everyone had turned aside into his own way, and Yahweh hath laid on him the iniquity of us all.   He was misused and crushed, and he opened not his mouth ; as a lamb led to the slaughter, and a sheep is dumb before her shearer, so he opened not his mouth.   He was taken away by torture and chastisement, and among those of his generation who hath believed that he was cut off out of the land of the living and struck for the wickedness of my people?   And he was given a grave among malefactors and his tomb was among the wicked. Although he hath not done any violence, neither was there deceit in his mouth.   And Yahweh was pleased to break him with suffering.   After having laid down his life for sin he shall see a multitude of children and his days shall be multiplied and the work of Yahweh shall be prosperous in his hand."   [*Is.* lii. 13-liii. 11.][1]

It seems very natural to see in this page of the prophet a prediction and as it were a preliminary description of our Saviour's death and of its atoning power.   Unfortunately that this is the case is by no means so certain as it looks.

The Servant of the Lord is held by many to be no more than a " poetic figure " of Israel, or rather of the faithful portion of the race ; this opinion was for many years common among our opponents, in fact it was considered as a first principle, but many critics to-day, following in the wake of Duhm, concede a real individual personality to the suffering Just One whom the prophet depicts, though they hesitate as to whom to apply the extraordinary description.[2]   Others even consider it as a literal Messianic prediction.[3]

All this shows clearly enough how difficult the matter is and how impossible it is at the present juncture to give any decisive answer to such questions.

[1] The translation is that given by Rose, *Études sur les Évangiles* (Paris, 1902), p. 240 *f.* [English ed. by Fraser.]

[2] *Cp.* Condamin, *Le livre d'Isaïe* (Paris, 1905), pp. 328-329.   *Cp.* p. 338.

[3] For the proof of this statement see Condamin, *op. cit.* pp. 329-330, and *cp.* p. 341.

But whatever the right answer may be, one thing is certain, critics have not yet succeeded in demolishing the traditional arguments. Hence if we now dismiss these arguments, this will not be because we consider them worthless, but because on the one hand we can claim no right to speak on a subject, which pertains to exegesis, and on the other because the question lies beyond the scope of our present work. It may be a fact that the ancient sacrifices and the prophecy of Isaias form a kind of providential foreword to the doctrine of the Atonement. As such they may be utilised by the apologist, but it is quite clear that this divine foreword does not belong to the history of the doctrine in question. From our point of view Old Testament ideas are interesting only by the traces which still remained of them at the time when Christianity first appeared, and by reason of the influence which they had on that Jewish world to which Christ preached and from which St. Paul received his training.

II

Now whatever may be the literal meaning of the texts in question, and even supposing that the traditional view of them is correct,[1] one thing is quite certain, and that is that the Jews themselves never understood them in this light and that the idea of suffering scarcely entered into their ideal of the Messias. "The common idea of the Messias," writes Bossuet, "stood for something wholly earthly, political, and national. The Messias was to be the powerful king of the latter days. It is quite exceptional to find, in the sources which we have examined, the

---

[1] This is the decided opinion of CONDAMIN, *op. cit.* p. 344.

slightest trace of anything transcendental in His personality or of any redeeming action, or expiating of sins."[1] So much so that Christ's humility was a scandal to the people, and not only His foes but even His own chosen disciples, and this in spite of the prophecies, could not bear to think of His death. Hence we are obliged to infer that the Jews rightly or wrongly did not read the prophecies as we do, and that the idea of a suffering Messias was by no means common among them. In fact the question arises : were they even acquainted with such an idea ?

We cannot state positively that they were.[2] A few rabbinical texts speak indeed of a suffering Messias, but their meaning is not clear and they may be interpolations. The only certain testimony which can be quoted is that of the Jew Trypho. According to Justin Martyr he allows as self-evident the fact that the sufferings of the Messias are predicted in Scripture.[3] He confines himself to protesting against the idea of the Messias dying on the cross. Now, even supposing that the dialogue is fictitious, the statements made in it by the Jew must correspond with ideas prevailing in the second century in certain Jewish circles. This fact leads Schürer to suppose that "it is not altogether impossible that even before this period certain individual Jewish teachers may have applied to the Messias the fifty-third chapter of Isaias." But we must not forget that Trypho's admissions had been called forth by the Christian polemics and that consequently it is quite possible that they do not

[1] *Die Religion des Judentums* (Berlin, 1903), p. 217. *Cp.* Holtzmann, *op. cit.* i. p. 85.

[2] The question is well handled by Schürer, *Geschichte des Jüdischen Volkes* (3rd ed.), ii. pp. 554-7.

[3] Justin, *Dial. cum Tryph.* 89.—*P.G.* vi. col. 689. *Cp.* 90, *ibid.* and 68, col. 636.

stand for the earlier and more spontaneous views of the Jews. These earlier views are more likely to be voiced by the Targum of Jonathan, which, though it applies the fifty-third chapter of Isaias to the Messias, carefully avoids applying to him the verses which deal with the sufferings of the Servant of the Lord.[1] Making use of an ingenious exegesis, "where the Scripture text alludes to atoning sufferings, the Targum speaks only of an atoning intercession (*Für-bitte*)." We have it also on Origen's authority that the Jewish third-century divines, anticipating present-day critics, applied the prophecy in question to their nation as a whole.[2] Another far more singular theory proves how deeply rooted were the old prejudices of Judaism. The Jews were finally driven by the Christian controversialists to admit the coming of a second Messias, a son of Joseph, who was to carry out the suffering portion of the Messianic programme.[3] But so far as the son of Juda was concerned they absolutely refused to believe that he could undergo any suffering other than that due to his own sins. This shows how far the Jews were from associating with the Messias of their dreams the idea of an atoning or redeeming death. "This idea was strange to Judaism as a nation, it never was more than a mere opinion held in the school"; if we add that the school which held it was a small one and that the opinion itself can scarcely be described as a genuine Hebrew growth, we may then accept the above conclusion of Schürer's.[4] It takes into account Trypho's testimony

---

[1] *Cp.* Weber, *Jüdische Theologie* (Leipzig, 2ᵉ edit., 1897), pp. 360-361.

[2] Origen, *Contra Cels.* i. 55.—*P.G.* xi. col. 761.

[3] *Cp.* Weber, *op. cit.* pp. 362-363, and Holtzmann, *op. cit*, i. p. 85.

[4] *Cp.* Stanton, in Hastings' *Dictionary of the Bible*, art. *Messiah*, iii. pp. 354-355.

and yet allows it to be clearly seen how very different was the view entertained by the majority of his countrymen. Whence we gather that the prophecies which seem so evident to us, even when insisted on by the early Christian apologists, never succeeded in altering the feelings of the Jews. Messianism and suffering—even atoning suffering—remained, in their eyes, two incompatible things.

III

This fact is all the more remarkable because the Jews had long been acquainted with the doctrine of the communion of saints (the anachronism is apparent only) ; Israel forms a body of which the members are inter-dependent and are consequently under the obligation of helping each other in attaining their common end. Israel's salvation was conceived of as a national work to which all, both living and dead, had to lend a hand. Hence the idea of the reversibility of merits and of acts of reparation is quite fundamental in Jewish theology. It is mainly here that historians perceive the lasting influence of the second Isaias.

The merits of the forefathers are shared by all and make up for the failings of the individual. *Nigra sum sed formosa*, I am black judged by my own deeds, such was the argument of the pious Jew, but I am beautiful through the good deeds of my fathers. Israel leans on the merits of its fathers as the vine leans on the supporting stake. It is wicked for a man to seek his reward here below, because . . . no merits will then remain over for his posterity. Such merits may most usefully be made use of in prayer ; the son of a just man has more assurance of being heard ; Moses prayed for forty days but he was not heard until he had mentioned the dead.[1]

The merits of the just whilst yet in life make their intercession all-powerful with God.   Jeremias and Baruch had to leave Jerusalem before God could destroy the city ; the mere presence of a just man staves off destruction (*cp. Gen.* xviii. 22 *ff*).   So long as Isaac of Modein lived and prayed for the people it was not possible to capture the stronghold into which Bar Kochba had retired to continue his struggle against the Romans.   The writer of the fourth book of Esdras alludes to the good result of the prayers offered by Moses and the other just men on behalf of sinners (vii. 36-41) ; and he himself prays God to regard "not the sins of His people but those who serve Him in truth" (viii. 26-31), and the Lord grants his petition (38-39.)

Any atoning act of a just man is as applicable to others as are his merits.   The idea of moral substitution was a common one among the Jews ; by means of it they explained the death of guileless children.   Pushing this principle to its very end the Rabbis had no hesitation in deducing all kinds of absurd conclusions.   Thus because Rabbi Juda the Saint suffered for thirteen years from toothache, during the whole of the period there occurred in Israel no miscarriage nor death in childbirth.   Above all, the death of the just was believed to be of great worth ; its efficaciousness being compared to that of the Day of Atonement.[2]

The Machabean history has preserved for us many precious data concerning these views.   "I, like my brethren," says the last of the Machabees,

---

[1] We take all these instances from WEBER, *op. cit.* pp. 292-302.
[2] WEBER, *op. cit.* pp. 326-330.

THE SUFFERINGS OF THE MESSIAS 43

"offer up my life and my body for the laws of our fathers, calling upon God to be speedily merciful to our nation ; . . . but in me and in my brethren the wrath of the Almighty, which hath justly been brought upon all our nation, shall cease" (ii. *Mach.* vii. 37-38). This declaration was enlarged upon in the apocryphal Machabean literature : " O God, be merciful to Thy people," says the young martyr, "and may the punishment which we suffer suffice Thee on its behalf. Grant that they be purified in my blood, and accept my life in lieu of theirs."[1] Farther on, the writer himself records his opinion : "Their death obtained for us victory over our enemies, the chastisement of the tyrants, and the purification of the people. By substitution they were burdened with the sins of the nation ; by the merits of their blood and of their atoning death God's Providence saved erring Israel"[2] (iv. *Mach.* xvii. 20-23. *Cp.* i. 11. and xviii. 4).

In the above clause we find expressed, as clearly as could be wished, the idea and the very terms of *vicarious Satisfaction.* If only we compare this with the idea of the suffering and death of the Messias, of *the* Just One, we see at once that the two ideas are harmonious and mutually complementary. But as a matter of fact this comparison was never made before we find it in the teaching of Christ and of His disciples ; hence the doctrine of the Atonement is entirely Christian in its origin.

[1] Ἵλεως γενοῦ τῷ ἔθνει σου, ἀρκεσθεὶς τῇ ἡμετέρᾳ περὶ αὐτῶν δίκῃ· Καθάρσιον αὐτῶν ποίησον τὸ ἐμὸν αἷμα καὶ ἀντίψυχον αὐτῶν λάβε τὴν ἐμὴν ψυχήν (iv. *Mach.* vi. 28-29).

[2] . . . ὥσπερ ἀντίψυχον γεγονότας τῆς τοῦ ἔθνους ἁμαρτίας καὶ διὰ τοῦ αἵματος τῶν εὐσεβῶν ἐκείνων καὶ τοῦ ἱλαστηρίου θανάτου αὐτῶν, . . . διέσωσεν. *Cp.* BOSSUET, *op. cit.* p. 181, and HOLTZMANN, *op. cit.* i. p. 68, and ii. p. 97.

CHAPTER IV

THE TEACHING OF ST. PAUL

IT is the merest commonplace to state that, among all the New Testament writers, St. Paul occupies an exceptional position on account of the number of his personal works and on account of his breadth of view. The Pharisee in coming over to Christ brought with him not only his generous and indomitable heart, but also a mind as remarkable for its width as for its depth; from that moment onwards he did not merely live after the fashion of the Christians, but he thought out and stated anew in his epistles, as occasion required, all the principal points of Christian doctrine, and this in such exact language that his formulæ are even now the basis of our theology. But of all the matters dealt with by the Apostle, that on which he lays most stress and which forms the very basis of his system is the mystery of the Atonement. As Harnack says: " Christ crucified and risen again is the central point, in fact the only source and the main principle of his teaching."[1] Holtzmann also has it that " St. Paul's Gospel consists essentially in the science of the Son of God's cross "[2]; and St. Paul himself writes to the Corinthians : " I judged not myself to know anything among you, but Jesus Christ, and him crucified " (1 *Cor.* ii. 2); and again : " We preach

[1] HARNACK, *Dogmengeschichte,* 3rd ed., i. p. 89.
[2] HOLTZMANN, *Lehrbuch der Neutestamentlichen Theologie,* ii. p. 97.

Christ crucified, unto the Jews indeed a stumbling-block and unto the Gentiles foolishness, but unto them that are called, both Jews and Greeks, the power of God and his wisdom " (*ibid.* i. 23-24 ; ii. 7).   Such statements as these are enough to show the necessity of examining first of all the doctrine of St. Paul on this matter, seeing that he considered it as the very mainspring of his Gospel.

I

The leading idea of St. Paul's theology on the Atonement is the reconciling of mankind to God through the cross of Christ.

The whole of mankind, Jews and Gentiles, had fallen into sin, and in consequence of this they were *ipso facto* condemned by God's Holiness and Justice to everlasting loss (*Rom.* ii. 2, 12 ; v. 16, 18) ; for it must be borne in mind that sin really made us foes of God (*Rom.* v. 10 ; xi. 28 ; *Col.* i. 21) and objects of His wrath (*Rom.* ii. 5, 8 ; *Eph.* ii. 3 ; 1 *Thess.* i. 10). Notwithstanding this, God had resolved to save us, and when the fulness of the time was come He made known to us the mystery of His will, which was to re-establish all things in Christ (*Eph.* i. 9-10).

St. Paul seems occasionally to describe the Atonement as the result of the Saviour's whole life-work. " God has reconciled us all to himself by Christ . . . for God indeed was in Christ reconciling the world to himself and not imputing to them their sins " (2 *Cor.* v. 18-19. *Cp. Eph.* ii. 4-8).   But the real act of reparation was Christ's death on the cross.   " When we were enemies we were reconciled to God by the death of his Son " (*Rom.* v. 10. *Cp.* 11).   St. Paul recalls to the Ephesians, how, before their conversion, being aliens from Israel, they were strangers to the Testament, having no hope of the promise, and without God in this world; 'but now in Christ Jesus, you, who some time were afar off, are made nigh by the blood of Christ; for he is our peace who *hath made both one, and breaking down the middle wall of partition*, the enmities in his flesh, making void the law of commandments contained in decrees, that he might *make the two in himself into one* new man, making peace, and might reconcile both to God in one body by the cross, *killing the enmities in himself*' (καὶ ἀποκαταλλάξῃ . . . τῷ θεῷ διὰ τοῦ σταυροῦ, ἀποκτείνας τὴν ἔχθραν ἐν αὐτῷ. *Eph.* ii. 11-16). It would seem that the " enmities," to which reference is made in concluding, are the same as those alluded to a moment before—*i.e.* the enmity constituted by the law separating the Jews from the Gentiles (λύσας τὴν ἔχθραν, ἐν τῇ σαρκὶ αὐτοῦ τὸν νόμον . . . καταργήσας) and not sin as it is sometimes thought. It would be wrong to give a double meaning to the expression used by the Apostle, for this could only result in ambiguity. What he is thinking of is the enmity between the Jews and the pagans. That they are also both enemies of God is not definitely stated though it is presupposed by the sequence of the argument; for we are told that Christ's death besides reuniting the two inimical portions of humanity, reconciles them both to God (*ibid.* 16) and that to this death they owe the recovery of peace and access to the Father (17-18).

To the Colossians St. Paul writes in a like strain: " In him [Christ] it hath well pleased the Father that all fulness should dwell, and through him to reconcile all things unto himself, making peace through the blood of his cross, both as to the things on earth and the things that are in heaven. And you, whereas you were some time alienated, and enemies in mind in evil works, yet now he hath reconciled in the body of his flesh through death to present you holy and unspotted and blameless before him ; if so you continue in the faith. . . ." (*Col.* i. 19-23). Here it is no longer a question of the Law but of sinful mankind, which by its sin had fallen away from God, but which has been restored and hallowed by the blood of Christ. In the next chapter the Apostle again expresses the same idea by means of a striking metaphor. " You, when you were dead in your sins and the uncircumcision of the flesh, he [the Father] hath quickened together with him [Christ], forgiving you all offences, blotting out the handwriting of the decree that was against us, which was contrary to us (τὸ καθ' ἡμῶν χειρόγραφον τοῖς δόγμασιν ὅ ἦν ὑπεναντίον ἡμῖν). He hath taken the same out of the way, fastening it to the cross " (*Col.* ii. 13-14). We incline to see in the *chirographum*, which has been so variously interpreted,[1] God's condemnation of sin. Some indeed have considered that it should be applied to the Mosaic Law ; but we must bear in mind that St. Paul is not addressing Jews, and that moreover, as all men are involved in the decree of which he speaks, it can be naught else than the sentence passed on sinners, that debt contracted by Adam in which we too become partakers by our sins. This fatal document was blotted out by Christ's death and attached to the cross just as any other cancelled deed might be stuck on a file. In yet another epistle St. Paul writes similarly, though here he omits the instance ; in his letter to the Thessalonians he speaks of " Jesus who hath delivered us from the wrath to come " (1 *Thess.* i. 10).

---

[1] CORNELIUS A LAPIDE gives seven several explanations.

It thus becomes apparent that according to St. Paul our reconciliation is due to a free act of God's love, but that in God's plans it required the death of Christ. God did not will to restore us to His grace by an act of free pardon ; in His goodness He willed to manifest His justice too, by making our reconciliation conditional on a complete and real atonement.

II

Under the olden dispensation God's Justice did not appear ; it was indeed there but it did not make its presence felt. God looked on seemingly unconcerned at the triumph of sin. (*Cp. Acts* xiv. 15 and xvii. 30.) Now however the time had come to make His Justice manifest to all, and this was the reason why He decreed the death of His Son. This is the teaching of the oft-quoted passage from the epistle to the Romans : " Being justified freely by his grace through the redemption that is in Christ Jesus, whom God hath proposed to be a propitiation (ὃν προέθετο ὁ θεὸς ἱλαστήριον) through faith in his blood to the showing of his justice for the remission of former sins ; through the forbearance of God for the showing of his justice in this time, that he himself may be just, and the justifier of him who is of the faith of Jesus Christ " (*Rom.* iii. 24-26). The expressions here used by St. Paul, being more remarkable for their strength than for their lucidity, have called forth numerous commentaries ; the majority of experts, whether Catholics or Protestants, have however finally come to the conclusion that by the word ἱλαστήριον St. Paul intends not (as Ritschl opined) the propitiation of the older Law, but a real atoning sacrifice by which

God was to be reconciled to sinners.[1] God, by Christ's work of salvation, intended to make satisfaction to His Justice [2] (προέθετο ἱλαστήριον . . . εἰς ἔνδειξιν τῆς δικαιοσύνης). There is no doubt that the Justice which is mentioned here refers to some action, taken by God regarding sin, which the Apostle contrasts with the forbearance shown by God in the past. This, however, does not necessarily imply, as Cornely has it, that the act in question was in the nature of that strict vindictive justice " which visits every sin with adequate punishment and thus restores the order which had been upset." [3] Such an interpretation of the word seems to us to be in conflict with the context and with the Pauline vocabulary. As used by St. Paul the word justice is taken in its most general meaning to signify the overflowing Holiness of God, which is ever opposed to sin and which by its overflow procures our justification (εἰς τὸ εἶναι αὐτὸν δίκαιον καὶ δικαιοῦντα τὸν ἐκ πίστεως Ἰησοῦ. *Ibid.* 26. *Cp.* 21-22). It stands to reason that vindictive justice is comprised in this as a part in the whole; but it is none the less evident that St. Paul's text excludes it. Rigorous justice demands that the guilty shall be requited with a proportionate penalty. Now this is just what God did not do, for He chose another means of manifesting His justice—viz. to atone by the blood of Christ for all the evil done. In this wise did God show His horror for sin without punishing the sinner. As Stevens rightly observes, " God in His grace adopts

---

[1] *Cp.* CORNELY, *In Ep. Rom.* (Paris, 1896), p. 190; HOLTZMANN, *op. cit.* ii. p. 103. SANDAY, *The Epistle to the Romans* (5th ed., Edinburgh, 1902), pp. 87-88. *Cp.* p. 91.

[2] Though He freely chose to do so. Holtzmann is wrong in insinuating the contrary.

[3] *Op. cit.* pp. 196-197. *Cp.* p. 193.

D

another course of procedure with sinful man than that
of retributive justice." [1]   If it be true, as Mgr. Simar
says, that "this sentence of the Apostle was the germ
of all subsequent speculations on the doctrine of the
Atonement," [2] care should have first been taken to
understand it rightly.

We find elsewhere similar views expressed by St.
Paul, but with no allusion to justice.   For instance
he says : " God sending his own son in the likeness of
sinful flesh, and of sin, hath condemned sin in the
flesh " (*Rom.* viii. 3), which means that the Son of
God became incarnate to offer His body as a sacrifice
for our sins ; at least this is the interpretation generally given to this obscure text of the Vulgate, one
which gave great trouble to ancient commentators. [3]
In another passage St. Paul says of God that "he
spared not even his own son, but delivered him up
for us all " (*Rom.* viii. 32).   And yet again : " Him
that knew no sin for us *he hath made sin* that we
might be made the justice of God in him " (2 *Cor.*
v. 21).   This strong expression is scarcely to the
liking of those rationalist theologians who are still
anxious to appear disciples of the Apostle.   One of
Ritschl's disciples, Ecklin, can see in the sentence last
quoted nothing more than " a piece of word-play or
kind of fugue performed by St. Paul." [4]   Those who
admit the realism of the Atonement do not find in it
any such difficulty.   Whether we translate the verse,
as many interpreters from St. Augustine down to

---

[1] *The Theology of the New Testament* (Edinburgh, 1901), p. 411.
Cp. HOLTZMANN, *op. cit.* p. 101.

[2] *Die Theologie des heiligen Paulus* (Freiburg, 2nd ed., 1883),
p. 119, n. 3.

[3] *Cp.* CORNELY, p. 401 ; SANDAY, p. 193 ; HOLTZMANN, p. 104.

[4] Quoted by GRÉTILLAT, *op. cit.* p. 344 *f.*

Franzelin have done, as 'God made him sin—*i.e.* a sacrifice for sin,' or whether we choose to render it like most moderns do, as 'God dealt with him as with a sinner—*i.e.* as the personification of sin'—an interpretation which by the way seems preferable, as it preserves the antithesis which St. Paul wished to make—in either case the "fugue" seems to us to be in thorough keeping with the tone of the whole Pauline teaching.

A parallel text to the last is the well-known one from the epistle to the Galatians. "Christ hath redeemed us from the curse of the law, being made a curse for us, for it is written: cursed is everyone that hangeth on a tree" (*Gal.* iii. 13). Here St. Paul is speaking to Jews, and he reminds them that because they have transgressed the Law, they have fallen under its curse (*ibid.* 10). This curse of the Law is a particular and more acute instance of the curse which through sin afflicts every man without exception. Hence the Apostle is careful to point out that this curse has been removed by a special act. The Law ordained (*Deut.* xxi. 22-23) that the body of the condemned should be hanged on the gibbet, and on such a death a curse was pronounced. Christ took upon Himself this outward curse to deliver us from the real curse that was upon us. Thus did St. Paul, by an *ad hominem* argument, turn the point of the objection of the Jews, who were scandalised at Christ's death on the cross.

We scarcely need point out that this curse on Christ was not real and that He remained all along the innocent Victim "who knew not sin" (2 *Cor.* v. 21), and who consequently, far from ever having been the butt of God's wrath, never ceased being precious in the sight of His Father (*Eph.* v. 2). His death was not the penalty of His own faults, but the punishment and Atonement for ours. "For our sins he was delivered," writes St. Paul, evidently alluding to *Isaias* liii. 4-5 (*Rom.* iv. 25). This is what is sometimes called the legal side of St. Paul's conception. A. Sabatier rightly calls our attention to it. "There is according to Paul's theology a positive substitution and exchange which takes place between Christ and the sinners whom He saves by His death ; He suffers and dies for them and in their lieu." [1] But it would be wrong to consider this aspect to the exclusion of the rest. St. Paul sees in the work of the Atonement much more than a mere transposal of a penalty. We have already pointed out that he does not speak of vindictive justice and that in his view Christ's death is not a mere punishment but a real Atonement. In other words, in his mind the idea of Christ's substitution for the sinner holds a secondary place. In order that God should be reconciled with man and His Justice appeased, the Apostle considers that something else is needed besides the legal formalities of substitution—namely, the self-devotion and the voluntary sacrifice of Christ. This is a matter which we shall now labour to make more evident.

III

So far we have confined ourselves to considering, in the plan of the Atonement, the work of the Father, whose sovereign Will presides over the whole affair of our Salvation. But the Son's Will also had its task to perform, by freely and generously accepting the Father's plan ; this it is which makes the merit of His sacrifice and the basis of our reconciliation.

[1] *Op. cit.* p. 28. *Cp. l'Apôtre Paul*, pp. 324, 357, 400 *f.*

St. Paul reminds us that Christ's life was a long-drawn act of self-denial. " Christ did not please himself" (*Rom*. xv. 3). " Being rich he became poor for your sakes, that through his poverty you might be rich." (2 *Cor*. viii. 9). " Who being in the form of God . . . emptied himself, taking the form of a servant, being made in the likeness of men " (*Phil*. ii. 6-7). His death especially was His highest act of obedience, for " he humbled himself, becoming obedient unto death, even to the death of the cross ; for which cause God hath exalted him, giving him a name which is above all names " (*ibid*. 8-9). Hence the death of our Saviour, which had been decreed from all eternity by the Father, was willingly consented to by the Son.

We thus understand better the meaning of that expression which in one form or another we meet so often in the Apostle's writings : Christ died for us. Christ's was no mere passive death, but a death actively willed and accepted. " Who died for us . . . that we may live together with him " (1 *Thess*. v. 10). " Christ died for all that they also who live may not now live to themselves but unto him who died for them and rose again " (2 *Cor*. v. 15). " Why did Christ when as yet we were weak according to the time die for the ungodly ; for scarce for a just man will one die, yet perhaps for a good man some-one would dare to die ; but God commendeth his charity towards us, because when as yet we were sinners according to the flesh, Christ died for us " (*Rom*. v. 6-9). And then the Apostle enters further into details. " Christ loved the Church and delivered himself up for it that he might sanctify it " (*Eph*. v. 25-26). He delivered Himself for the sake of each of our brethren, and this accounts for the grievousness of scandal. " Destroy not him with thy meat for whom Christ died " (*Rom.* xiv. 15 ; 1 *Cor.* viii. 11). The Apostle even goes on to apply this to himself. " Christ Jesus came into this world to save sinners, of whom I am the chief " (1 *Tim.* i. 15) ; He " loved me and delivered himself for me " (*Gal.* ii. 20), and to those who inquire for the ultimate reason of this death St. Paul replies that it was our sin ; He died for our sins, generously giving His life for our deliverance (1 *Cor.* xv. 3 ; *Gal.* i. 4).

One and the same idea clearly emerges from all these texts—namely, that Christ's death was an act of loving obedience and at the same time a willing gift. Here we touch the very bottom of the mystery ; Adam's rebellion was repaired by the submission of the Son of God. " For as by the disobedience of one man many were made sinners, so also by the obedience of one many shall be made just " (*Rom.* v. 19). The Atonement which had been decreed by God's Justice was performed by a sublime act of obedience and love. If Christ's death was " a sacrifice to God for an odour of sweetness," this was because Christ loved us so much as to deliver Himself for our sakes (*Eph.* v. 2). If His death has a right to be called a sacrifice, this is first and foremost because it was an act of the highest moral worth.

Holtzmann, who at all costs wishes to bring St. Paul's doctrine down to a merely legal proceeding, naturally refuses to see in the Apostle's texts any idea of voluntary sacrifice. He considers this idea as a convenient integration (*eine wohlthätige Ergänzung*) due in the first instance to the author of the epistle to the Ephesians and afterwards adopted in the writings attributed to St. John and St. Peter.[1] Yet St. Paul

[1] *Op. cit.* ii. p. 105. *Cp.* p. 113.

in two passages tells us clearly enough (*Gal.* i. 4 ; ii.
20) that Christ delivered Himself for us, and according to the principle laid down in the epistle to
the Philippians (ii. 8.   *Cp. Rom.* v. 19), he everywhere
takes it for granted that Christ's death was a willing
one.   Holtzmann simply shuts his eyes to these facts ;
they are sufficient to dispose of his system, for what
he considers as a novelty appearing for the first time
in the epistle to the Ephesians is simply a new expression of the Apostle's fundamental idea.   If we only
consent to see things as they are, there can be no
question of any shortcomings which were made up
for in the subsequent apostolic writings.

If we have succeeded in showing how, according to
St. Paul, the Atonement was accomplished, not by
a merely penal substitution, but by a free act of
Christ's love, we shall have already disposed implicitly
of a verbal difficulty with which Catholic theology
has been far too long occupied.   Critics have pointed
out that in the rendering of the sentence 'Christ
died for us' the Greek preposition used is in one
instance περί (1 *Thess.* v. 10) and everywhere else
ὑπέρ, and that both are translated by the Vulgate as
"*pro.*"   From Socinus down to Ritschl our opponents
have used these words as arguments against us ;
they argue that these prepositions mean "on account
of," "on behalf of," whereas to denote "instead of"
the Greek preposition should be ἀντί.   Hence what
the Apostle means is not that Christ died "in our
stead," but rather that His death was for our profit
and instruction.   If this be so, what becomes of
vicarious Satisfaction ?   The objection is all the more
striking in view of the fact that the other New
Testament writers and all the Greek Fathers use
almost exclusively the self-same preposition ὑπέρ.

Theologians have naturally endeavoured to retain for this word its traditional meaning, but their efforts were not attended with equal success. Thus Perrone, utterly forgetful of the Greek, in order to prove that "*pro*" may stand for a substitution, quotes one doubtful text (1 *Cor.* i. 13), and others such as Luke xi. 11; Matthew ii. 22; xvii. 26, where evidently "*pro*" has the meaning he gives it, but where the Greek word used is ἀντί.[1] Bertrand—for we must remember that orthodox Protestants have also an interest in the question—quotes a few better-chosen texts (2 *Cor.* v. 15; *Philem.* 13), and whilst fully admitting that "ὑπέρ has a less exact and narrow meaning," he nevertheless considers that "generally speaking in the New Testament ὑπέρ is synonymous with ἀντί."[2] He lays great stress on 2 *Cor.* v. 14: "*Si unus pro omnibus* (ὑπὲρ πάντων) *mortuus est, ergo omnes mortui sunt,*" and argues as follows:—Since all died by the death of one, He must have died *in their stead*; this conclusion is rendered necessary by logic; were it otherwise Paul's conclusion should be: If one died for all (for the good of all) therefore all live. This rather subtle argument is to be found in other writers, but unfortunately it is based on a wrong translation. The original text can be, and in fact must be, rendered: One died for all, therefore all were dead[3]; taken in this light the words fit the context and agree with the general trend of the Apostle's thought.

Moreover against the few texts which allow of the

---

[1] Perrone, *Prælect. Theol. De Incar.* pars IIᵃ, c. vi. Obj. 1ᵃ, ad 3ᵐ.

[2] *Op. Cit.* p. 333.

[3] This is the meaning given to the text by Chrysostom, 2 *Cor.* Hom. xi. 1-2—*P.G.* lxi.; col. 474-476.

meaning in question being given to ὑπέρ—we might add *Heb.* v. 1 to those referred to by Bertrand—we must set the many others which formally exclude this meaning.[1] We can only infer that the meaning of the word is rather complex and that it might with fair accuracy be rendered as "in behalf of." This however does not make our position untenable. Even Billuart was early in the field to point out that the idea of substitution is found less in the Apostle's words than in the trend of his thought.[2] At any rate, as we have seen, it is so clearly expressed that we have no reason to tarry longer over its vocabulary.

We should moreover be losing our time and our labour, for doubtless if the Apostle never made use of the preposition ἀντί, this was because he did not wish to express the idea which this word conveys. In effect it would be inexact to state without qualification that Christ died in our stead. As Stevens rightly observes, the idea of substitution is too delicate a one to be expressed in so brief and brutal a formula.[3] Hence in the New Testament—and the same is also usually true of the Fathers—we find the preposition ἀντί used only when its use is demanded by the word "ransom" (λύτρον ἀντὶ πολλῶν. MARK x. 45; MATT. xx. 28). Everywhere else ὑπέρ is the technical word used. Indeed it would be difficult to find a better, for this preposition pre-eminently befits a voluntary action entered on with due consideration of the end. Ἀντί would rather mean a material equivalence, ὑπέρ on the other hand denotes an intention and implies

---

[1] *Gal.* i. 4; *Heb.* vii. 27; x. 12; *Rom.* viii. 31, 34; ix. 3; 2 *Cor.* xii. 10, 15, etc.

[2] "Nos non facere vim in particula *pro* seu ὑπέρ præcise, sed cum adjunctis et circumstantiis." *De Incarn.* Diss. xix. art. iv.

[3] *Op. cit.* p. 410.

an act of the will. We are thus led back to the Apostle's deepest thought by understanding aright his vocabulary. The Socinian objection, which might be valid when used against a narrower conception of the Atonement, is of no avail against us ; far otherwise, we profit by it for it enables us to see how the very *minutiæ* of St. Paul's language hint at the entirely voluntary character of Christ's sacrifice. Grammar and logic meet in harmony, and inform us that Christ died for us—*i.e.* for the sake of us and of our sins ; this act of love it is which saves us.

IV

Christ's sacrifice gained its end ; it was efficacious ; St. Paul describes for us its principal results. The first, one which comprises all the others, is God's reconciliation with mankind generally, a reconciliation which applies to each of us individually. We are made partakers of Christ's righteousness just as we had been made partakers in Adam's sin (*Rom.* v. 18, 19) ; we have been reconciled and justified by Christ's blood (*Rom.* v. 9-10.) It is not our business to show here that this justification involves in St. Paul's thought an inner cleansing of the soul.

In other passages St. Paul uses in a like meaning the word "redemption." All are justified freely by his grace "through the redemption that is in Christ Jesus" (*Rom.* iii. 24); unto all of us Christ is made " wisdom, and justice, and sanctification, and redemption" (1 *Cor.* i. 30). It is impossible not to notice how the two ideas, of sanctity and of the liberation from bondage signified by the word redemption, are brought together, and this collocation of the two ideas suggests that in St. Paul's mind Christ redeems us by sanctifying us.

St. Paul, as though dissatisfied with such weak expressions, goes further and uses literally the metaphor of redemption : " You are bought with a great price " (1 *Cor.* vi. 20), and the context even increases the force of the statement. The Apostle is striving to show the wickedness of fornication. " Know ye not that your members are the temple of the Holy Ghost who is in you, whom you have from God, and that you are not your own but have been bought with a great price ? " Farther on St. Paul argues likewise when endeavouring to show how faith has transfigured the old social ranks. " He that is called in the Lord being a bondman, is the freeman of the Lord ; likewise he that is called being free, is the bondman of Christ ; you are bought with a price, be not made the bondslaves of men " (1 *Cor.* vii. 22-23).

This great price is Christ Himself, " who gave himself a redemption [1] for all " (ὁ δοὺς ἑαυτὸν ἀντίλυτρον ὑπὲρ πάντων. 1 *Tim.* ii. 6).

The bondage whence we are redeemed by Christ is that of sin. Echoing the words of Christ, " whosoever committeth sin is the slave of sin " (JOHN viii. ; 34), St. Paul teaches that sin is a real bondage (*Rom.* vi. 16-17, 20 ; vii. 14). Hence in his language redemption is synonymous with the remission of sins ('Εν ᾧ ἔχομεν τὴν ἀπολύτρωσιν, τὴν ἄφεσιν τῶν ἁμαρτιῶν. *Col.* i. 14 ; *Eph.* i. 7). " Christ gave himself for us that he might redeem us from all iniquity and might cleanse to himself an acceptable people " (*Tit.* ii. 14). This " acceptable people " is the " Church . . . which

---

[1] Stevens is right in observing that this expression must not be taken literally, that it should be looked on as a forcible and touching figure of Christ's love for us. *Op. cit.* p. 412.

he purchased with his own blood" (*Acts* xx. 28), and sanctified, presenting it to himself as a spouse without blemish (*Eph.* v. 25-27).

According to the Apostle's well-known teaching, the Mosaic law aggravated the slavery of sin; hence he takes care to point out that Christ's death delivers us from this other bondage also (*Rom.* vii. 4; *Gal.* iii. 13; iv. 5) and bestows on us true freedom (*Gal.* iv. 31; v. 13). Sin too had made us captives of the devil (2 *Tim.* ii. 26). Christ overthrew this sovereignty, and His cross was as it were a triumphant chariot behind which He dragged his vanquished foe (*Col.* ii. 15). Lastly, death too reigned over us, and this frequently serves the Apostle as a figure comprising all the dreadful results of sins. By His death and resurrection Christ destroyed also death (2 *Tim.* i. 10). Victory however will not be complete until the day of the last resurrection, when the devil and death having received their finishing blow, Christ will establish His kingdom with the elect (1 *Cor.* xv. 24-27), and our bodies will receive incorruptibility (*Rom.* viii. 23; 1 *Cor.* xv. 54-58), a complete redemption of which here below grace gives us only the promise and the assurance (*Eph.* iv. 30). Such is the power of Christ's death; it redeems us, and sanctifies us, and restores us to favour and to the hope of everlasting life, and obtains for our very bodies a state of immortality. St. Paul shows us that Calvary occupies the centre of God's plan. Sin had established between God and man an obstacle which the latter could not remove. This obstacle it was which Christ removed by offering as a dutiful act of obedience to His Father the expiation of His death. This sacrifice of the Innocent was needed to bring men again into contact with God, but, once offered, the pardon of the guilty was immediately assured, and Salvation became something which all could secure.

But for us to secure our Salvation and the application of Christ's merits, some labour is required of us; it remains for us to make our own that Atonement of which God has furnished us the means.

The principal way of applying to ourselves the benefit of the Atonement is Faith (*Rom.* iii. 25. *Cp. Col.* i. 23), and, as we know, by Faith the Apostle means no mere trust or fruitless belief, but a life fruitful with works of Salvation; for Christ died for us not only to give us life (1 *Thess.* v. 10) but also that we might give Him ours (2 *Cor.* v. 15). St. Paul sees in our Saviour's death the spring of all virtues; by an example stronger than any preaching it teaches us the love of God (*Rom.* v. 8; 2 *Cor.* v. 14); confidence in His goodness (*Rom.* viii. 32); conjugal love (*Eph.* v. 25); forgiveness of injury (*ibid.* iv. 32); and especially the spirit of sacrifice, which should lead us to fill up what is wanting in Christ's Passion (*Col.* i. 24); in a word, it teaches us to devote our whole soul to God and to our brethren (*Gal.* ii. 20; *Phil.* ii. 4-5). Christ dead and risen again becomes in the eyes of St. Paul a kind of type with which we must make ourselves one; the Christian is "buried together with him by baptism into death"; in words, none the less striking for all their mixture of metaphors, he tells us that, "having been planted together in the likeness of death," the Christian must rise again and lead a new life; that as Christ died once and now dies no more so also must His follower be dead to sin (*Rom.* vi. 3-15). St. Paul never tires recalling this transformation, this resurrection of the Christian soul which becomes its duty as soon as it "puts on Christ" at baptism (*Gal.* iii. 27; *Col.* iii. 1-3; *Eph.* iv. 22-24; *Rom.* vii. 6; viii. 9-13; 2 *Cor.* v. 17).

Modern Protestants willingly make use of this moral teaching, but at all costs they would separate it from its dogmatic basis. Thus Holtzmann admits that this conception of the individual Christian's work is not in disagreement with the Apostle's conception of a quasi-legal Atonement, but he maintains that the former conception is independent of the latter (*nicht über und nicht untergeordnet*). He believes that the " Apostle's mysticism makes up for his legal reasoning."[1] But as a matter of fact St. Paul's thought stands in no need of correction provided only it be rightly understood; it is all one, and its mysticism is the outcome of its reasoning; if the believer should lead a new life, this is because his sins have been remitted, and this is effected by baptism, which applies to us the results of Christ's death by rehearsing it symbolically. How can we see in Christ's resurrection the type of our own, unless we admit that His death is the cause of our restoration?

" The so-called ' juristic ' and ' ethical ' theories of the Atonement are complementary to each other. Paul passes from one to the other with no sense of discrepancy,"[2] and the reason is that if Christ's death fulfilled the conditions which had been fixed by God for our salvation, it did so only because His death was the outcome of a moral act, and thus became a source of moral life. The objective reality of the Atonement is the condition of its subjective efficaciousness, and this is the reason why St. Paul, more than any other, laid stress on the cross.

[1] HOLTZMANN, *op. cit.* ii. pp. 116-120.

[2] G. FINDLAY, in HASTINGS' *Dictionary of the Bible*, art. *Paul the Apostle*, iii. p. 724.

Our summary of St. Paul's doctrine will have sufficed to show how rich and complex it is. He does not confine himself to reiterating the fundamental article of our faith by stating that salvation is in the cross; he wishes also to explain its supernatural potency, and this he does by making use of the ideas of ransom, sacrifice, reconciliation, and vicarious Satisfaction. There is no doubt that the Apostle was fond of showing these different aspects of penal substitution, but we cannot point out too often that he did not limit himself to doing this but that he rose to the idea of Satisfaction through obedience. Besides the legal aspect of the Atonement he knew how to discern in it a moral aspect; perhaps indeed the moral side of the matter was uppermost in his mind, for if Christ voluntarily substituted Himself for us this was not only to pay our debt, it was rather to make by His obedience amends for our rebellion, thus restoring to law and order in God's sight mankind, whose head He is. No doubt the mystery remains, but the Apostle has at least shown us how to find in it both love and wisdom.

To conclude, we cannot say that St. Paul had any theory properly so-called regarding the Atonement, though as occasion arose he suggested the principal schemes of doctrine which were later on to be used to express the reality of the Atonement. But he left us, what was better than any theory, certain simple and striking ideas which were as living and fruitful as the mystery they served to express; it is consequently not surprising that it was from St. Paul's principles, as from an unfailing spring, that both the piety and the theology of later generations continued to draw their inspiration.

CHAPTER V

THE BELIEF OF THE EARLY CHURCH—THE EPISTLE TO THE HEBREWS, ST. PETER, ST. JOHN

THE apostolic writings, other than those of St. Paul, are few in number and most of them convey moral instruction rather than explanations of doctrine. Hence, we find in them only slight indications of the belief prevalent among the earliest Christians concerning the Atonement; in fact, were it not for the framework furnished by St. Paul we should find it very difficult to cast the other apostolic dicta into doctrinal shape. There is however one exception; the epistle to the Hebrews deals professedly with Christ's Priesthood and Sacrifice; on this account it has a special importance for us and deserves to be dealt with apart, hence we shall first of all seek out the distinguishing mark of the doctrine embodied in this epistle.[1]

1

The object of the epistle to the Hebrews is to establish the superiority of the new Law over the old. The latter had indeed been instituted by God, and the writer is speaking to Jews who were thoroughly convinced of this; but he reminds them

[1] In dealing with the epistle to the Hebrews apart from the epistles of St. Paul we have no intention of prejudicating the question of authorship, we simply do so in order to conform ourselves to the views now held by Catholic scholars.

that this law "brought nothing to perfection" and that it was only the "bringing in of a better hope by which we draw nigh to God" (vii. 19). In proclaiming by the voice of His prophets the coming of a new covenant in which each one should have the law written in his heart and receive forgiveness of sins, God had already implicitly declared that the older Law was destined to pass away (viii. 7-13). Now, this setting aside is already a matter of the past, the Law having been rejected "because of the weakness and unprofitableness thereof" (vii. 18), and a new one established in its stead by Christ (viii. 6). The superiority of the new covenant is due more especially to the perfection of its Priesthood which is evinced by the grandeur of its Priest and the power of His Sacrifice.

Jesus Christ is the Priest; the first portion of the epistle proves and describes His Priesthood. "Every priest taken from among men is ordained for men in the things that appertain to God, that he may offer up gifts and sacrifices for sins; who can have compassion on them that are ignorant and that err, because he himself also is compassed with infirmity, and therefore he ought, as for the people, so also for himself, to offer for sins" (v. 1-4). Christ fulfilled these conditions; He who was the brightness of His Father's glory and the figure of His substance (i. 3), who by His Sonship was better even than the angels (i. 4-14), placed Himself below the angels and abased Himself even to us that He might die for all (ii. 9). His own children being partakers of the flesh, He also in like manner took flesh (ii. 14) and was made in all things like His brethren "that he might become a merciful and faithful high priest before God, that he might be a propitiation for the

E

sins of the people " (ii. 17-18. *Cp.* iv. 14). A priest must indeed be a man, but must be called by God. Christ too awaited His Father's call (v. 4-7).

For this reason Christ is a priest according to God's own mind, and we can approach the throne of grace full of confidence in His compassion (iv. 16) and in the power of His intercession, "for whereas he indeed was the Son of God, he learned obedience by the things that he suffered and became to all that obey him the cause of eternal salvation " (v. 8-9).

Not only is Christ a priest, he stands far above all others. This He owes not alone to the excellence of His person by which He is above Moses and the angels (iii. 3-7 ; i. 13-14 ; ii. 5-9), but also to the character of His priesthood. He is priest according to the order of Melchisedech (v. 10 ; vi. 20). This ancient and mysterious patriarch, who was " without father, without mother, without genealogy," is the perfect figure of the eternal priesthood of the Son of God (vii. 3). Melchisedech by receiving tithes of Abraham, showed that he was above the Levitical priesthood (vii. 4-11) ; still more so is this perfection exhibited in Christ, who owes His Priesthood to no law of carnal descent but to the power of indissoluble life (vii. 11-18). Christ, otherwise than the priests of the old Law, is immortal, " always living to make intercession for us " (vii. 23-26) ; He is the Holy Priest " who needeth not daily (as the others do) to offer sacrifices first for his own sins and then for the people's " ; in a word, the priests of the Law were men of infirmity, but, since, God has given us His Son, " perfected for evermore " (vii. 26-28).

The super-eminence of the new covenant may be perceived more especially in the sacrifice of its high Priest. The writer of the epistle describes with great

force the efficaciousness of this Sacrifice, but unfortunately with such lack of logical sequence that
Western minds can scarcely follow him.

The old covenant had been established in the blood
of victims which Moses sprinkled over the people,
over the tabernacle, and the sacred vessels ; moreover,
"almost all things, according to the law, are cleansed
with blood, and without shedding of blood there is
no remission " (ix. 16-22) ; Jesus established the new
covenant in His own blood; the old Law "had justifica-
tions of divine service and a worldly sanctuary " (ix. 1) ;
but whereas the priests entered each day into the
former tabernacle, the high priest only entered once
a year into the Holy of Holies, carrying in his hand
the blood of the victims offered for his sins and for
those of the people.   This proves that the perfect religion was not yet come and that the way to the Holy
of Holies was not yet manifest (ix. 2-9).   Christ showed
us this way when he entered into the more perfect
tabernacle not made with hands (ix. 11), where He now
appears for us in the presence of God (ix. 24. *Cp.* viii. 2).
The Jewish high priest offered the blood of imperfect
victims, which were unable to cleanse the conscience
(ix. 9), and which only resulted in the cleansing of
the flesh (ix. 13) ; it was not thus, with the blood of
goats and heifers, but with His own blood that Christ
entered into the Holies (ix. 12), for He ' offered himself unspotted unto God to cleanse our conscience.'
" Therefore he is the mediator of the new testament,
that by means of his death for the redemption of those
transgressions which were under the former testament,
they that are called may receive the promise of eternal
inheritance " (ix. 14-15).

The high priest was obliged to renew his offering
each year (ix. 25), but Christ offered Himself once

only, and this one offering was sufficient " to exhaust
the sins of many " (ix. 26, 28.   *Cp.* vii. 27).   Nothing
shows more clearly the impotence of the Law than
the frequent need of sacrifice and the absence of result ;
the sacrifices served rather to keep up the memory of
past sins than to obtain their remission (x. 1-4. *Cp.* 11) ;
the reason of this is that " it is impossible that with
the blood of oxen and goats sins should be taken
away " (x. 4).   Hence Christ, seeing that material
holocausts were no longer sweet to God, and obeying
His Father's will, offered Himself in lieu of them ;
" in which will we are sanctified by the oblation of
the body of Jesus Christ once for all " (x. 10).   After
this single offering Christ sits for ever on God's right
hand, " for by one oblation he hath perfected for ever
them that are sanctified " (x. 12-14. *Cp.* 18).   In this
wise we have secured through Christ's death that
forgiveness of sins and that sanctification of our souls
which had been vainly promised by the Law.   To
complete our summary we may remind the reader
of what the writer had said in beginning, that Christ
through His death destroyed " him who had the
empire of death, that is to say the devil," and delivered
them " who through fear of death were all their life-
time subject to servitude " (ii. 14-15).   But now our
redemption is secured to all eternity (ix. 12) ; our sins
are wiped out and we have the right of entry unto
God.   The writer is now free to draw his moral conclusions ; and to exhort his readers to trust in God
(x. 19-21. *Cp.* iv. 14-16), to fly sin (x. 26-30. *Cp.* vi.
4-10), to practise both faith and good works (x. 22-25.
Cp. vi. 1, 11-12), and to cultivate patience and self-
denial by following in the footsteps of the saints and
of our Saviour Himself (x. 35-36 ; xii. 1-4).
   Such are the leading ideas of the epistle to the

Hebrews. Much has been said of the mysterious relationship which the writer perceives between the old Law and the new, between the Levitical sacrifice and that of the Cross, between the shadow and the reality, of that mystic symbolism which has led most critics to believe that this epistle was addressed to Jews by an Alexandrine writer probably distinct from St. Paul. As Holtzmann well puts it : " Whereas Paul confines himself to dealing with the centre of the idea of sacrifice, the writer of the epistle to the Hebrews works round the periphery of the same idea and applies his symbolic interpretations to matters which are more or less accidental to the notion of sacrifice."[1] However this may be, both writers agree in contending for the reality of the sacrifice of the cross and of its effects. Hence we shall know what to think of the following statement of M. Sabatier :—
" What is most noticeable in the conception of this epistle [to the Hebrews], and what will be most fruitful in the future development of doctrine, is the fact that the *propitiation for sin is transferred from earth to heaven.* . . . Christ's death thus leaves the realm of history and assumes the character of a metaphysical act. . . . Instead of a drama enacted in the midst of human history and in the conscience of each believer, by means of which moral crisis the individual man or mankind in general is born anew, we here find merely a priestly function, a transcendent act of ritual purification performed outside of the world and connected by no link either with man's moral state nor with his development or end."[2] It is curious to note how these statements are traversed by Holtzmann. He writes : " Here [in *Hebrews*] expiation does not assume the

[1] *N.T. Theologie,* ii. p. 105.
[2] A. Sabatier, *op. cit.* pp. 36-37.

character of an act taking place between God and Christ, outside of sinners, but rather of the giving to man of a special power of sanctification."[1] Both Sabatier and Holtzmann are wrong in making no account of Christ's earthly and historical sacrifice, the reality of which they diversely explain away to make it fit into their respective systems, thereby robbing the Scripture of its true meaning. For if Christ continues to exercise in heaven, into which He entered by His own blood, that priestly function which M. Sabatier compares to " *the offering of a kind of ideal and divine Mass*," and if too He gives to our souls a power of sanctification, this is all because He offered Himself once for all as a sacrifice on the cross. M. Sabatier sees " plainly enough how this differs from the theory of St. Paul," but he wonders " why it took so long for exegesis to distinguish two ideas so radically different." We have a right to wonder both at M. Sabatier's astonishment and at his discovery. In effect, according to the writer of the epistle to the Hebrews, as according to St. Paul, salvation consists in the remission of sins, and this is only obtained by Christ's death. In *Hebrews* stress is laid on the voluntary, spontaneous side of this death and little is said, at least directly, as in St. Paul, concerning the legal view of expiation. It would however be wrong to see in this an essential difference,[2] for as we saw the Apostle does not stop short at the narrower idea of penal substitution, but enlarges it and explains it— he, too, by the idea of a voluntary offering.

What is really new in the epistle to the Hebrews is its making the whole scheme of the Atonement to

---

[1] *N.T. Theologie*, ii. p. 304.

[2] *Cp.* JACQUIER, *Histoire des livres du N.T.* i. p. 474 (Paris, 3rd ed., 1904). [English trans. by J. DUGGAN. London : Kegan Paul, 1907.]

tend towards the purification and sanctification of the individual soul, whereas St. Paul considers it rather as a reconciling with God of the whole of mankind generally. The epistle to the Hebrews is also particularly attached to the symbolism of the Levitical ritual, which the Apostle almost ignores ; putting aside certain rather far-fetched allegorical similes, we may say that *Hebrews* was the pioneer of traditional apologetics concerning the religious worth and prophetic meaning of the olden sacrifices. Thus the framework of the two writers is different, the ideas which occupy a secondary position in St. Paul's mind are here found to the front, but the underlying idea is the same in both, both writers maintain the unique and decisive character of Christ's death and its necessity in the economy of Salvation. The grand theology of the Apostle is in the epistle to the Hebrews commented on and enlarged, and is brought before the Jews under the rather one-sided aspect of Levitical symbolism. In this epistle the doctrine of the Atonement is restated for a special class of people in terms which they shall be able to grasp. We have in *Hebrews* an echo and a type of the early Christian preaching, or if the expression be preferred, the first *Passion*.[1]

II

After having considered the doctrinal synthesis contained in *Hebrews* it is now our duty to examine the meagre details to be found in the epistles of St. Peter and St. John ; in so doing we must avoid ascribing to these apostles a system which they

[1] [A local term denoting a sermon on Christ's sufferings preached on Good Friday. *Trans.*]

never expressed, but at the same time we must neglect none of the elements which lie scattered throughout their epistles.

According to St. Peter, Christ's blood cleanses us, and the faithful are blessed because they are pre-destined by the Father to be sprinkled with the blood of Christ (1 *Peter* i. 1-2). Christ is also our ransom: "You were not redeemed with corruptible things as gold and silver, from your vain conversation of the tradition of your fathers, but with the precious blood of Christ, as of a lamb unspotted and undefiled" (1 *Peter* i. 18-19). Elsewhere in the second epistle we are told that Christ is the master who bought us (2 *Peter* ii. 1). The allusion is evidently to our being freed from sin, of which we had been slaves, "for by whom a man is overcome, of the same also he is the slave" (*ibid.* 19).

Christ's death was also the expiation of our sins. He died for us, and doubtless His death forms an example which we are called upon to follow; St. Peter says this to induce the faithful to be patient especially under undeserved injury; nor does he stop short here, but proceeds to apply to Christ the words of Isaias concerning the Servant of the Lord. "Who did no sin, neither was guile found in his mouth. Who when he was reviled did not revile, when he suffered he threatened not, but delivered himself to him that judged him justly.[1] Who *his own self bore our sins in his body upon the tree*, that we being dead to sins should live to justice, by whose stripes you were healed" (1 *Peter* ii. 21-24). Of this text Beyschlag retains only the first portion, and thus reduces Christ's work to "the moral impression"

---

[1] Παρεδίδου δὲ τῷ κρίνοντι δικαίως. The Vulgate wrongly renders this as: "*Tradebat iudicanti se iniuste.* Who judged him unjustly."

aroused by His sufferings and death.[1] It is no doubt true, as St. Peter tells us, that Christ left us in His death an example of self-sacrifice, but then he also tells us that Christ bore our sins in His body on the cross. To take this expression otherwise than realistically we should have to do violence to the literal meaning of the text. Ritschl was nearer the truth when he said that the expression used is "very mechanical,"[2] but even putting aside what in the metaphor is too gross or 'mechanical' the meaning remains the same—namely, that Christ underwent on the cross the penalty of our sins in order to cure us of them. We have here the same penal substitution which we noticed in St. Paul, though here it is without the legal form which it had there. We again find the same idea farther on, and this time it is quite free from any imagery which might cause misunderstanding, the words used even suggesting the idea of reconciliation : "Christ died once for our sins, the just for the unjust, that he might offer us to God, being put to death indeed in the flesh, but enlivened in the spirit" (1 *Peter* iii. 18).

Hence St. Peter looks on Christ's death as the real cause of our salvation, and this because it furnished the expiation of our sins. What is new in this text is the applying of *Isaias* liii. to Christ, for it is thus evinced that the chapter in question was one of the sources drawn upon by the earliest theology on the Atonement.

In the writings of St. John we find the idea of a redemption effected by the death of Christ. In the canticle sung by the elect to the Lamb we find :

[1] *N.T. Theologie,* i. p. 396, quoted by STEVENS, *op. cit.* p. 302, note 1.

[2] E. BERTRAND, *op. cit.* pp. 109 and 355.

"Thou wast slain and hast redeemed us to God in thy blood out of every tribe" (*Apoc.* v. 9. *Cp.* xiv. 3-4). The very image of the Lamb which is so familiar to the Apocalypse—however it may have originated—is as it were a summary of the Atonement, "the Lamb being the symbol of obedient and self-denying love." [1] Christ's blood has yet another virtue, it cleanses us from our sins (1 *John* i. 7). We read in the Apocalypse: "Who hath loved us and washed us from our sins in his own blood" (i. 5); likewise in this same blood of the Lamb, as in a bath of Salvation, the elect had "washed their robes" (vii. 14. *Cp.* xxii. 14).

Christ came into the world to destroy sin. The Fourth Gospel has preserved the saying of St. John the Baptist: "Behold the Lamb of God, behold him who taketh away the sin of the world" (JOHN i. 29. *Cp.* 36). The writer of the epistle uses similar expressions: "He appeared to take away our sins" (1 *John* iii. 5). He appeared "that he might destroy the works of the devil" (*ibid.* 8). "He hath laid down his life for us and we ought to lay down our lives for the brethren" (*ibid.* 16). The writer of the Fourth Gospel had reported the involuntary prophecy of Caiaphas: "It is expedient for you that one man should die for the people and that the whole nation perish not." The high priest had unwittingly spoken under Divine inspiration, for, as the Evangelist adds, Jesus was to die for the nation, "and not only for the nation, but to gather together in one the children of God that were dispersed" (JOHN xi. 50-53. *Cp.* xviii. 14). In his epistle St. John takes up the same idea, explaining more fully the meaning of this death. "God is charity; by this hath the charity of God

[1] STEVENS, *op. cit.* p. 536.

appeared towards us, because God hath sent his only begotten Son into the world that we may live by him. In this is charity, not as though we had loved God, but because he hath first loved us and sent his Son to be a propitiation for our sins " (ἱλασμὸν περὶ τῶν ἁμαρτιῶν ἡμῶν. 1 *John* iv. 8-11). The Apostle had already written: " He is a propitiation (ἱλασμός) for our sins, and not for ours only, but also for those of the whole world " (*ibid.* ii. 2).[1] According to St. John also the world owes its salvation to Christ's death, and the Apostle, combining the data furnished by St. Paul and *Hebrews*, sees in His death a sacrifice which is at once an expiation and a purification.

III

We have thus found among the other apostolic writers of the New Testament precisely the same ideas on the Atonement as we found in St. Paul ; here and there we have even found like expressions. All of them agree in putting Christ's death in an essential relationship with the forgiveness of sins ; all of them agree in speaking of it as a ranson which delivers us, as an expiatory sacrifice which sanctifies us and brings us nearer to God. Indeed, on account of this similarity, it has been argued that all these ideas were really derived from St. Paul. We are told that it was St. Paul who, with his paradoxical mind and fearless faith, first excogitated and, heedless of Jewish susceptibilities, put before the faithful the doctrine of

---

[1] By comparing together the two texts, that of the Gospel and that of the Epistle, it will be easy to see the parallelism between the different expressions which convey the same idea. Whence it will appear that " voluntary and salutary death " was ever synonymous with " expiatory death."

the cross ; that it was from St. Paul that St. John and
St. Peter derived their ideas, and that backed up by
their authority, St. Paul's view ultimately became that
of the Church. This opinion has been recently adopted
by M. Loisy : " The earliest Christian community
was aware that Christ died on the cross. . . . But
His death and resurrection could be diversely understood, and we must beware of ascribing these different
views of the matter indiscriminately to the earliest
disciples, to Christ Himself, and to the Apostle of the
Gentiles. The statement we find in the epistle to
the Corinthians (1 *Cor.* xv. 3) does not at all prove
that the idea of an expiatory death existed from the
beginning *as clearly as we find it expressed in the
teaching of St. Paul.*" [1] With this qualification M.
Loisy's statement might be accepted as true, but a
little farther on he drops it when he writes : " The
first Christians softened the hard fact of Christ's death
by the glory of His resurrection. *Paul discovered* in
His death a meaning and an efficaciousness, which,
though co-ordinate with His resurrection, retain their
value independently of it." [2]

If by this M. Loisy only meant that St. Paul's
figures and vocabulary were adopted by the subsequent writers, then we might agree. The writer of
Hebrews, St. Peter, and St. John were acquainted
with St. Paul's writings and may well have made use
of them ; though this has not been conclusively proved
to be a fact, we should have no objection to accepting
Holtzmann's view on the matter.[3] But if it is M.

[1] *L'Évangile et l'Église*, 2nd ed., pp. 112-113. [English trans. by
HOME, *The Gospel and the Church*. London, 1903.]

[2] *Ibid.* p. 117. *Cp. Autour d'un petit livre*, p. 122.

[3] *Op. cit.* ; this writer speaks of *Hebrews* in ii. p. 286 ; of St. Peter
in ii. pp. 312-315 ; of St. John in ii. p. 477 *ff*.

Loisy's intention to insinuate that St. Paul is the originator of the doctrine itself, then we may appeal to history against the insinuation.   As Archbishop Mignot says [1]: "Judging from a merely human standpoint, can we believe that St. Paul's (and St. John's) religious ideas, in spite of the special character which the writers owed to their time and their education, were not a reflection of what was generally felt, a living echo of apostolic tradition?   How could St. Paul's personal ideas have become those of the Church? We must not forget that the Apostle's influence was far less than some fancy . . . and that his efforts received a set-back which lasted for a considerable time after his death."   Hence, even though we had no other proof, if we find both in St. Paul and the other Apostles the doctrine of an Atonement by the cross, we may safely conclude that they all derive their teaching from early tradition.

It is true that in *Acts* the forgiveness of sins is ascribed to Christ's whole mission rather than to His death in particular.   "Him hath God exalted with his right hand to be prince and saviour, to give repentance to Israel and remission of sins" (v. 31).   The same idea is expressed by St. Peter in all his discourse (ii. 38 ; iii. 19.   *Cp.* 26 ; iv. 12 ; x. 43), and curiously enough St. Paul too expresses himself likewise, though his grand view of justification is already becoming apparent.   "Through him forgiveness of sins is preached to you, and from all the things from which you could not be justified by the law of Moses ; in him everyone that believeth is justified" (xiii. 38-39. *Cp.* xxvi. 18 and 20).   Such sayings only inadequately express the mystery of the Atonement, but then is it

---

[1] *Tradition et Critique* in the *Correspondant,* 10th January 1904, p. 25.

right to seek a complete theology in a series of popular discourses? What was needed just then was not a scientific definition of the Atonement, but that souls should be made acquainted with the salvation procured by Christ and the forgiveness of sins which He had made possible. Inspiration by its action on the Apostles made them good preachers indeed; it was not a part of their ministry to be also theologians.

Moreover Christ's death, even in *Acts*, is something more than a common fact. The Apostles do not consider it merely in the light of a murder committed by the Jews; they see in it an event decreed by Providence (ii. 23; iv. 28) and predicted by the prophets (iii. 18; xiii. 27; xxvi. 23), and consequently a necessary part of the Messiah's career. It was the prophecies of the Old Testament, interpreted by means of the new faith, which deprived the " scandal of the cross " of its sting, and among all the older prophecies, that of *Isaias* liii. (*Acts* viii. 33-36) exerted a preponderating influence; for from it it was inferred that Christ died for our sins. This is the belief which St. Paul, far from having invented it himself, declares to have received (παρέλαβον ὅτι Χριστὸς ἀπέθανεν ὑπὲρ τῶν ἁμαρτιῶν ἡμῶν. 1 *Cor.* xv. 3).

Hence by unbiassed historians it must be accepted as an undeniable fact that the Apostle drew his doctrine of the Atonement from the traditions current among the early Christians [1]; in their turn these had drawn it from the teaching of Christ.

---

[1] Contra EVERETT and BEYSCHLAG ita STEVENS, *op. cit.* p. 270 *f.* HOLTZMANN, *op. cit.* p. 366 *f.*, who also quotes, as favouring the same view, WEIZSÄCKER and JOH. WEISS. Harnack is particularly categorical, he writes : " There is no historical fact more certain than that the Apostle Paul was not, as we might perhaps expect,

the first to emphasise so prominently the significance of Christ's death and resurrection, but that in recognising their meaning he stood exactly on the same ground as the primitive community. . . . Paul did, it is true, make Christ's death and resurrection the subject of a particular speculative idea, and, so to speak, reduced the whole of the Gospel to these events; but they were already accepted as fundamental facts by the circle of Jesus' personal disciples and by the primitive community " *Das Wesen des Christentums* (English trans. p. 154), *Dogmengeschichte* (1894), p. 80, also *Die Mission und Ausbreitung des Christentums* (1902), p. 64, note 4 [English trans. by Moffatt, *Expansion of Christianity*.   London, 1904].

CHAPTER VI

THE GOSPEL DATA

THE idea which pervades the whole Gospel is the idea denoted by the very word Gospel: the good tidings; similarly the work accomplished by Christ is all summed up in the very name He bears amongst us, that of *our Saviour*. The reason why this latter word is dear to every Christian heart is that no other is capable of expressing so well the mission which Christ undertook on earth. These terms were not chosen simply on account of their verbal fitness; but because there is in them a deeper meaning, and as we shall have occasion to see, the philosophy of language is here, as it so often is elsewhere, that of reality itself.

I

Christ nowhere expresses any view on the nature of sin, but we gather from His words that mankind had gone astray and that He came to save it. The shepherd leaves his ninety-nine sheep in the fold and goes to seek for the one which was lost (MATT. xviii. 12-13; LUKE xv. 1-8), in this parable Christ is manifestly describing Himself. He too came from afar to seek and save that which was lost (LUKE xix. 10).[1] When the Pharisees find fault with Him for consort-

---

[1] John records similar words: "God sent not his Son into the world to judge the world but that the world might be saved by him," iii. 17. *Cp.* xii. 47; MATT. xviii. 11; and LUKE ix. 56.

ing with sinners He merely replies : " They that are
well have no need of a physician, but they that are
sick " ; and in case this figure should be beyond the
comprehension of His hearers He adds : " For I came
not to call the just, but sinners " (MARK ii. 17 ;
MATT. ix. 12-13 ; LUKE v. 31-32).

The " sickness " from which men suffered was sin.
All men were affected by it though all were not
equally conscious of it. Those who felt it most were
the just ; they were no longer satisfied with the legal
purifications and they already long ago had been in-
structed by the prophets to seek a perfect forgiveness
of their sins in the future, when God would establish
a new covenant with His people (*Isaias* xxxiii. 24 ;
Jeremias xxxi. 33, 34). Hence though the majority
of the lower classes set their hopes on an earthly
reign of the Messias, more highly wrought minds had
already risen to the idea of a purely moral Kingdom
of God, and the deliverance they looked forward to
was, above all, the deliverance of their soul. " A
portion of the people had undoubtedly awakened to
the feeling that the kingdom of God presupposed a
moral condition of a corresponding character and that
it could come only to a righteous people. Some
looked to acquiring this righteousness by means of a
punctilious observance of the law, and no zeal that
they could show for it was enough ; others, under
the influence of a deeper self-knowledge, began to
have a dim idea that the righteousness which they so
ardently desired could itself come only from the hand
of God, and that in order to shake off the burden of
sin—for they had begun to be tortured by an inner
sense of it—divine assistance and divine grace and
mercy, were needful." [1]

[1] HARNACK, *Das Wesen des Christentums,* p. 86 [in English trans. p. 135].

F

St. Luke, in the persons of the old man Simeon
and the prophetess Anna, shows us types of such
souls who looked forward to the " consolation " and
" redemption " of Israel (LUKE ii. 25, 38) ; Zachary had
already greeted the dawn of this redemption in the
birth of his son. " Blessed be the Lord God of Israel
because he hath visited and wrought the redemption
of his people " (LUKE i. 68-69). No doubt Salvation
is to consist in Israel's deliverance from the hand of
its foes (*ibid.* 71, 74), but this ill-defined political character of the approaching deliverance is completed by
a much clearer allusion to its spiritual side : " That
being delivered from the hand of our enemies we
may serve him without fear, in holiness and justice
before him all our days. And thou, child, shalt be
called the prophet of the Highest for thou shalt go
before the face of the Lord to prepare his ways, to
give knowledge of salvation to the people unto the
remission of sins " ($\gamma\nu\hat{\omega}\sigma\iota\nu$ $\sigma\omega\tau\eta\rho\iota\alpha\varsigma$ . . . $\dot{\epsilon}\nu$ $\dot{\alpha}\phi\dot{\epsilon}\sigma\epsilon\iota$ $\dot{\alpha}\mu\alpha\rho\tau\iota\hat{\omega}\nu$
$\alpha\dot{\upsilon}\tau\hat{\omega}\nu$. LUKE i. 74-78. *Cp.* 16-17).

This was why the Baptist began by preaching the
baptism of penance for the remission of sins (MARK i.
4 ; LUKE iii. 3). The result of his preaching was
that the Jews, roused by his strange words, came to
be baptised confessing their sins (MARK i. 5 ; MATT.
iii. 6).

But the Baptist was only a forerunner ; and his
baptism in water was only a figure of the true
baptism in the Holy Ghost and fire (MARK i. 8 ;
MATT. iii. 11 ; LUKE iii. 16). The true Salvation,
God's own chosen one, was near at hand but still
all unknown. Inspired by the Holy Ghost, Simeon
had recognised the Saviour in the little child brought
by Joseph and Mary to be presented in the Temple
(LUKE ii. 30) ; the angels too had announced Him to

the shepherds of Bethlehem as the Saviour (LUKE ii. 11), and the archangel had imposed on Him a name symbolic of His mission: "Thou shalt call his name Jesus, *for he shall save his people from their sins*" (MATT. i. 21).

When Christ's public life began, the purport of His preaching was the promise of an approaching deliverance from sin. This is the weight of which He promises to relieve those who come to Him: "Come to me all you that labour and are burdened and I will refresh you" (MATT. xi. 28). The cures which He performed on ailing bodies were not merely tokens of His kindness but also symbols of the cure of souls; we all know how after-tradition delighted in drawing out this symbolic meaning. It was to show this that He applied to Himself the text of Isaias: "The spirit of the Lord is upon me, therefore he hath anointed me, to preach the gospel to the poor he hath sent me, to heal the contrite of heart. To preach deliverance to the captives and sight to the blind, to set at liberty them that are bruised, to preach the acceptable year of the Lord and the day of reward" (LUKE iv. 18-19. *Cp. Isaias* lxi. 1-2; lviii. 6).

All these figures of speech are used more especially to indicate the healing of sin, man's great spiritual ailment. Christ Himself took pains to point this out when He healed the paralytic, and His words are recorded by the three synoptists. Being moved by the man's faith He declared his sins forgiven; and when the Jews affected to be scandalised at this usurpation of Divine power, He immediately healed his bodily ailment also; "that you may know that the son of man hath power on earth to forgive sins, he saith to the man sick of the palsy, 'I say to thee,

arise, take up thy bed and go into thy house'" (MARK
ii. 5-12; MATT. ix. 2-7; LUKE v. 20-25). In like
manner He forgave the sins of the repentant woman
because of the great love she had shown (LUKE vii.
47-48. *Cp.* JOHN v. 14; viii. 11).

Thus we see that Christ does not, like the Baptist,
merely promise forgiveness of sins, He actually gives
it. At the same time He also teaches the conditions
of remission. By the parable of the publican He
shows that the sinner must have humility (LUKE
xviii. 10-15); by that of the prodigal son He shows
how the sinner may trust himself to God's kindness
(LUKE xv. 11-35); by that of the unmerciful servant
He shows that the sinner must himself be forgiving
(MATT. xviii. 35). He lays great stress on this latter
condition and warns us that God will measure His
pardon to us by the amount of forgiveness which we
ourselves bestow on our enemies (MARK xi. 25-26;
MATT. vi. 14-15; LUKE vi. 37). Indeed so much
did Christ hold to this idea that He even incorporated
it in the Lord's prayer (MATT. vi. 12; LUKE xi. 4);
lastly, all the dispositions pre-requisite for forgiveness
are summed up in " penance "—*i.e.* repentance and
heartfelt conversion (MARK i. 15; MATT. iv. 17. *Cp.*
LUKE xiii. 3-5 and MATT. xi. 20-21).

In fine all that Christ demands as a condition of
pardon for sin is a certain disposition of the will. It
was our duty to point out this peculiarity of the
Gospel preaching, but we shall see later on whether it
is true, as certain critics hold, that such a teaching
excludes any real atoning death. At any rate, from
the texts to which we have alluded, it is evident that
the world was waiting for Salvation and the remission of sins; and that Christ came to fill this need,
bringing with Him the hoped-for Salvation and

forgiveness. This is the first Gospel doctrine which must be borne in mind.

II

Another doctrine which we must now examine is the important position occupied in Christ's mind by the thought of His death. It seems certain that He foresaw it and accepted it beforehand as an essential part of His mission. Until lately the fact had not been controverted. No doubt historians had not been wanting who were willing to see in this a merely human anticipation, but even these considered that He freely and generously sacrificed His life for His cause. Recently, however, certain critics have ventured to express opinions at variance with this universal belief. According to these Christ had no wish to die ; being aware of His enemies' plans, even at the last moment He hoped to escape from them by fleeing to Galilee ; but His intention was spoilt by the treachery of Judas. We shall not tarry over this fanciful hypothesis which is wholly built on a wilful distortion of facts.[1] If our Gospels have the slightest value as historical documents, then one thing is certain, viz. that the presentiment of a violent death appears quite early in Christ's mind and that in the latter portion of His ministry it was never for a moment absent.

When beginning His preaching in Galilee, Christ had, however, avoided acquainting His disciples with

[1] Even M. Sabatier, who would have been pleased to welcome this hypothesis, is obliged to reject it for psychological and historical considerations. See ROSE, *Études sur les Évangiles,* pp. 244-248. [English translation by FRASER, *Studies on the Gospels.* London : Longmans, 1903.]

the tragic end in store for Him, fearing no doubt that this would be a source of scandal to them ; we only find a scarcely perceptible allusion in that sentence of His which the three Evangelists have preserved : " Can the children of the marriage fast so long as the bridegroom is with them ? . . . but the days will come when the bridegroom shall be taken away from them, and then they will fast " (MARK ii. 19-20 ; MATT. ix. 15 ; LUKE v. 35). Had they been so minded they might have seen in this a sign of the coming storm.

After the failure of the Galilean mission His predictions become more numerous and definite. Holtzmann opines that Christ made progress, and, under the pressure of historical circumstances, gradually rose to the idea of His death.[1] But there are no texts by which such a supposition could be proved ; on the other hand everything goes to show that the idea appeared suddenly and that at the moment of its appearance it was already perfect.[2] It first came on the scene after St. Peter's memorable confession ; Christ being now assured of the faith of His disciples thought the time come to disclose to them His future passion : " And he began to teach them that the son of man must suffer many things and be rejected by the ancients and by the high priests and the scribes, and be killed, and after three days rise again " (MARK viii. 31 ; MATT. xvi. 21 ; LUKE ix. 22). That this was Christ's first clear allusion to the matter is evident from the astonishment and dismay of the disciples : " And Peter taking him began to rebuke him ; who turning about and seeing his disciples,

[1] *N.T. Theologie*, i. p. 287.
[2] *Cp.* LEPIN, *Jésus Messie et Fils de Dieu d'après les Synoptiques* (Paris, 1904), p. 125.

threatened Peter, saying: Go behind me, Satan, because thou savourest not the things that are of God but that are of men" (MARK viii. 32-33; MATT. xvi. 22-23).

The three synoptists also record two other of Christ's predictions of His death. When all the people were in admiration at His deeds He chose the occasion to take His disciples apart and remind them of the coming catastrophe: "The son of man shall be betrayed into the hands of men and they shall kill him and after that he is killed he shall rise again the third day" (MARK ix. 30-31; MATT. xvii. 21-22; LUKE ix. 44-45). These words conveyed no intellegible meaning to the disciples, yet they forbore to ask Him for a fuller explanation; St. Matthew merely tells us that they became sad. Finally, when about to go up to Jerusalem for the last time, Christ took His disciples apart and told them again more clearly than ever what they were to expect: "Behold we go up to Jerusalem and the son of man shall be betrayed to the chief priests and the scribes; they shall condemn him to death and shall deliver him to the Gentiles, they shall mock him and scourge him and spit on him and shall put him to death and the third day he shall rise again" (MARK x. 32-35; MATT. xx. 17-20; LUKE xviii. 31-35.) It is easy to see that the last prophecy contains no more than the first. All these predictions are fundamentally, and in fact almost verbally, the same. The coming event is emphasised once more, but of real progress we find none.

Besides the threefold solemn prediction just alluded to, Christ made many allusions to His approaching end; thus the Baptist's death seemed to Him to forebode His own (MARK ix. 11; MATT. xvii. 12).

When the sons of Zebedee are smitten with ambition he tells them of the cup he has to drink (MARK x. 38; MATT. xx. 22). Even on Thabor He still seems obsessed with the same thought, for in the midst of the transient glory of the Transfiguration He spoke with Moses and Elias of His coming end (LUKE ix. 31). When He was told that Herod sought to put Him to death, he told the messengers to tell "that fox" that His hour had not yet come and that He must die at Jerusalem (LUKE xii. 32-33). He seems to long for this coming baptism of blood (*ibid.* 50). When the great week comes at last, He depicts Himself under the form of the Son whom the faithless husbandmen put to death (MARK xii. 7-8; MATT. xxi. 38; LUKE xx. 14-15); He informs His disciples that this will be His last Passover (MATT. xxvi. 2); in the ointments with which Magdalene anointed His feet He perceived a preparation for His burial (MARK xiv. 8; MATT. xxvi. 12); lastly, after having foretold Judas's treachery and Peter's denial (MARK xiv. 18; MATT. xxvi. 21; LUKE xxii. 21; *Cp.* JOHN xiii. 21; MARK xiv. 27-32; MATT. xxvi. 31-36; LUKE xxii. 34), and after having drunk the parting draught of the "fruit of the vine" (MARK xiv. 25; MATT. xxvi. 29; LUKE xxii. 15-16), in His agony, He, in spite of its bitterness to His nature, accepted willingly the cup proffered by His Father (MARK xiv. 34-42; MATT. xxvi. 37-47; LUKE xxii. 40-47) and delivered Himself of His own accord into the hands of His foes.

At least this is what we read in the Gospels, but maybe for some reason or other these texts are not esteemed sufficient by critics. In effect M. Loisy says[1]: "After Simon Peter's profession of faith

---

[1] *L'Évangile et l'Église,* 2nd ed., p. 85.

Christ is *supposed* to have spoken on several occasions with His disciples concerning the fate which awaited Him as Messias. But in these passages we find no saying which is formally stated to have been uttered by Christ." The "general purport" of these texts is moreover "moulded on past events and on the theme of the early Christian preaching." M. Loisy therefore considers himself justified in setting aside a whole series of texts to be found throughout the Gospel story. As his conclusion appears to us to be hardly warranted, and until cause can be shown for a different view being adopted, we prefer to believe on the authority of the Gospel that Christ foresaw His death and that He foretold it to His disciples as an event which had to come to pass.

It is not unusual for historians to explain this necessity by the concatenation of circumstances, thereby bringing the prophecy down to a mere human premonition. At the outset of His ministry Christ had hoped to convert the people quite easily, but the passive resistance of the stationary mass of public opinion and the active hostility of the Pharisees soon undeceived Him. He then began to understand that He would have to struggle and suffer and that death would be the "historically inevitable end of His career owing to the turn which His life and work had taken." With the generosity of every hero He accepted this outcome of His mission, nevertheless "Jesus felt that He was still in the contingent realm of history and to the very end He sought the removal of the bitter chalice." [1] But there are other possible explanations of the episode during Christ's Agony which are not only nobler but more consonant with that perfect submission "when in the presence of

[1] SABATIER, *op. cit.* p. 23 *f.*

God's mysterious ways" which M. Sabatier kindly concedes to Christ; our author, without leaving historical ground, had he but used a less commonplace psychology, might have perceived in it an instance of the painful struggle which accompanies sacrifice even in the most generous will. Holtzmann, who sets out from a like historical point of view, has at least the merit of stating explicitly that the obligation of dying was taken by Christ as part of the Divine will and that He accepted it as such not only freely but affectionately. He however maintains that this death must not be considered as an "*a priori* necessity" of the Messiah's calling, but as a merely "contingent and *per accidens* necessity" depending mainly on the circumstances in which Christ took upon Him this mission.[1] This hypothesis which preserves all the importance and moral worth of Christ's sacrifice would be of a nature to satisfy Christian piety and would at a stretch be sufficient for our purposes. But judging by the Gospel texts it is quite clear that, as understood by Christ, the thought of His death had just that character of which Holtzmann seeks to deprive it.

If it be true that in the latter two predictions Christ only uses the future: "The son of man shall be delivered," it is a point worthy of notice that in the first prediction He had used a term implying necessity. "The son of man *must* [δεῖ] suffer many things . . . and be killed" (*Cp.* LUKE xvii. 25). Whence arises this necessity? Christ's answer to St. Peter already implies that there is here a mystery of God (οὐ φρονεῖς τὰ τοῦ Θεοῦ), a fact which is more manifestly hinted at in the words given by St. Luke. "All things shall be accomplished which were written by the prophets

[1] *N.T. Theologie*, i. p. 288 *f. Cp.* p. 291.

concerning the son of man" (LUKE xviii. 31). We also find in St. Mark: "It is written of the son of man that he must suffer many things" (ix. 11). And on the threshold of the Passion Christ several times repeated words to a like effect: "The son of man indeed goeth as it is written of him" (MARK xiv. 21; MATT. xxvi. 24). He warned His disciples of the approach of His foes by saying: "I say to you that this that is written must [δεῖ] yet be fulfilled in me, 'and with the wicked was he reckoned'" (Luke xxii. 37). He also gave a similar reason to prevent St. Peter from using his sword: "How then shall the scriptures be fulfilled that so it must be done" [οὕτως δεῖ γενέσθαι] (MATT. xxvi. 54. Cp. MARK xiv. 49).

All these texts point to the source of the obligation being in the sayings of the prophets, in which the Messias could read beforehand God's will with respect to Himself. According to St. Luke's account Christ Himself after His resurrection expounded to the disciples of Emmaus the meaning of these writings. "O foolish and slow of heart to believe in all things which the prophets have spoken. Ought not Christ to have suffered these things and so to enter into his glory? And beginning at Moses and all the prophets he expounded to them in all the scriptures the things that were concerning him" (LUKE xxiv. 25-28). He also used similar words when speaking to the assembled Apostles: "These are the words which I spoke to you while I was yet among you, that all things must needs [δεῖ] be fulfilled which are written in the law of Moses, and in the prophets and in the psalms concerning me. Then he opened their understanding that they might understand the scriptures, and he said to them, Thus it is written, and thus it behoved Christ to suffer and to rise again from the dead

the third day " (LUKE xxiv. 44-47).   Hence, whenever
Christ assigns a reason to His death, this is always
found in the fulfilling of God's will, as shown by the
Scriptures ; nowhere does He hint at any other reason.
As we have no right to put our own hypotheses in
lieu of facts we can only conclude as follows :—In
Christ's mind the thought of death was not a merely
human presentiment, nor was it bound up with a mere
contingency of His Messianic mission, rather, it was,
as Father Rose puts it, "an essential phase" of His
career.[1]   The Jews of course read these prophecies
otherwise, but Christ understood their real meaning
and saw in them God's injunction and the pre-arranged
program of His life.[2]   For this reason He had always
considered His death necessary, not *metaphysically
necessary*, as M. Sabatier makes us say—a necessity
which would here be devoid of meaning—nor merely
historically necessary, but as a necessary part of His
mission, as a duty inseparable from his functions as
Messias.   Not only did the death of the Messias seem
to impose itself on Him as a fact, it seemed also
obligatory as a duty.

III

Must we go further and bring His death into some
relationship with the salvation of mankind ?—two
series of ideas which we have seen developing so far
independently of one another.   Did Christ ever express any opinion as to the Atoning value of His
sacrifice ?   We must admit that the Gospel gives us

---

[1] *Op. cit.* p. 252.

[2] See ROSE, *op. cit.* p. 250.   *Cp.* 257.   " This duty is bound up with
the office of Messias which had devolved on Christ.   To die is one
of the duties of His life-giving mission."

little information on the subject; among the many passages in which Jesus speaks of His death, two only speak of its use : the narrative of the Last Supper and the well-known text of MARK x. 45; MATT. xx. 28. With these two passages criticism has played havoc; and M. Loisy, to mention but one critic, has called their authenticity into question.

" The idea . . . that there is in the sufferings of the Just a cleansing expiation . . . is a symbolic conception in which *we must not be in too great a hurry* to see a statement of absolute truth abiding permanently, in this particular form, in man's consciousness. This conception is indeed found in the Second Isaias, but *it has yet to be proved* that it belongs to Christ's teaching. . . . The passage in St. Mark (x. 45) *may very likely* have been influenced by Pauline theology, and *we may say the same* for the narratives of the Last Supper. According to the primitive text of St. Luke (xxii. 18-19a.—Verses 19b and 20 were taken from 1 *Cor.* xi. 24 *f*, and *seem* to have been added later on) it *seems* that Christ gave the chalice and the bread to His disciples, foreseeing the imminence of His death, but without laying any stress on its expiatory or atoning character. Mark's narrative also *seems* to be based on a similar report into which the words concerning the blood of the new testament *may have been* introduced later." [1]

This extract has frequently been quoted as an instance of M. Loisy's tortuous methods of reasoning. It has been pointed out that we do not find in it a single categorical statement, and unkindly people have not been slow to perceive in it the shuffling of a thought which seeks to hide itself; it would however

[1] *L'Évangile et l'Église*, 2nd ed., p. 115 *f*. *Cp. Autour d'un petit livre*, p. 237 *f*.

be more just to see in all this the groping of a mind which is seeking after and striving to express aright the truth.   Others, with better reason, have expressed their surprise that a mere bundle of possibilities and insinuations, which at the most can only engender a probability, should be given us as a proof.   For these halting premises all point to an inference which, though nowhere expressed, is everywhere apparent— viz. that Christ never spoke of, and consequently never had an inkling of, the idea that His death had any atoning value.

At any rate it is easy to see that the present state of criticism is not such as to allow M. Loisy to speak at all dogmatically on the subject, and this is sufficient to relieve our minds.   But his arguments are there awaiting an answer, and as they tend to weaken the authority of a text which is of supreme importance to the doctrine we are treating, it is now high time for us to deal with them.   So weighty is the question that it well deserves a digression.

To prevent any misunderstanding as to the nature of the discussion, we think it necessary to print in parallel columns the four accounts of the Last Supper which have been preserved in the New Testament.

1 Cor. xi. 23-26	Luke xxii. 19-20	Mark xiv. 22-25	Matt. xxvi. 26-:
;. Ἐγὼ παρέλαβον ἀπὸ τοῦ Κυρίου καὶ παρέδωκα ὑμῖν, ιὁ Κύριος' Ἰησοῦς, τῇ νυκτὶ ᾗ παρε-δίδετο, ἔλαβεν ἄρτον			
ι. καὶ εὐχαριστή-σας ἔκλασεν	19. (a) λαβὼν ἄρτον, εὐχαριστήσας ἔκλασεν καὶ ἔδωκεν αὐτοῖς,	22. λαβὼν ἄρτον, εὐλογήσας ἔκλασεν καὶ ἔδωκεν αὐτοῖς	26. λαβὼν ἄρτς καὶ εὐλογήσας, ἔκλασεν καὶ, δοὺς τοῖς μαθηταῖς,
καὶ εἶπεν	λέγων·	καὶ εἶπεν· λάβετε·	εἶπεν· λάβετε, φάγετε·
τοῦτό μου ἐστὶν τὸ σῶμα τὸ ὑπὲρ ὑμῶν·	τοῦτό ἐστιν τὸ σῶμά μου (b) τὸ ὑπὲρ ὑμῶν διδόμενον·	τοῦτό ἐστιν τὸ σῶμά μου.	τοῦτό ἐστιν τὸ σῶμά μου.
τοῦτο ποιεῖτε ς τὴν ἐμὴν ἀνά-μνησιν.	τοῦτο ποιεῖτε εἰς τὴν ἐμὴν ἀνά-μνησιν.		
;. Ὡσαύτως καὶ τὸ ποτήριον ιετὰ τὸ δειπνῆσαι	20. Καὶ τὸ ποτή-ριον ὡσαύτως μετὰ τὸ δειπνῆσαι	23. Καὶ λαβὼν ποτήριον	27. Καὶ λαβι ποτήριον
		εὐχαριστήσας ἔδωκεν αὐτοῖς καὶ ἔπιον ἐξ αὐτοῦ πάντες	καὶ εὐχαριστήσι ἔδωκεν αὐτοῖς,
λέγων·	λέγων·	24. καὶ εἶπεν αὐ-τοῖς·	λέγων·
			πίετε ἐξ αὐτ πάντες·
ὑτο τὸ ποτήριον	τοῦτο τὸ ποτήριον	τοῦτό ἐστιν τὸ αἷμά μου	τοῦτο γάρ ἐστιν ι αἷμά μου
καινὴ διαθήκη ἐστὶν	ἡ καινὴ διαθήκη	τῆς διαθήκης	τῆς διαθήκης
τῷ ἐμῷ αἵματι·	ἐν τῷ αἵματί μου, τὸ ὑμὲρ ὑμῶν ἐκχυννόμενον.	τὸ ἐκχυννόμενον ὑπὲρ πολλῶν.	τὸ περὶ πολλά ἐκχυννόμενον εἰς ἄφεσιν ἁμα τιῶν.
τοῦτο ποιεῖτε, σάκις ἐὰν πίνητε, ς τὴν ἐμὴν ἀνά-μνησιν.			

At first sight it is clear that these narratives fall into two categories, on one side those of St. Paul and St. Luke, on the other those of St. Mark and St. Matthew. On looking more closely, we see that LUKE 19b-20 is the same—like ideas, and almost the identical words—as St. Paul's parallel passage. This curious similarity between the texts would, of itself alone, afford exegetists a legitimate ground for doubt, and this suspicion is confirmed and strengthened by an argument from textual criticism to which M. Loisy does not indeed allude, but which lies at the basis of his argument. These verses of St. Luke's are wanting in the Greek *Codex Bezæ* and in three recensions of the Old Latin version. They are also left out by the Cureton Syriac version, which in their place gives verses 17 and 18, an arrangement which is also found in two MSS. of the Old Vulgate. Have we not then every reason to suppose that verses 19*b*-20 are a later gloss? Hence M. Loisy's note, that these verses " were taken from the epistle to the Corinthians and added later on."

But the verses in question are preserved by all existing Greek codices, nor can the *Codex Bezæ*, of which the Greek is manifestly modelled on the Latin version, be alleged as an exception. This practical unanimity of the Greek MSS. has been considered by the best textual critics a sufficient proof of the authenticity of the reading, and though Wescott and Hort put the passage in brackets, Gebhardt and Nestle give it without any qualification, and the omission of the two verses is commonly set down to " an accident "[1] in the old Latin and Syriac tradition.

At any rate it is certain that the clause in question is authentic ; to deprive St. Luke of it we should have to favour a small group of codices against the testimony of all the others, a mode of proceed-

---

[1] MGR. BATIFFOL, *Études d'histoire et de théologie positive.* 2nd scrics : *L'Eucharistie,* p. 27 *f.* We may explain the " accident " by the difficulty of accounting for the *two* chalices in LUKE 17 and 18. Some copyists may have solved it by suppressing the latter passage. *Cp. ibid.* p. 30, *f.*

ing which would be no longer critical but merely fanciful.[1]

M. Loisy is at a loss to find in textual criticism a pretext for dismissing St. Mark's narrative ; he consequently confines himself to examining the purport of the narrative. "Mark's account seems to be based on a report, similar to that embodied in St. Luke, into which the words concerning the 'blood of the new testament' may have been slipped later on, in order to bring it into agreement with St. Paul's teaching. . . . It is scarcely reasonable that Christ should have said : 'This is my blood,' after the disciples had already drunk ; this was felt by Matthew, for he makes these words to accompany the presenting of the chalice. But the redactor of the second gospel[2] refrained from altering the primitive narrative, merely adding to the words which followed the drinking of the chalice those which he found in St. Paul concerning this chalice."[3]

There undoubtedly exists in St. Mark's text a difficulty of which, moreover, olden commentators were well aware. St. Mark upsets the order of Christ's actions. "He gave them the chalice, *and they all drank of it*, and he said to them : This is my blood. The latter words, uttered after the drinking of the chalice, seem to have lost their *raison d'être*. We may, however, observe that the objection, though it has a bearing on the Eucharistic doctrine, cannot be used against us. It was time enough, even after the drinking of the chalice, to point out to the disciples the relation which existed between the chalice and

---

[1] [See, however, WESTCOTT and HORT, *The N.T. in the original Greek*, Introduction, p. 274.—*Trans.*]

[2] [That which stands second in our Bible—*i.e.* St. Mark's.—*Trans.*]

[3] *L'Évangile et l'Église*, 2nd ed., p. 116 *f.*

G

the blood which was about to be shed for them.
Even discarding this interpretation, it is still possible
to answer M. Loisy's argument. Mark's little clause
may well be a parenthesis suggested by a natural
association of ideas between the presenting of the
chalice and the drinking, as it were an anticipation
slipped in between two breaths, and without breaking
the sequence." [1] This answer will seem all the more
reasonable if we bear in mind that the Hebraistic
Greek sentence in question does not necessarily imply
that the acts were successive. Again, the parallelism
with verse 22 seems to require that Christ, after
having said : " This is my body," should say : " This
is my blood." The primitive narrative, as it is
hypothetically reconstituted by M. Loisy, has the
appearance of being wanting in logic and complete-
ness.

Whatever our explanations may be worth, and even
granting that no reason can be assigned for the
anomaly in St. Mark, have we a sufficient reason for
believing that it embodies two different stories?
Much is wanting to render M. Loisy's system complete;
we are asked to believe in a " primitive narrative,"
a " proto-Mark " whose existence M. Loisy elsewhere
establishes on no better basis than a supposed analogy
with a " proto-Luke " who himself is little better than
a hypothesis with no footing in reality. We are
asked to believe that St. Mark was acquainted with
the epistle to the Corinthians, and that he derived
from it (we are not told why he should have used this
particular source) the words which were there found
concerning the giving of the chalice, but which he
nevertheless read very differently from the fashion in

[1] This was the traditional explanation from CORNELIUS A LAPIDE
down to M. FILLION.

which we now find them. Lastly, we must believe that Matthew having before him the second gospel and feeling the lack of sequence in the narrative, introduced into the body of his account the words which the more scrupulous Mark had simply given as an appendix. Hence St. Matthew's text, far from being primitive and spontaneous, is to be considered as a carefully elaborated synthesis. Now has this all been proved ? And do we not find greater simplicity in the traditional account which looks on Matthew's as the true order which for some reason or other has been inverted by St. Mark ?

We have accordingly no right to state that St. Mark's text, any more than that of St. Luke, has been textually derived from the epistle to the Corinthians. But it may be asked whether doctrinally it has not been influenced by Pauline theology. For this view no proofs are forthcoming, and in default of textual arguments it can only be based on *a priori* considerations.

In effect, we have yet to learn that a critic is content with a mere resemblance of texts. In the case in point besides certain similarities we find some notable divergencies ; moreover, can it be a matter for surprise that Evangelists who were relating the same fact—a particularly memorable one to boot, which had already been consecrated by liturgical usage—should agree in using similar ideas and expressions ? Surely it would be more astonishing were it otherwise. Besides, why should we stop short here and not extend the hypothesis indefinitely ? Thus, as there is a striking resemblance between LUKE xxii. 19b-20 and its parallel in the epistle to the Corinthians, why not argue that it was St. Paul who discovered the Eucharistic symbolism of the Last Supper, and that here again the Synoptists were influenced by Pauline theology ?

But there is more; the hypothesis of a Pauline influence is not only a gratuitous assumption, it is in opposition to all the probabilities of history.

It is admitted that St. Luke was not acquainted with St. Paul's epistles; a fact which some consider "a commonplace of New Testament criticism."[1] Were Mark and Matthew any better acquainted with them than St. Luke ? It might be argued that the Apostle's teaching had already so permeated the Christian communities that it had first been confounded with, and had afterwards replaced, the earliest tradition.   Eye-witnesses of the events connived at these alterations, even if they did not actually make them their own, so that ultimately the original picture was entirely obliterated by later accretions, but nevertheless still continued to be accepted as the real work of the Master.   For this reason the Evangelists, without making any distinction between the two elements when recounting the scene of the Last Supper, put into Christ's mouth the words and ideas first broached by St. Paul.   But there is surely some difficulty in the way of our accepting such a view as correct.

It is interesting to see that the Pauline tradition which we must needs believe to have been unanimous, influenced unequally the three Synoptists.   St. Luke accepts it fully; just like St. Paul, he speaks of the "body delivered for us"; he too reports Christ's command that the act should be renewed for a memory of the Lord.   He even enlarges on the theme, and, whereas St. Paul only writes: "This chalice is the new testament in my blood," St. Luke, led on no doubt by parallelism or by the grandeur of

[1] BATIFFOL, *op. cit.* p. 29.

the Pauline thought, or thinking to interpret the Apostle's mind more clearly, adds : " My blood which shall be shed for you." Now what is exceedingly remarkable is that the other two Evangelists, of all this Pauline tradition, have only preserved just that latter portion which is, strictly speaking, not Pauline at all.

But there is, between the different Gospel accounts, more than a diversity of words, there is a diversity of ideas. Mark and Matthew are thinking more of the Eucharist than of the new covenant. On the contrary, this latter idea is uppermost in Paul's mind, expressing as it does the relation between the Last Supper and the cross, which is characteristic of the Pauline theology on the Eucharist. St. Paul is before all a witness to the sacrificial character of the Eucharist.[1] This character is hinted at in the formula pronounced over the bread : " This is my body which shall be delivered *for you*," but more clearly still in the words used for the chalice : " This chalice is the new testament in my blood." Here the idea of the covenant is more prominent, whilst the Eucharist as such passes into the background. Hence in the Synoptists as in St. Paul we find the same fundamental ideas, but they are considered from different view-points and differently combined. All these differences may be easily explained by admitting that under these slightly divergent personal interpretations there lies some primitive datum ; on the other hand, if these ideas are derived from an exclusively Pauline source, how can we explain that St. Paul should have been so badly understood or so completely transformed ?

Nor can we forbear observing that the sentence as

[1] *Cp.* BATIFFOL, *op. cit.* pp. 8, 20 *f*, 56.

recorded by St. Paul, with all its precision—which by the way does not exclude a certain incoherence—has every look of being a technical formula, one of those striking word-forms in which the Apostle was fond of condensing the deepest substance of his thought; on the contrary, in both Mark and Matthew, the words run easily. If it be true that simpler ideas and expressions usually precede in time the more synthetic and complicated views, then there is reason to suppose that in Mark and Matthew we have Christ's own words,[1] which St. Paul restates in the categories of his systematic theology. If this be true, then St. Luke gives us a combination of the two texts; for in the narrative of the latter Evangelist it is easy to perceive a breach of sequence; τοῦτο τὸ ποτήριον ἡ καινὴ διαθήκη ἐν τῷ αἵματί μου, τὸ ὑπὲρ ὑμῶν ἐκχυννόμενον, so we read in verse 20. The last member of this sentence, τὸ ὑπὲρ ὑμῶν ἐκχυννόμενον, which according to grammatical rules refers to τὸ ποτήριον, ought logically to refer to τῷ αἵματι, for to be sure it was not the chalice but the blood which was to be " shed." [2] Logic and grammar too would have led us to expect something like the following :—τοῦτό ἐστιν τὸ αἷμά μου . . . , τὸ ὑπὲρ ὑμῶν ἐκχυννόμενον—i.e. like the grammatically and logically more correct sentence preserved by Matthew and by Mark. For this simple sentence St. Luke, who was St. Paul's immediate disciple, substitutes the Apostle's formula without however modifying the latter portion of the clause, which had already been stereotyped by traditional

---

[1] " Christus videtur potius dixisse eo modo, ut narrant Marcus ot Matthœus, quia illa phrasis clarior est." CORNELIUS A LAPIDE, In Matt. xxvi. 28.

[2] This anomaly is already indicated by HOLTZMANN, Hand-Commentar zum N.T. : die Synoptiker (Leipzig, 1901), p. 410.

usage. Thus it is not in St. Matthew's but in St.
Luke's Gospel that we find a synthesis of the traditions on the Last Supper; the artificial character of
the latter account betrays that it is a piece of
patchwork.

At a stretch, and in spite of all these difficulties, we
might still maintain that the Synoptists were acted
on by the Pauline theology; but we are also asked
to believe that St. Paul himself was affected by it:
"St. Paul was the theologian of the cross and of the
Atonement by death, and he manifestly expounds
the Last Supper in the light of his theory of universal
expiation."[1] But to us it appears that St. Paul does
nothing of the sort; he is exposing no pet theory, nor
his own personal theology, he is testifying as a witness
to an account which he expressly describes as traditional (ἐγὼ παρέλαβον . . . ὅ καὶ παρέδωκα).[2] We are
asked either to call into question the Apostle's good
faith and say that he is putting his own ideas in the
Master's mouth to make them more acceptable, or
to believe that he deceived himself and embraced as
the traditional account a view which he himself had
helped to form. Personally, we prefer to take the
Apostle at his word; and, to conclude, we may state
it as our opinion that the narrative of the Last Supper
as it is given by St. Paul is no recollection of his own
preaching, but a really traditional datum which in its
purport, if not in its actual words, belongs to Christ
Himself. The Evangelists drew their teaching from
the same source, and it is worse than useless to imagine that they depended on each other for their

---

[1] *Autour*, p. 237.

[2] Harnack confesses that it is only the evidence of this text
which stands in the way of his adopting Spitta's enticing view.
Dogmengesch. i. p. 64, note 1.

information; all we need do is to admit, as everyone does, that all the writers depend on an earlier tradition.

We think we have said enough to prove the historicity of the narratives of the Last Supper and to explain why M. Loisy's exegesis was severely handled in certain quarters. M. de Grandmaison[1] described it as a piece of special pleading; Mgr. Le Camus[2] not only considered it false and fanciful, but believed its author to have been actuated by fell designs. We have no intention of setting ourselves up as judges of our author's purpose, but we cannot but state that in our humble opinion his arguments are insufficient to overthrow the traditional interpretation. There is nothing to prove that St. Paul's theology had any influence on the synoptic accounts; but there is everything to show, and the epistle to the Corinthians indeed explicitly states, that we have here so many mutually independent accounts drawn from one original source. Criticism teaches us no more so long as it remains what it should be, " a species of applied logic . . . which proves what it puts forward and is not ashamed of often confessing its own ignorance." [3]

Thus " St Paul's testimony may be said to strengthen rather than complete that of the Evangelists." We cannot do better than end with these words, which are M. Loisy's own.[4]

---

[1] *Études*, 20th Jan. 1903, p. 172.

[2] *La vraie et la fausse exégèse* (Paris, 1903), p. 31.

[3] A. HOUTIN, *La question biblique et les catholiques*, pp. 263 and 265 (2nd ed., 1902).

[4] *L'Évangile et l'Église* (2nd ed.), p. 1. [M. Loisy's reply to the strictures embodied in the above will be found in the *Revue de l'histoire des religions*, Mars-Avril 1906.—*Trans.*]

IV

We must now turn to the thought expressed by these texts. After having established their authenticity it is now time to investigate their meaning.

The sons of Zebedee had just made their vainglorious request, and Jesus improved on the occasion by giving a lesson to His disciples: "You know that they who seem to rule over the Gentiles lord it over them, and their princes have power over them. But among you it shall not be so, but whosoever will be greater shall be your minister," and to substantiate His words He quotes His own example: "For the son of man also is not come to be ministered unto, but to minister, and to give his life a redemption for many " (οὐκ ἦλθεν διακονηθῆναι ἀλλὰ διακονῆσαι καὶ δοῦναι τὴν ψυχὴν αὐτοῦ λύτρον ἀντὶ πολλῶν. MARK x. 45 ; MATT. xx. 28).

Some have sought in vain to render allegorically the word λύτρον ; but there can be no doubt that it is used here, as elsewhere in the Bible, in the strict sense of "ransom." No doubt this expression involves a metaphor, but we must retain the essential meaning of the word. Now a ransom involves some kind of captivity ; in what does this captivity consist ? Interpretations are not wanting, but unfortunately most of them are bound up with some theory or other.

According to some, Christ by the generosity and the deep humiliation of His death delivered us from moral anguish, from the fear of death, or possibly from the worldly spirit which is in very deed the spirit of sin ; such ideas are characteristic of the vague moralism of Ritschl and his school.[1] M.

[1] Cp. ROSE, op. cit. pp. 253-257.

Sabatier's exegesis is less commonplace. In Christ's concluding words he sees " a figure, and, as it were, an abbreviated parable," which he thus explains : " Jesus could lay the foundation of the Kingdom of God only by first overthrowing the kingdom of Satan ; He could only save men by delivering them from Satan's bondage. Now a slave cannot be redeemed save at a price. Hence if we wish to keep to the metaphor taken from the demoniacal mythology, which then dominated all minds, we shall have to say that *Jesus considered the giving of His life as a ransom paid to the devil.*" [1] The syllogism is rigorous and serves at least to show how well M. Sabatier can embroider a text with the products of his own fancy.

On the other hand, orthodox theologians prefer to compare these words of Christ with those in MARK viii. 37 ; MATT. xvi. 26. " If any man will follow me let him deny himself . . . whosoever shall lose his life for my sake . . . shall save it. For what doth it profit a man if he gain the whole world and suffer the loss of his soul ; or what shall a man *give in exchange for his soul?* " (τi $\gamma \grave{a} \rho$ $\delta o \hat{\iota}$ $\mathring{a} \nu \theta \rho \omega \pi o s$ $\mathring{a} \nu \tau \acute{a} \lambda$-$\lambda a \gamma \mu a$ $\tau \hat{\eta} s$ $\psi v \chi \hat{\eta} s$ $a \mathring{v} \tau o \hat{v}$). Upon this they reason as follows :—" Man is helpless to regain everlasting life once he has lost it ; he is no longer able to give a price proportionate to the ransom required. . . . Jesus therefore gives His life as an exchange and as a

---

[1] SABATIER, *op. cit.* p. 25. To corroborate his argument the learned writer refers us in a note to MARK iii. 27 ; MATT. xii. 29 ; LUKE xi. 22, where in masked words Christ speaks of the warfare which He has come to wage against the prince of this world ; He overcomes him, takes away his armour, and binds him : M. Sabatier expounds these texts as follows :—" He will vanquish him . . . though He must first die in the fight."

ransom "[1]; hence we find in these two passages of
the Gospel the whole theology of the Atonement.
Unfortunately this interpretation is rather too comprehensive, and the least that can be said of it is that
it lays us open to the charge of expounding the
Gospel by means of theological data belonging to a
later period. We may also point out that this interpretation does not keep to the text. When Jesus
speaks of man's inability of giving an exchange for
his soul, what He has in His mind is our Salvation,
on the strictly individual character of which He
insists by means of this figure. There is here no
question of a ransom paid to God's Justice, nor does
Christ, farther on, state that He gives to God a
ransom for us. The two ideas, which an effort is
made to explain by each other, have, as a matter of
fact, nothing in common.

For our own part, we believe that we must seek
the meaning in the context. Jesus sets His own
conduct against that of kings ; the latter give orders,
He gives Himself ; He comes to serve and not to
be served. This " service," which is the end and
object of His mission, will be performed until the
last day of His earthly life, and the yielding up of
His life will be again a redemption for many. By
these words—reminiscent of those good servants who
are so attached to their masters as to give their life
for their safety—Christ expresses his life-long devo-
tion to men which was to be crowned by His death ;
His death will not be without use, for it too will
deliver many. But what exactly is this deliverance
and from what bondage does it set us free ? We
should feel inclined to believe that it is the servitude

---

[1] Rose, *op. cit.* p. 257. *Cp.* Knabenbauer, *Com. in Matth.* ii. p.
189 *f.* (Paris, 1893).

of sin to which elsewhere the Gospel alludes (JOHN
viii. 34), but it must be admitted that the text does
not say so ; the word λύτρον, standing, as it does, all
alone, does not allow of our ascribing to it any special
meaning, still less of our building on it a whole
theory. On the whole, we prefer to leave Christ's
expression in its primitive indefiniteness and to see in
it just that matter which He was wishing to impress
on His disciples—viz. the generosity and utility of
His sacrifice, and nothing more. "Jesus began to
give His life when He undertook His ministry, and
He ended by wholly surrendering it on the cross.
His outward actions were different, but their promot-
ing cause was ever the same—viz. faith and charity."
M. Sabatier's words, though possibly they may have
been intended against us,[1] admirably express the
Catholic doctrine, and we can find no better in which
to condense our own thought.

Holtzmann too comes nearer to us than he sus-
pects. No doubt he sees a Pauline influence in
the synoptic text : " One of Jesus' thoughts expounded in the light of a recollection of the Pauline
theory on the Atonement." But all the same he
holds to the idea of the great usefulness Christ
attached to His death. Holtzmann is even willing to
retain the word " redemption " provided it be understood to signify the " price paid for delivering a
captive." And so far as we are concerned, this is all
we want ; but we do want this much, and we can
only say that Holtzmann is getting away from the
text and evading its real meaning when he further
explains himself as implying that " Jesus saw in His
death—which He accepted for the good of His brethren,
a personal act on account of which He might demand

[1] *Op. cit.* p. 24.

of His disciples the sacrifice of brotherly love as the basic law of the Kingdom."[1] If we understand aright this somewhat involved clause, the only value which Christ attached to His death was that of an example. But, as a matter of fact, we find nothing of the kind in the Gospel text ; there Christ speaks of a real service He owes to His brethren and of an effective deliverance secured by the giving of His life. It is true that He says nothing of the manner, and we have no right to be more definite than the text. But whilst refusing to credit Christ with theological accretions which were strange to His thought, we must nevertheless retain the main idea He expresses—viz. the salutary and liberating character of His death.

On this character stress is laid at the Last Supper. According to all the four narratives, the chalice was presented by Christ to His disciples as the blood which was to be shed for them and in which the New Covenant was to be established. Some indeed would reject this idea of a New Covenant as a later addition, but Holtzmann considers it essential, and believes it to contain Christ's most prominent idea.[2] He explains it by comparing it with the narrative of the olden covenant which is contained in Exodus. Here we read that Moses, after the people had promised to obey the words of the Lord, proceeded to seal the covenant by a sacrifice of blood. At that time a sacrifice was considered of binding force, after the fashion of a signature, or like the seal affixed to a contract to show the good faith of the two parties, and to ensure the legal soundness of the compact. This was why Moses sprinkled both the book and the people with blood, saying meanwhile : " This is the

---

[1] *N.T. Theologie*, i. pp. 292-295. *Cp. Die Synoptiker*, p. 160.
[2] *Ibid.* i. pp. 296-300. *Cp. Die Synoptiker*, p. 100.

blood of the covenant which the Lord hath made
with you concerning all these words" (*Exod.* xxiv.
4-9. *Cp. Heb.* ix. 18-21). There was manifestly in
this rite not the slightest trace of anything like an
expiation. Similarly Christ considered Himself as
the mediator of the new covenant, and gave His blood
to seal it.

Learned critics have rightly pointed out how
fancifully exclusive this theory is, and how inexact it
is to say that "the narrative of Exodus, of itself
alone, gives the key to the narrative of the Synoptics."[1] But there is even more to be said against
the theory; it is noteworthy that Holtzmann himself
is not able to keep to it consistently, and in reading
his works we soon perceive how hard put he is to
justify his view and how the qualifications which he
is obliged to use finally lead him to something peril-
ously like self-contradiction.

With regard to St. Matthew's text εἰς ἄφεσιν ἁμαρτιῶν,
Holtzmann easily gets rid of it. This expression is
in evident contradiction with Christ's whole teaching,
according to which forgiveness of sins depends wholly
on God's mercy and requires no other condition
except penance. " Every qualification of this master-
thought of Christ's is an anticipation of later
theorisings on the Atonement." In spite of this,
several scholars are of opinion that Christ, being under
the influence of prevalent ideas concerning expiation,
and recollecting the sayings of the Second Isaias, may
have, even though merely accidentally, considered His
death as a true sacrifice. Holtzmann agrees that we
"cannot call in question the possibility" of such a
view,[2] especially since Christ's words: τὸ ὑπὲρ ὑμῶν

[1] BATIFFOL, *op. cit.* p. 70.
[2] *N.T. Theologie,* i. p. 300. *Cp. ibid.* note 3.

ἐκχυννόμενον, would naturally allow this to transpire. This much is conceded by Holtzmann, but he nevertheless sticks to his point, arguing that there is " always the possibility of this passage having been rounded off according to Pauline ideas." We cannot help feeling that this "possibility" is a poor argument to use against an evident text, nor would Holtzmann's honesty allow him to conceal that all scholars do not share his view regarding the influence of St. Paul. Looking at his conclusion, we cannot but suspect that his best argument is an *a priori* one. " Let us not seek in the establishment of the new covenant for any more allusion to sin or to the forgiveness of sins than is to be found in the sacrifice on Sinai."[1] Unhappily, this is just the question at issue.

M. Sabatier, who has put into an elegant French dress certain ideas akin to those of Holtzmann, has an easier way of solving the difficulty, he simply rules it out of court. Of the four narratives of the Last Supper he retains only St. Mark's version, " the shortest," and even this version he is careful to abbreviate ; thus of MARK xiv. 24 he omits the latter portion, τὸ ὑπὲρ ὑμῶν ἐκχυννόμενον ; the remaining portion, of course, adapting itself quite easily to the biblical rite of the covenant.[2]

What part exactly was played by Christ and His death in establishing the new covenant ? Holtzmann avoids telling us, but in the unfolding of his system he occasionally seems to go beyond the narrow formalism of the ancient covenant, and appears to ascribe to Christ's blood some real influence and efficacy. Not only was it a bond of union (*das richtige Bindemittel*) between God and the new com-

[1] *N.T. Theologie*, p. 302. *Cp. ibid.* note 1.
[2] SABATIER, *op. cit.* p. 26 *f.*

munity, but His blood was a salutary sacrifice (*heilstiftendes Bundesopferblut*), and " was shed for the good of many," of those, to wit, " who, as disciples of Jesus, will become—what they never could have become as disciples of Moses and servants of the Law—children of God." [1] Holtzmann thus returns by a tortuous path to the correct and obvious meaning of the Gospel text ; for certainly the new covenant was established in Christ's blood, but His blood was not merely the seal and the signature of the new dispensation, it was in very deed its creative cause. [2] Here we might well stop, but the Bible allows us to describe more clearly than in Holtzmann's words the character of this new covenant. It was sin which placed an obstacle between God and His people (*Isaias* lix. 2, 12). The new covenant was destined to take away this obstacle and forgive the sin (*Isaias* xxxiii. 24 ; lix. 20 ; lx. 17-22 ; lxi. 8 ; *Jeremias* xxxi. 34). Hence Christ in giving His life to establish the new covenant also gave it " for the forgiveness of sins," which is a necessary condition of the new covenant ; this is why the words we find in St. Matthew, εἰς ἄφεσιν ἁμαρτιῶν, far from being a later interpretation, have every appearance of being according to the mind of Christ. They are simply a natural explanation and a normal growth, of which the germ is found in Christ's other allusions to the new covenant. [3]

Here again we shall abstain from giving to Christ's

---

[1] HOLTZMANN, *op. cit.* i. p. 303 *f.*

[2] *Cp.* BATIFFOL, *op. cit.* p. 73.

[3] We can certainly not agree with Holtzmann when he maintains that this text has been transposed from MARK i. 4. *Cp. N.T. Theologie*, i. p. 300, and *Die Synoptiker*, p. 290 ; this view is wholly fanciful.

simple saying any rigorously theological meaning ; we shall not inquire whether He considered His death as an expiatory sacrifice and whether we should not see in this text " the juridical and legal theory of vicarious Sacrifice." [1]   Christ Himself did not theorise, nor did He state what relation He perceived between His death and the forgiveness of sins ; but that He did see some relation between the two things is quite clear, and this is sufficient to justify the later theological developments.

True it is that we are charged with putting Christ in contradiction with Himself.   Did He not promise forgiveness on the one condition of doing penance ? Did He not depict God under the guise of a loving Father who is ever ready to forgive the prodigal on his return ?   Undoubtedly ; and this we have already acknowledged.   Christ never posed as a theologian discoursing on Salvation ; He spoke to souls in that loving language which they needed, and strove to excite them to acts of filial trust and penance.   In His sermons He was thinking of the individual preparation which is ever needful, and to use an expression of the Schools, He taught the subjective conditions of forgiveness, without prejudice however to the objective conditions which He was to reveal later on.

One result of this is—we do not fear to assert it against M. Sabatier—that the Gospel parables are " doctrinally incomplete," [2] the reason being that they do not pretend to teach a " doctrine."   M. Sabatier has, moreover, no right to state that " historically there is nothing more certain than that they (the parables) contain all that Jesus understood by His gospel " ;

---

[1] ROSE, op. cit. p. 268.
[2] Op. cit. p. 22 f.   Cp. p. 101.

H

for, as we can see, Christ's doctrine involves something more.

The forgiveness of sins and the Messianic necessity of our Saviour's death, the two ideas which we have seen growing side by side in the Gospel, are found together in the narratives of the Last Supper. It was Christ Himself who bound them together, thereby allowing us to perceive the ultimate reason of His sacrifice, at which until then He had only hinted darkly. There is no discrepancy concerning this matter until we bring *a priori* views to the consideration of the Gospels ; whoever takes them as they are will find them perfectly harmonious. Let us not strive to put asunder what God has joined together ; and far from bringing Christ's doctrine down to our human level, let us rather endeavour to fathom its height and its depth. The Atonement effected by Christ's blood is no doubt a mystery and we need not hope to make it clear ; but without sounding it to the very bottom we may at least convince ourselves that its beginning and end is simply charity.

V

According to St. John's Gospel, Christ was the " Word made Flesh " ; hence He constantly describes Himself in this gospel as the Light, the Resurrection, the Life, expressions which later on were to furnish a fertile field for the speculations of the Greek Fathers. But it is noteworthy that here, as in the Synoptists, we find stress laid on the special benefits accruing to us through His Atoning death.[1]

[1] We have already dealt with the Johannine theology ; here we shall confine ourselves to considering the words which the fourth gospel puts into Christ's mouth. It will readily be perceived how

Christ sums up in a few words the whole mystery of Salvation. " God so loved the world as to give his only begotten Son, that whosoever believeth in him may not perish but may have life everlasting " (iii. 16. *Cp*. 36). In His turn the Son carried out the work principally by His death ; this was part and parcel of His mission ; though He does not explicitly predict it, He gives us to understand that it is the end and aim of His life ; it was the commandment which the Father had given Him and which He had willingly accepted. " Therefore doth the Father love me, because I lay down my life that I may take it again ; no man taketh it away from me, but I lay it down of myself, and I have power to lay it down and I have power to take it up again " (x. 17 *f*). Yet He is stricken with fear at the thought. " Now is my soul troubled, and what shall I say : Father save me from this hour ; but for this cause I came unto this hour " (xii. 27). Hence He lovingly resigns Himself to suffer. " As the Father hath given me a commandment, so do I " (xiv. 31). And when the fatal hour comes He recognises everywhere and blesses the hand of Providence (xviii. 11 ; xix. 11). Thus His life of suffering is a manifestation of God's will, or rather of a special act of God's will with regard to His Son, which the Son considers in the light of a precept. This mission was accepted by the Son in a spirit of loving obedience. The work of Atonement, which took its beginning in the love of the Father who sent His only Son, ends with the love of the Son, to whose love His own definition applies : " Greater love than this no man hath, that a man lay down his life for his friends " (xv. 13).

the testimony of the fourth gospel agrees with that of the synoptics.

As we might expect, this death of His will be of great service to us. Speaking to Nicodemus, Christ compares Himself to the brazen serpent: " As Moses lifted up the serpent in the desert, so must the Son of man be lifted up " ; and just as the sight of the serpent restored the ailing to health, so does belief in Christ procure us life everlasting (iii. 14 *f*). According to this text what saves us is belief in the Son of God, and as yet nothing has been said of His death. But soon this too makes its appearance. Christ came " that they may have life, and may have it more abundantly. I am the good shepherd . . . and I lay down my life for my sheep " (x. 10-11, 15). Elsewhere, He states that He gives Himself to us as the bread coming down from heaven which gives life everlasting, and that the bread which He will give is His flesh " for the life of the world " (vi. 52). His sacrifice will be fruitful. " The grain of wheat falling into the ground unless it dieth remaineth fruitless, but if it dieth it bringeth forth much fruit," a similar law rules in the world of the spirit, and to save our soul we must first lose it (xii. 24 *f*) ; when He dies He will draw all men to Himself (xii. 32. *Cp.* viii. 28). And as the Evangelist informs us in a parenthesis: " This he said speaking of his death " (xii. 33).

Lastly, when He prays God for His own, He says: " For them I sanctify myself that they also may be sanctified in truth " (ὑπὲρ αὐτῶν ἀγιάζω ἐμαυτὸν ἵνα ὦσιν καὶ αὐτοὶ ἡγιασμένοι, xvii. 19). Now the verb ἀγιάζω rendered according to Old Testament ritual means " I offer in sacrifice." Maldonatus states that all the authors known to him interpret thus the word, and this interpretation is still common among Catholics. The only difficulty this rendering encounters is the fact that in the latter portion of the above sentence (and also in verse 17) the same verb is used in a different sense. Maldonatus himself noticed and pointed this out—it is a pity that his successors do not always do likewise—and answers it by saying that Christ " as was His custom plays on the double meaning " of this verb, which in biblical language means either the person or thing sanctified, or the rite by which it is sanctified—*i.e.* either holiness or the efficient cause of holiness.[1] As M. Loisy writes: " The twofold meaning of the word 'to sanctify' permits of a sort of word-play; Christ sanctifies Himself—*i.e.* He gives His life as a victim, that His disciples may be sanctified,"[2] and this sanctification is in truth (ἐν ἀληθείᾳ)—*i.e.* real and inward, not merely legal and outward, as that which resulted from the olden sacrifices. Thus did Christ repeal the old law and its useless works and declare Himself to be the perfect Victim by whose death alone man could secure holiness.

It matters little whether Christ's death, as M. Loisy believes, is not here represented as " an expiation for sin "[3]; or whether, as Holtzmann thinks, "it is a sacrifice of sanctification rather than of propitiation,"[4] we have no wish to put into the sentence more than it contains; we are quite content to learn from it that Christ offered Himself as a victim for man's sanctification, a thought similar to that expressed by St. Matthew. The brief formulæ used at the Last Supper are here enlarged upon by St. John with the aid of His own mystic vocabulary, but the idea expressed remains the same.

[1] MALDONATUS, *In Ioan.* xvii. (Paris, 1668), col. 1832 *f.*
[2] *Le 4ᵐᵉ Évangile* (Paris, 1903), p. 809.
[3] LOISY, *ibid.* Cp. *l'Évangile et l'Église* (2nd ed.), p. 190.
[4] *Das Evangelium des Johannes* (Leipzig, 2nd ed., 1893), p. 203.

To sum up, the Gospel according to St. John brings to the fore two characters of our Saviour's death; it was laid on Christ by God and was freely accepted by the latter, and it facilitates the salvation of souls, though we are not told the motive which regulated this choice of means, or the exact relation in which this Sacrifice stands to man's sanctification. That the death was at once necessary and free, and that it benefited and hallowed us, such are the data of this Gospel; St. John's doctrine is similar to that of the Synoptists, and strictly speaking it betrays no progress.

From the Gospels we gather that Christ, who all along had foreseen His death, little by little, as their faith grew firmer, allowed it to become known to His disciples that this death was to be the crisis of His career as Saviour and Messias. On two occasions when He expressed Himself more clearly than was His wont, He made use of the ideas of ransom and sacrifice to show the hallowing and re-deeming character of His death. Though these words contain no theory, it was in their depth and simplicity that all latter theories took their rise.[1] St. Paul was the first to attack the problem of the cross; to him "the Gospel appears in the light of a datum and Jesus in that a principle,"[2] and his wonderfully active mind laid the foundation of all future speculations on the Atonement. But the Apostle's doctrinal system is that of the Gospel, and though it is true that he penetrated more deeply into the Master's thought, it is not true that he sub-stituted his own thought for that of Christ. Jesus was the first to connect our salvation with His own

[1] STEVENS, op. cit. pp. 131-134.
[2] BATIFFOL, Six leçons sur les Évangiles, 5th ed. (Paris, 1902), p. 92.

death, and He willed to give His life for us and our sins. In this lies the whole mystery of the Atonement, and whatever efforts Christian thinkers may make to fathom its meaning, they will never exhaust the sublime though simple reality expressed by the Gospel.

PART THE SECOND

THE ATONEMENT AMONG THE GREEK FATHERS

CHAPTER VII

THE APOSTOLIC FATHERS AND THE APOLOGISTS

It is quite certain that the doctrine of the Atonement did not, among the Fathers, hold the position of importance which it has in our theology. Far from being considered the last word of the providential plan and the very centre of salvation, it was scarcely dwelt upon at all for its own sake. To discover what the Fathers thought of it we have to hunt through their homilies and commentaries for the casual texts, in which we find indeed allusions to the traditional data, but which, even when we can reduce them to some sort of unity, seldom trench on the deepest elements of the mystery. In a word, as every historian is forced to admit, the Fathers were mostly satisfied with fragmentary, we might almost say superficial, views of the Atonement; they never made this doctrine the special subject of their inquiries.

Possibly the reason of this may have been that they were too familiar with this truth; it was as Döerholt expresses it, " the solid ground under their feet; the atmosphere in which they lived. . . ." [1]

There was also another reason—viz. the fact that

[1] Op. cit. p. 62 f.

their attention was engaged elsewhere. All heretics from the Gnostics to Nestorius concentrated their efforts on our Saviour's personality, and naturally enough the defence followed the attack. Only later on did Christian thought rise above the immediate needs of controversy to consider those simpler truths which form the very food of the Christian, but which until then had not been seriously studied, just because nobody had seen fit to deny them. This is the reason why the theology of the Atonement was comparatively late in developing. As Harnack aptly puts it, among the early Christians " faith in Christ was Christianity in brief." [1] Hence it is not difficult to see why Christology long made up the whole of theology.

But does this mean, as M. Sabatier thinks, that all else was considered of little account, and that " the meaning and worth of Christ's sufferings were points which might freely be debated " ? [2]—Nothing falls shorter of the truth. No doubt, as M. Sabatier says, " the Apostles' Creed speaks of the death of our Lord and of the forgiveness of sins in different places," and the same is true of the other creeds, which are all more or less modelled on the Roman form. [3] But we must not forget that the creed does not pretend to be more than a summary of the principal articles of faith, so much so, in fact, that our faithful may, whilst remaining perfectly orthodox, still recite it even now. It is also true that the Niceno-Constantinopolitan creed connects man's salvation quite

---

[1] *Dogmengesch.* i. p. 174.   [2] *Op. cit.* p. 44.

[3] *Cp.* HAHN, *Bibliothek der Symbole* (3rd ed., Breslau, 1897), pp. 22-127. The formula " died for us " occurs only in St. Epiphanius's text (p. 135) and in the Syrian and Egyptian creeds (pp. 140 and 157).

generally with the Incarnation, the Passion, and Resurrection of the God-Man, but it also contains the
words : "Was crucified for us."[1] Did this article of
the creed escape M. Sabatier?

To prove his point our learned author in addition
quotes a few Patristic texts. He refers us to a passage
in which Origen defines the position and scope of
theology as distinct from faith, but in which there is
not the slightest allusion of any kind to any controversy
on Christ's sufferings.[2] The other texts, though more
to the point, are scarcely stronger.

To show that the Church is heir to the teaching
of the Apostles, St. Irenæus first epitomises the
articles of faith held by the Catholic Church ; amongst
these we find this one : "The Son of God *became flesh
for our salvation*."[3] Besides these great universal
and necessary truths, the essential oneness of which
Irenæus describes in grandiloquent language, he
mentions certain others ; or, to be more exact, he says
that each one may investigate according to his wisdom
each of these truths and seek their why and wherefore.
Among the questions which St. Irenæus proposes
to Christian thought is this one : "Why did the Word
become flesh and suffer?"[4] From this M. Sabatier
rather hastily infers that Irenæus considered the
answer as of little account.[5] But if we bear in mind
that Irenæus had just classed the object of the
Incarnation among the necessary truths, and that he
puts the question we are now considering between

---

[1] *Cp.* DENZIGER, No. 47. HAHN, *op. cit.* No. 144, p. 164.

[2] ORIGEN, *De Princip. præf.* 1-5 ; *P.G.* xi. 116 *f.*

[3] IREN. *Adv. Hær.* i. 10, 1 ; *P.G.* vii. 549. *Cp.* i. 9, 3 ; col. 541.

[4] Διὰ τί ὁ Λόγος τοῦ Θεοῦ σὰρξ ἐγένετο καὶ ἔπαθεν ; i. 10, 3 ; col. 556.

[5] SABATIER, *op. cit.* p. 44, note 1. In this he follows LICHTENBERGER,
op. cit. p. 137, and HARNACK-CHOISY, *Précis*, p. 90.

two others—Why did God give mankind two Testaments and what is the characteristic of each? and why did Christ come at the end and not at the beginning of the world?—we shall be forced to infer that this passage of Irenæus is the first defence of theology and of reasoned faith as contrasted with the faith of the little ones. But it remains the same faith of which Irenæus had already said: "Neither does he who can say much of it increase it, nor does he who can say less diminish it." [1]

M. Sabatier lays special stress on St. Gregory Nazianzen. In one of his discourses this Father speaks as follows:—" Philosophise as you will on the world and the worlds, on matter and the soul, on reasonable creatures good and evil, on the resurrection, the judgment, and rewards, or on the *sufferings of Christ*. For if it be not profitless to succeed in such matters, so neither is there any risk in failing." [2] Gregory is speaking here to people who had brought their love of discussion with them into the Church, a love which he describes as the "new malady 'glossalgy.'" [3] Nevertheless, he is quite willing to allow them to discuss freely the older philosophical theories, which he describes in bitter words. But some would not be content with this, and to satisfy them he gives a list of metaphysical and dogmatic subjects, amongst which figures Christ's Passion. What does this text mean? A timid footnote of the Benedictine editors suggests that he is thinking of apologetics, and that we should read "to convince" after the words

---

[1] *P.G.* vii. ci. 10, 2; col. 553.

[2] Φιλοσόφει μοι περὶ . . . Χριστοῦ παθημάτων. Ἐν τούτοις γὰρ καὶ τὸ ἐπιτυγκάνειν οὐκ ἄχρηστον καὶ τὸ διαμαρτάνειν ἀκίνδυνον. *Orat.* xxvii. 10.—*P.G.* xxxvi. 25.

[3] γλωσσαλγία καινὴ νόσος. *Ibid.* 7, col. 20.

"risk in failing." But this suggestion besides being gratuitous is not in accordance with the trend of the discourse. Though we should not lay too much stress on a sentence uttered in the heat of an oration, the truth is that St. Gregory gives the rein to philosophical speculations concerning the manner and circumstances of several of our mysteries in which he considers that theoretical error could lead to no evil results. But though he does not say so, he makes an exception for the actual data of the traditional faith, unless indeed we are prepared to say that in his eyes Christianity teaches nothing whatever concerning the resurrection and the judgment.

Moreover, we are confronted by facts which show the existence of a single progressive doctrine concerning Christ's atoning sufferings, which, though it occupies but little room in tradition, yet often served as a basis for Christology, or at any rate made progress concomitantly with it.

Another matter to be noticed is that the word Satisfaction, which is now technically used to describe Christ's Atonement, is not found once among the Fathers, and appears for the first time in the works of St. Anselm in the twelfth century. Some writers, more especially of that Protestant school whose orthodoxy consists in a slavish literalism, laboured much to find at least some trace of it, but succeeded in discovering nothing better than an inaccurate translation of St. Athanasius, two wrongly rendered passages from St. Hilary and St. Ambrose, and a text of Tertullian's which may now be sought for in vain.[1] We shall meet those texts in the course of our work ; suffice it to say that we consider ourselves in no wise obliged to set both grammar and good sense at naught

[1] The texts are quoted and dealt with by DÖERHOLT, *op. cit.* p. 63 *f.*

simply in order to ascribe to the Fathers of the Church a word which they never used, just because their use of the word might assure to our dogma a deceitful identity of formulæ. It matters little to us whether we find the word or not, provided we find the idea.

After these general remarks it is now high time to seek the earliest glimpses of this idea in the works of the Apostolic Fathers.

I

Some writers make it a point to be very harsh with these early exponents of Christianity. Thus M. Grétillat speaks of the "power of platitude peculiar to the time of the Apostolic Fathers,"[1] and even Harnack complains of finding scarcely anywhere any original thoughts on the relations existing between "Christ's atoning work and the facts heralded by the Gospel preaching."[2] Personally, we are not at all sorry on this account, and are only too glad to find in these writings of the early Church a faithful echo of the teaching we have already found in the Gospels.

The *Didache* contains nothing whatever concerning Christ's atonement, and only thanks God in vague words "for the knowledge and faith and immortality which He revealed to us by Jesus, His servant."[3] We may say the same of the *Shepherd* of Hermas; though its object is to teach penance, we only find this one single far-off allusion to our Saviour's Atonement: "He cleansed their sins at the cost of much work and sufferings."[4] Comparing these two texts, Harnack

---

[1] *Essai de Théologie systématique,* iv. p. 370.

[2] HARNACK-CHOISY, *Précis,* p. 14. *Dogmengesch.* i. p. 190 *f.*

[3] *Didache,* x. 2.

[4] *Sim.* v. 6, 2. We quote the Apostolic Fathers according to FUNK's edition (Tübingen, 1901).

believes he is right in surmising that at a certain early stage Christians ascribed salvation to Christ generally and not to any particular act of His life[1]; and, in fact, there would be nothing surprising if such a view really prevailed among the early Christians, who made up for the shallowness of their theology by the strenuousness of their practical Christian life; nevertheless, we do not think it right to compare together two writings which differ so greatly in their character, origin, and date. We should almost be justified in considering their silence as due to individual idiosyncracies, especially as other early Fathers, whose testimony Harnack does not attempt to conceal, clearly make the Atonement to depend on Christ's death.

"Christ's blood," writes St. Clement, "was given on our behalf,"[2] and farther on the same Father writes: "God reunited us to Himself through love; it was through the love He had for us that Christ delivered His blood for us according to the will of God, and His flesh for our flesh, and His soul for our souls."[3] We owe our salvation to His self-sacrifice. "Let us ever keep our eyes on Christ's blood and know how precious in the sight of God, His Father, is this blood, which, being shed for our salvation, procured for the whole world the grace of penance."[4] St. Clement sees a figure of this blood in the scarlet cord which saved the house of Rahab, "a sign that the Saviour's blood would be a redemption to all who believe and hope in God."[5]

---

[1] *Dogmengesch.* i. p. 191, note 2.

[2] Clem. *Ad Cor.* xxi. 6.

[3] Τὸ αἷμα αὐτοῦ ἔδωκεν ὑπὲρ ἡμῶν . . . ἐν θελήματι θεοῦ, καὶ τὴν σάρκα ὑπὲρ τῆς σαρκὸς ἡμῶν καὶ τὴν ψυχὴν ὑπὲρ τῶν ψυχῶν. xlix. 6.

[4] *Ibid.* vii. 4.

[5] Διὰ τοῦ αἵματος αὐτοῦ λύτρωσις ἔσται πᾶσιν τοῖς πιστεύουσιν. xii. 7.

St. Ignatius considers that the object of the whole of Christ's mission was our salvation, and he thanks Him who, " being immortal and invisible, became visible for our sake ; who, being incorruptible and exempt from pain, became subject to pain for our sake, and for our sake suffered every manner of torments." [1]   But he especially dwells on our Saviour's death.   Thus at the very commencement of his letter to the Church of Philadelphia, he says that it " rejoices unceasingly in the Passion of our Lord Jesus," and, likewise to the Church of Tralles, that it " possesses peace through the flesh and blood and passion of Jesus Christ, who is our hope."   He also writes to the Romans : " I seek Him who died for us, I wish for Him who rose from the dead for us." [2] Writing to the faithful of Smyrna, he speaks of Christ " crucified for us " and of the " fruits which accrue to us from this Divine and blessed Passion. . . . For He suffered all this for our sake and for our salvation "; farther on he speaks also of " Christ's flesh which suffered for our sins." [3]   The result of Christ's death was the salvation of our souls, which the saintly bishop describes under the figure of life.   " Christ is our Saviour . . . we were restored to life by His divine blood," [4] whilst elsewhere he implores the faithful to " keep no longer the Sabbath, but the Lord's day, on which Life rose again for us, thanks to Him and His death." [5]   Lastly, to the Christians

---

[1] Ignat. Ad Polyc. iii. 2. δι' ἡμᾶς ὁρατόν . . . δι' ἡμᾶς παθητόν . . . κατὰ πάντα τρόπον δι' ἡμᾶς ὑπομείναντα.

[2] Rom. vi. 1. 'Εκεῖνον ζητῶ τὸν ὑπὲρ ἡμῶν ἀποθανόντα.

[3] Ad Smyrn. i. 2—ii. ταῦτα πάντα ἔπαθεν δι' ἡμᾶς ἵνα σωθῶμεν. . . . vii. 1. σάρκα . . . τὴν ὑπὲρ τῶν ἁμαρτιῶν ἡμῶν παθοῦσαν.

[4] Eph. i. 1. ἀναζωπυρήσαντες ἐν αἵματι Θεοῦ.

[5] Magn. ix. 1.

of Tralles he says explicitly : " Let us live according to Christ, who died for us, that by faith in His death we may be delivered from death." [1]

In his brief epistle to the Philippians, St. Polycarp, the friend of Ignatius, several times alludes to Christ's wholesome death. He speaks of Christ, " who consented to suffer for our sins even unto death." Farther on, expounding St. Peter's well-known text, he writes : " Let us be steadfast in our hope and the pledge of our justice, who is Christ Jesus, who also bore our sins in His body on the cross, who committed no sin, and in whose mouth there was found no guile ; but who suffered for us that we might have life in Him." He also exhorts the faithful to imitate this great example of patience. A few lines farther, he, like Ignatius and St. Paul, puts in apposition Christ's death and resurrection and beseeches the Philippians to give their whole-hearted love " to Him who died for us and whom God raised again for our sake." [2] Again, the Church of Smyrna in its letter to the other Churches dealing with Polycarp's martyrdom, speaks of Christ, " who suffered for the salvation of the elect throughout the world, the sinless for the sinful." [3]

We should certainly hesitate to build up a theory on such brief and scattered texts, but one thing plainly emerges from them—viz. that Christ's death brings salvation to the world, destroys sin, and quickens

---

[1] *Trall.* ii. 1. Τὸν δι' ἡμᾶς ἀποθανόντα, ἵνα πιστεύσαντες εἰς τὸν θάνατον αὐτοῦ τὸ ἀποθανεῖν ἐκφύγητε.

[2] Polyc. *Ad Philipp.* i. 2. ὃς ὑπέμεινεν ὑπὲρ τῶν ἁμαρτιῶν ἡμῶν ἕως θανάτου καταντῆσαι.—viii. 1. δι' ἡμᾶς, ἵνα ζήσωμεν ἐν αὐτῷ, πάντα ὑπέμεινεν. . . . see also ix. 2.

[3] *Mart. Polyc.* xvii. 2: τὸν ὑπὲρ τῆς τοῦ παντὸς κόσμου τῶν σωζομένων σωτηρίας παθόντα . . .

souls.   We shall find clearer texts in the epistle of
Barnabas and in the epistle to Diognetus.

St. Barnabas, or whoever else may be the writer of
the epistle, writing to Jews, is manifestly seeking to
justify in their eyes Christ's death, which was a scandal
to them.   As was to be expected, he does so by
appealing to the Old Testament prophecies of which
it was the fulfilment, and which our author, using his
subtle allegorism, has no difficulty in expounding
agreeably to his views.   After having pointed to the
figure of Isaac's sacrifice, he dwells at length on the
symbolism of the scapegoat, and then shows in Moses
on the mountain and in the brazen serpent two other
types of the cross and its benefits.   The writer then
plunges deeper into the real meaning of the mystery.
" If the Son of God, He who is the Lord and shall
judge the living and the dead, suffered, it was to give
us life by His stripes " ; and he continues : " Be sure
that *the Son of God could not undergo suffering save
on our account* "; even more than Isaac, " He gave
His own body as a sacrifice for our sins." [1]   The real
object of His passion was no other.   " The Lord
willed to deliver His body that by the forgiveness of
our sins we might be sanctified, which is effected by
the aspersion of His blood ; for it is written : He was
wounded for our iniquities and bruised for our sins,
by his bruises we are healed.   He was led as a sheep
to the slaughter, and was dumb as a lamb before the
shearer."   And yet again the writer returns to the
point : " If He suffered, it was for our souls . . . to
destroy death and bring about the resurrection of the
dead, and to fulfil the promise made to our fathers

---

[1] vii. 2. πιστεύσωμεν ὅτι ὁ υἱὸς τοῦ θεοῦ οὐκ ἠδύνατο παθεῖν εἰ μὴ
δι' ἡμᾶς and *ibid.* 3.   αὐτὸς ὑπὲρ τῶν ἁμαρτιῶν ἡμῶν ἔμελλεν . . .
προσφέρειν θυσίαν.   Cp. *Mart. Polyc.* 5.

I

that He would prepare unto Himself a new people," [1] " a people born again by the forgiveness of sins, and possessing the other quality of being children of God, who has fashioned us again " [2]; in a word, a nation of heirs adopted by suffering. [3]

If all this is somewhat obscure, it is nevertheless quite clear that forgiveness of sins was the object and result of Christ's sacrifice. In fact, the Incarnation itself was productive of immense good. " Had He not come in the flesh how could men have been saved to see Him [in His glory], those men who cannot even bear to look on the sun, a corruptible thing made by His hands ? " [4] Hence God drew nigh to us by His Incarnation and drew us to Him by His Passion ; this, in a nutshell, is the Saviour's work as understood by Barnabas.

In the epistle to Diognetus we find the same theme. God, who was unknown to men, willed to manifest Himself to them. To this end He conceived " a grand and unspeakable thing "—i.e. the Incarnation of His Son, to whom we owe it that " we not only share His goods, but see and touch Him. Who of us would have ever expected such a favour ? " [5] The writer then proceeds to epitomise the data of St. Paul and St. Peter in that eloquent ninth chapter, which we shall now quote in full. " God having decided in His eternal decrees to manifest Himself to the world, in olden times allowed men to give themselves over freely to their ill-ordered passions. Not indeed that He took pleasure in our sins, but He endured them, not that He approved iniquity, but He was preparing for present justice. Thus did He act that we, being

---

[1] BARNAB. *Epist.* v. 1-2, and 6-7.
[2] *Ibid.* vi. 11.
[3] *Ibid.* xiv. 4.
[4] *Ibid.* v. 10.
[5] *Epist. ad Diogn.* viii., passim.

convinced of our inability to make ourselves, by our own efforts, worthy of life, might be favoured by the gratuitous goodness of God, and that, after having shown ourselves powerless to enter God's kingdom, we might receive this power from the Almighty. Hence when our iniquity had filled the cup and when we could only expect its wage in punishment and death—O the boundless love of God—He hated us not, nor did He cast us away, nor did He take revenge. On the contrary, He suffered us to be, and, yet more, moved by mercy, He loaded Himself with our sins, and gave His own Son as a redemption for us, the Holy for the wicked, the Blameless for the guilty, the Righteous for the unrighteous, the Incorruptible for the corruptible, the Immortal for mortal men; *for what else could have blotted out our sins save His righteousness? Who could have justified us impious sinners save only the Son of God?*" [1] The singular boldness of the latter sentence cannot but impress us. Barnabas had told us that the Son of God could suffer only for our salvation; here we read that our salvation could be effected only by the Son of God. These are the two fundamental principles on which little by little the whole theology of the Atonement will be constructed.

Our author continues, giving vent to his admiration at the mystery he has just described. "What a sweet exchange; how unsearchable are the ways of providence and how unexpected are its favours! That the iniquity of many should be taken away by

---

[1] *Epist. ad Diogn.* ix. 2-4. . . . ἐλεῶν αὐτὸς τὰς ἡμετέρας ἁμαρτίας ἀνεδέξατο, αὐτὸς τὸν ἴδιον υἱὸν ἀπέδοτο λύτρον ὑπὲρ ἡμῶν, κτλ. . . . Τί γὰρ ἄλλο τὰς ἁμαρτίας ἡμῶν ἠδυνήθη καλύψαι ἢ ἐκείνου δικαιοσύνη; ἐν τίνι δικαιωθῆναι δυνατὸν τοὺς ἀνόμους ἡμᾶς καὶ ἀσεβεῖς, ἢ ἐν μόνῳ τῷ υἱῷ τοῦ θεοῦ;

the righteousness of one and that one's righteousness should justify many sinners. Thus God in ancient times proved the powerlessness of our nature to restore life unto ourselves, and in the latter times He has given us a Saviour able to save those who were unable to save themselves; on either hand God leads us to trust in His kindness." [1]

The epistle to Diognetus manifestly draws its inspiration from St. Paul; we feel this by the depth of its doctrine. As we saw, the other Apostolic Fathers consider the proximate cause of Salvation, which is the death of Christ, or else the immediate effect of this death, which is our Salvation. Our sins caused Christ's sacrifice, and in its turn this sacrifice obtained the forgiveness of our sins. But here they stop short, nor do they give any reason for the salutary results of Christ's action. Now it is just this matter which the writer of the epistle endeavours to probe; according to him the real cause of our salvation is the righteousness of the Son of God, which alone can compensate for our shortcomings. In other words, we here again meet the great Pauline principle of the substitution of Christ for guilty mankind, and indeed it will be long before we find it again put forward so vigorously as it is by the anonymous writer of this epistle to Diognetus. But if he explains in some sort the Divine plan of Salvation, he has less to say of its carrying out. He was not unmindful of Christ's death, but at the same time he does not expressly mention it; it would almost seem that from the transcendent standpoint whence the writer views the whole matter, such a contingency appeared of small account. He gives us the ultimate reasons of a pro-

---

[1] *Epist. ad Diogn.* ix. 4-6. ὦ τῆς γλυκείας ἀνταλλαγῆς, . . . ἵνα ἀνομία μὲν πολλῶν ἐν δικαίῳ ἑνὶ κρυβῇ, δικαιοσύνη δὲ ἑνὸς πολλοὺς ἀνόμους δικαιώσῃ.

blem of which the other sub-apostolic writers only enlarged upon the appearances. The two methods are equally, though inversely, incomplete, and should be combined to account for the whole mystery of Salvation, but it will be ages before this combination is effected.

II

The early Apologists, owing to the character of their work and the object at which they aimed, could not be expected to have much to say concerning the Atonement. Their first concern was to defend Christianity against the objections of the populace or of the learned. Occasionally indeed they felt themselves called upon to explain the new religion. But even then, recollecting that their pagan audience was an utter stranger to their philosophy, they had to leave mysteries aside and confine themselves to what we might call the outward aspect of Christianity. Hence they usually describe the Christian revelation as the highest development and perfection of Natural Religion; in fact we know one *Apologia*—that of Minucius Felix—in which even the name of Christ does not occur. Popular ignorance prevented the Apologists from trenching on the ground of theology.

Likewise, when they wished to paint pagan immorality they stood in no need of discussing the nature, gravity, and remedies of sin. They had only to point out the evils and disorders to which paganism conduced and the ignorance in which the pagans were concerning even the most elementary truths, an ignorance leading them to continue in that gross idolatry which to the Apologists seemed to be the very reign of Satan. Hence when they would fain show how Christianity is a freedom, they describe it as bringing with it truth—even that complete and Divine truth for which philosophers had sought in vain—and as destroying in consequence the deceitful rule of the devil.

Thus whilst no Apologist prescinds altogether from the idea of the Atonement,[1] they reduce it to the fact that Satan's tyranny was abolished by the Word and could be abolished only by Him ; that, moreover, it was mainly by His teaching that He gained His victory, "it was as a Divine master that Christ obtained for us salvation."[2] This is quite characteristic of the early apologetic literature ; their exposition of Christian doctrine undoubtedly lacked much, but its poverty in dogma may be easily explained by the circumstances which called forth the Apologists' efforts.

But, as Harnack admits, St. Justin is an exception to this general rule, for he "holds the widespread Christian doctrine that Christ's blood cleanses believers and that we have been saved by His wounds."[3] According to Ritschl, however, St. Justin's views do not differ from those of the other Apologists. Christ had for His mission to bring back men to their former destiny, which had been spoilt by sin, and this He does in two ways : as a teacher He taught them faith and obedience, as a judge He will at His return give everlasting life to the just and damnation to the wicked.[4] We shall now see how the facts com-

---

[1] This is admitted by HARNACK, *Dogmen.* i. p. 459.   *Cp.* p. 496 *f*, and *Précis,* p. 71.

[2] HARNACK, *Dogmen.* i. p. 499.

[3] *Ibid.* p. 500.

[4] RITSCHL, *op. cit.* i. pp. 4-5

pletely justify Harnack's contention as opposed to that of Ritschl.

There can be no doubt that Justin sets great stress on the good work wrought by Christ's teaching, and there is no need to remind our readers of his theory of the λόγος σπερματικός, which enables him to perceive fragments of truth in all the philosophical systems of ancient Greece. But he by no means confines himself to this. Even his Apologies contain some summary allusions to the Passion of Christ and to the Atoning power of His sufferings : " The Word of God became man for our sakes, that becoming a partaker of our sufferings He might also bring us healing." [1] " He took flesh and blood in view of our salvation." [2] He did not merely become man, He also suffered. " Having become man for the human race He endured all the sufferings which the devils instigated the senseless Jews to inflict on Him." [3] Justin had already quoted at length *Isaias* liii. to show that these sufferings had been foretold ; it is true that he merely records it as a prediction and does not point out in any way its doctrinal meaning.[4] Lastly, in the text of *Genesis* xlix. 11 : " He shall wash his robe in the blood of the grape," Justin again sees a prediction of the Passion, and he adds : " Christ had to suffer to cleanse in His blood those who believe in Him." [5]

But this doctrine of St. Justin's comes out much more clearly in the *Dialogue with Trypho*. To answer the objections of the scandalised Jewish

---

[1] JUSTIN, ii. *Apol.* 13. [2] *Ibid.* i. 66.
[3] *Ibid.* 63. [4] *Ibid.* 50.
[5] *Ibid.* 32. . . . τοῦ πάθους οὗ πάσχειν ἔμελλε, δι' αἵματος καθαίρων τοὺς πιστεύοντας αὐτῷ. See a similar interpretation in the *Dialogue with Trypho*, ch. 54.

Rabbi, Justin shows that Christ's Passion was the fulfilment of the prophecies and the reason of the forgiveness of our sins.

He first tells us that Christ frees us because He is our defence against the demons whose kingdom He came to destroy (ch. 30, 41, 45). Entering more into detail, he adds that it was His " Passion which saved men " (ch. 74), that it was His cross which restored them to life (ch. 138). Jacob served Laban for his flocks, " Christ too served—a service which He maintained even to His death on the cross—but for men whom He purchased at the price of His blood " (ch. 134). For which reason He has since become the prince of a new nation, and reigns, powerful and glorious, over all the earth (ch. 135). But He had first to die, according to the prophecy of Isaias, that sinners might be healed by His sufferings (ch. 43). The Old Testament swarms with figures of this wholesome Passion. The scapegoat stands for Christ, " who offered Himself in sacrifice for all sinners who wish to do penance." The flour of the sacrifices pre-figures the Eucharist, and the latter is a commemoration of the Passion undergone for us (ch. 40 *f*). The Paschal Lamb was a figure of the " salvation which Christ's blood would obtain for mankind," and likewise the scarlet cord of Rahab (*Jos.* ii. 18) was a sign of this blood, " by which those who were formerly adulterers and sinners obtain forgiveness of their sins and are saved" (ch. 111). The Jewish sacrifices and oblations were but an empty show, true forgiveness of sins is to be secured only " by the blood of Christ, who died for this end," and to prove this Justin quotes *Isaias* liii. (ch. 13).

Christ's death appears to St. Justin not only as a benefit and source of justification, he also represents

it, though he does not do so very clearly, as a penal
expiation, and in this his doctrine is novel. It was
the people's sins, he says, repeating Isaias, which
brought Christ unto death (ch. 89) ; it was for us
that He suffered His Passion (ch. 117). But a more
explicit passage is in chapter 95. Trypho had just
adduced the old rabbinical objection that Christ had
incurred the curse of God by hanging on a tree.
On the contrary, replies Justin, we it was who were
cursed for our sins ; pagans for their crimes, Jews for
their unfaithfulness, and then to deliver men from
this malediction " *God willed that His Christ should
take upon Himself this curse of all,*"[1] and Christ
obeyed His Father's wish. Here we find expressed
that idea of substitution, which in later days was to
prove so fruitful.

To sum up, according to St. Justin, as according
to the Apostolic Fathers, Christ's death was the
efficacious cause of Salvation. To explain its action
we as yet find no theory properly so-called ; but the
sacrificial symbolism and the ideas of St. Paul and of
Isaias, which later on were to become classical, are
already in the field. Thus did the brief and fitful
statements of the earliest churchmen prepare the
way for the dogmatic theology of a later age.

[1] Χριστὸν ὑπὲρ τῶν ἐκ παντὸς γένους ἀνθρώπων ὁ Πατὴρ . . . τὰς
πάντων κατάρας ἀναδέξασθαι ἐβουλήθη.—*P.G.* vi. col. 701.

CHAPTER VIII

THE DIFFERENT LEANINGS OF GREEK THEOLOGY—SPECULATION AND REALISM

ST. IRENÆUS, ORIGEN

IN the Apostolic Fathers and Apologists we found dogmatic statements, but little real theology. Their minds were indeed bent on the problem of the Atonement, but regarding its nature and cause their answers are somewhat shallow. Salvation, which they usually identify with the forgiveness of sins, comprises an ill-defined conglomeration of spiritual benefits present and future; and it is ascribed to Christ's mission in general and to the person of the Saviour, but more especially to His death upon the cross. Such are the basic truths which were handed down to the Christian Doctors for them to digest and analyse and classify according to the ever stricter rules of the nascent science of theology.

It was to be expected that a development would ensue in two alternative directions. Some reflecting on the severity of the conditions of Salvation would naturally be led to define the grievousness of sin, which is its obstacle, and the efficaciousness of our Saviour's death, by which grace is restored. Others would prefer to seek how they might best fit Christ's work into the general plan of God. No doubt these two sides of the question are inter-connected; but it is easy to consider one rather than the other, and history will show us that this is what really happened. No doubt we too must reunite the two aspects to see completely the mystery of the Atonement, but it is in the nature of things that the synthesis should be preceded by a more or less perfect analysis, nor, in fact, is it a matter of indifference from which side the question is approached.

By studying man's sin and Christ's atoning death we enter straightway into the very heart of the question; hence it is not to be wondered at that it was by reflecting on the Scriptural realism that little by little the doctrine of Satisfaction, which we explained in beginning, was built up. On the other hand, the second aspect of the question lends itself more readily to abstract reasoning and to the speculations which were the especial delight of the Greek mind. From the consideration of the latter aspect of the question arose a view of the Atonement which some have wrongly deemed the only theory of the Greek Fathers, and which we must now describe.

Salvation consists in restoring man to the destiny for which he was created, that everlasting and Divine life which he had lost through sin. Now sin shows itself especially in its consequences, and of these the most visible and grievous, the one which pierces our nature most cruelly and is the most in opposition to God's ultimate designs, is surely death. Hence Christ's work before all consists in destroying death; that of the soul by restoring us unto God's grace and love, that of the body by giving us the promise of the resurrection to come. Mankind will thus recover the double immortality which had originally belonged to it, and return to that sublime degree of resemblance with God in which it had been first constituted by the goodness of the Creator; mankind is thus made God-like. Given this view, the terms life, immortality, incorruptibility, deification, which are already met with in St. John and his disciples, will naturally be in constant use to describe Salvation as wrought by Christ, and naturally too the Saviour's death, though it will not disappear altogether, will be thrown into the background. What is all-important is the Incarnation, for it was necessary that Christ, in order to accomplish His work of restoration, should be at once God and man. This is why the Fathers always laid great stress on the conception of the Atonement as a deification when fighting the heresies which successively called into question the reality of Christ's human nature and that of His Divinity. But, once the mystery of the Incarnation of the Word had been accomplished by God Almighty, nothing more seemed requisite; human nature had been deified by its union with the Logos, and a similar process will take place in the individuals who unite themselves to Him by faith in, and faithfulness to, His teaching. In this fashion the Person of the Word-made-Flesh becomes not merely the cause, but also the type and the concrete realisation of Salvation, and the Atonement tends to be confounded with the Incarnation.

This theory now goes by the name of "mystical" or "physical" Atonement. It is not for us to say how much room it affords for speculations on the supernatural world, but it is clear that, if taken rigidly, it leaves no place for Christ's atoning death. As a matter of fact, in this absolute form it has been held by nobody, but it did provide the ideal framework in which the thought of several of the Greek Fathers moved. As a natural consequence, though these Fathers maintained the traditional data concerning Christ's death and its good results, they did not sufficiently show its importance nor penetrate its meaning; it is unfortunately too often the case that a broadening of the mental horizon is only gained at the expense of the precision, if not of the exactitude of the details. Whilst we have no desire to under-value these speculations of the Greeks, we wish that their failings and doctrinal imperfections should also not be lost to sight. We must also point out that modern historians of the Atonement have erred doubly, first by exaggerating the theory, and then by declaring that it was the only one known.[1] For even among the Greek Fathers there was another school of theologians—and the more numerous one to boot—which, basing itself on the realism of St. Paul and the Scriptures, was fully conscious of the decisive im-portance of our Saviour's death and devoted its best efforts to entering more thoroughly into its meaning.

Speculation and realism, such we believe are the two words which best characterise the two drifts which are perceptible in the Greek Fathers' theology on the Atonement. Of this twofold current of opinion we shall find two accredited exponents in the founders of Greek Theology—St. Irenæus and Origen.

I

In St. Irenæus's vocabulary a word which is fre-quently used to express Christ's work is *recapitulatio* (ἀνακεφαλαίωσις), a word which is exceedingly vague in its meaning by reason of the complexity of the ideas for which it stands. Usually meaning a " summary," it sometimes signifies a " restoration "; both these meanings are allowed or even suggested by ety-mology, and thus it is used, now in the one, now in the

[1] *Cp.* RITSCHL, *op. cit.* p. 4 *ff.* HARNACK-CHOISY, *Précis,* pp. 144-146. SABATIER, p. 45 *f.*

other sense. For Christ indeed sums up in Himself all mankind, but He does so only to form it anew, and restore it, and lead it back to the way from which it had strayed. One and the same word thus stands for both the result and the reason of the Atonement, and serves as the mantle to shroud the somewhat unstable thought of the Doctor of Lyons, affording us a glimpse of its general form without however allowing us to be quite sure of its elements.

According to St. Irenæus, ever since Adam, men have been ruled by sin, which puts them in the devil's power and makes them foes of God, whom they have offended.[1] But our Doctor dwells by preference on the ravages which sin has wrought in our nature. Man had been made to God's image to enjoy incorruptible and everlasting life, a sublime and gratuitous destiny which he was to acquire by voluntary obedience. " Submission to God gives incorruptibility, and perseverance in incorruptibility gives everlasting glory " (iv. 38, 3). On the contrary, " to separate oneself from God is death " (v. 27, 2). This is why Adam by his sin incurred death and passed on this fell legacy to his descendants (iii. 18, 7 and passim). Man being unable to come out of this state, God in His goodness gave him a Saviour (iii. 20, 1 and 3),[2] in whom we find that which we lost in Adam—viz. the image and likeness of God.[3] This sentence contains the general principle

---

[1] IREN. *Adv. Hær.* v. 14, 1. *Cp.* v. i. 1 ; v. 17, 1, etc.

[2] Nevertheless, as a motive of Adam's salvation, Irenæus bids us consider God's Majesty, which cannot allow itself to be overcome by the devil (iii. 23, 1). But this principle, if pressed, would in addition make the Atonement *necessary.*

[3] " *In compendio nobis salutem præstans,* ut quod perdideramus in Adam, id est secundum imaginem et similitudinem esse Dei, hoc in Christo Iesu reciperemus." iii. 18, 1.—*P.G.* vii. ; col. 932.

and almost a summary of St. Irenæus's theology on
the Atonement.

Christ's positive work, the more important, consists
in restoring our corrupt nature by giving it the Divine
likeness which it had lost; and this work demands a
real union between God and mankind. When arguing with the Docetæ, St. Irenæus always takes his
stand on this idea: "*Christ became what we are to
make us what He is*" (v. præf.). "The Word of God
became man, the Son of God became the Son of Man
that man by being thus brought into contact with the
Word of God, might receive adoption and become a
son of God. For it were not possible for us to receive
incorruptibility and immortality were we not united
with incorruptibility and immortality. And how
could we be united with incorruptibility and immortality, unless He of His own accord had become
what we are, in order that what, in us, is corruptible
might be swallowed up in incorruptibility, and what
is mortal in immortality, and we ourselves might receive the adoption of the children of God." For this
reason those who deny Christ's Godhead "are still in
their mortal flesh and debtors to death because they
will not receive the antidote of life" (*antidotum vitæ
non accipientes.* iii. 19, 1). Elsewhere St. Irenæus,
quite as energetically, and for a like reason, maintains
the real human nature of the Saviour: "He has not
truly redeemed us if He did not truly become man"
(v. 2, 1. *Cp.* v. 14, 2 and 3).

But does it not seem to follow from this that our
salvation was wrought by the mere fact of the Word
taking on Him our nature—*i.e.* by the very fact of the
Incarnation?—"It used to be said that man was
created to God's image, but this was not shown, for
the Word of God, to whose image man was made,

was invisible. That is why man so quickly lost the likeness of God. But when the Word of God became flesh, He confirmed all; He showed that the image was true; He restored and strengthened the likeness, by the visible Word leading man to resemble more and more the invisible Father" (iii. 16, 2). Thus, by His union with our human nature, the Incarnate Word restores all things and renews them in Himself.

But reparation was yet to be made for Adam's fault, and this was the object of Christ's whole life, which is a kind of reversed summary of that of our first father. Christ was born of a virgin mother, as Adam out of the virgin soil (iii. 21, 10). But what most impresses St. Irenæus is the steadfast obedience manifested by Christ, which he never tires of contrasting with Adam's disobedience.[1] Christ's temptations are in every respect the counterpart of the circumstances which accompanied the Fall. Because man had sinned through food, Christ abstains from food; because man had waxed proud at the bidding of the serpent, Christ humbled Himself. "Adam had infringed God's precept, this infringement was repaired by Christ, who obeyed all the precepts of the Law and all His Father's commands" (v. 21, 2). Especially does this obedience appear in His death on the cross, a form of death which was necessary "to heal that disobedience which had been through the wood" (*Eam quæ in ligno facta fuerat inobedientiam, per eam quæ in ligno fuerat obedientiam sanans.* v. 16, 3). Nor is Irenæus slow in finding in the Old Testament many figures

---

[1] "Nostram inobedientiam per suam obedientiam consolatus." v. 17, 1. *Cp.* iii. 18, 7, and iii. 21, 10. Eve's disobedience was likewise repaired by Mary's obedience. iii. 22, 4.

of the wood of the cross by which we are saved (v. 17, 3 and 4).[1]

Shallow parallelism of this kind is a poor development of the great Pauline idea that the moral disorder of sin must be repaired by the infinitely meritorious submission of the Son of God. But there are reasons to believe that St. Irenæus had not altogether lost sight of the main principle, in spite of his imperfect manner of expressing it, for he goes on to say that we are united with the second Adam, as we were with the first, by a union amounting to identity. " In the first Adam we offended God by disobeying His command, in the second Adam we have been reconciled by becoming obedient even to the death of the cross " (*Deum in primo quidem Adam offendimus non facientes eius præceptum ; in secundo autem Adam reconciliati sumus obedientes usque ad mortem facti.* v. 16, 3).

Nor does St. Irenæus confine himself to speaking of Christ's Atoning obedience, he also repeats the traditional sayings concerning His expiatory death. Christ died for us (iii. 16, 6 ; iii. 20, 2 ; iv. 27, 2) ; quoting the better-known texts of St. Paul, St. Irenæus tells us that this death redeems[2] and reconciles[3] us. Once at least he speaks of this death as a sacrifice—pre-figured by that of Isaac—in which God offers His own dear Son for our redemption.[4] Lastly, in another passage St. Irenæus ascribes to the Passion

---

[1] Irenæus points out that Christ's death occurred on the same day as Adam's Fall (v. 23, 2).

[2] iii. 16, 9 : " Pro nobis mortuus est et sanguine suo redemit nos." *Cp.* v. 1, 1 and 2 ; v. 2, 1 and 2 ; v. 14, 3-4.

[3] iii. 16, 9 : " Per passionem *reconciliavit* nos Deo " ; col. 929. " Iusta caro eam reconciliavit carnem, quæ in peccato detinebatur et *in amicitiam adduxit Deo.*" v. 14, 2 ; col. 1162.

[4] Τὸν ἴδιον μονογενῆ καὶ ἀγαπητὸν Υἱὸν θυσίαν παρασχεῖν εἰς λύτρωσιν ἡμετέραν. iv. 5, 4 ; col. 986.

K

the very benefits we have just seen him attributing to the Incarnation. " By His Passion He destroyed death, chased away error, corruption and ignorance, manifested both life and truth, and gave incorruptibility." [1]

Unfortunately St. Irenæus makes no attempt to harmonise these views of his on the Passion with his general principles concerning the necessity of the Incarnation, so much so that in the passages which seem to render his thought most completely, for instance Chapter xviii. of Book III., it is on the Incarnation that most stress is laid.

Irenæus here begins by standing out for the reality of Christ's sufferings, which had been impugned by the Gnostics. "If He did not really suffer, He deceives us when He tells us to imitate Him . . . and we ourselves are above Him when we suffer what He would not suffer." But this is not the case, for Christ is our perfect leader. " He fought and gained His victory, *making up for our disobedience by His obedience* ; He vanquished the devil and set free his captives, and gave salvation to His creature by destroying sin." Irenæus does not tell us how sin was destroyed, but he goes on to speak of the qualities of the Redeemer. " God, who is good and merciful and who loves mankind, willed to unite man to God [in Christ's Person]." For it was necessary for our Saviour to be both God and man ; man, because otherwise the fight against the Enemy would not be fair, and because so long as our nature was not united to God it could not possess incorruptibility ; and God

---

[1] ii. 20, 3. " *Per passionem mortem destruxit,* et solvit errorem, corruptionemque exterminavit et ignorantiam destruxit; vitam autem manifestavit, et ostendit veritatem, et incorruptionem donavit " ; col. 778.

too, otherwise our salvation would not be sure. "In a word, what was needed was a mediator between God and man who should be able, by His connection with both parties, to bring them again into peace and friendship, presenting man to God and revealing God to man. How could we share the adoption of the children of God were it not that the Word had united us to God by becoming flesh and communing with our nature? He therefore came and passed through every age, restoring all to communion with God."[1] Hence the Docetæ, who deny the reality of the Incarnation, are still under the old condemnation, for all the Mosaic Law does is to show sin without destroying it. It was therefore necessary that He who was to destroy sin and deliver man from death should become man like the man He wished to save. "Man had allowed himself to be carried off into bondage by sin, and had since remained the captive of death; it was also by a man that it behoved sin to be destroyed and death lose its power." This is exactly what happened: "Just as by the disobedience of one man, who had been fashioned out of the virgin soil, a great many became sinners and lost their life, so it was by the obedience of one man, who was born of a virgin, that many were justified and received Salvation." For this reason the Word of God became truly man, "*recapitulating mankind in Himself* that He might destroy sin, bring death to naught, and men to life."[2]

Full as this passage is of reminiscences of St. Paul,

---

[1] Elsewhere Irenæus says that He became elderly (senior) to sanctify old age (ii. 22, 4).

[2] iii. 18, 5-7; col. 935-938. "*Deus hominis antiquam plasmationem in se recapitulans,* ut occideret quidem peccatum, evacuaret autem mortem et vivificaret hominem."

Christ's death is not even mentioned. In other passages it is indeed alluded to, and put into some relation with the Incarnation, but without its transpiring which of the two is the principal cause of our Salvation. " Christ redeemed us by His blood; He gave His soul for our soul, His flesh for our flesh; by pouring over us the Holy Ghost He restored union between man and God; He made God to come down to man by the Spirit and made man to come up to God by His Incarnation; by His coming He gave us true and permanent immortality, uniting us to Him; these great truths are the refutation of all heresies." [1] Here the picture of our doctrine is complete indeed, only it is lacking in perspective. Elsewhere, speaking of reconciliation, Irenæus is no more precise. " Only those can be reconciled who were enemies. We were foes of God since Adam's fault, but by assuming our nature Christ reconciled mankind to God the Father; for He reconciles us to Him by His fleshly body and redeems us by His blood." [2] And a little farther on: " Having become by His Incarnation the mediator between God and man, He restored us to God's love, appeasing on our behalf the Father against whom we had sinned, and repairing our disobedience by His own obedience." [3]

These texts seem to show fairly clearly that our Doctor was inclined to put Christ's Incarnation and death on the same level; his thought is lacking in order and system, but there can be no doubt that according to him the Atonement meant the repairing of the havoc wrought in our nature by sin and the reconciling of man with God, and that for this the In-

[1] v. i. 1 ; col. 1121.
[2] v. 14, 3 ; col. 1162.f.
[3] v. 17, 1 ; col. 1169.

carnation, Passion, life, and death of the God-Man
was needed. He seems to hold strongly to both
these ideas, but he never succeeded in fitting the two
together. At any rate we know now what to think
of Ritschl's statement that Irenæus, " in agreement
with his predecessors, gave eminence to, and in fact
followed as his leading thought, the idea that Christ
is a master who gives us the full knowledge of God,
in order that by imitating His works and following
His injunctions we may enter into perfect communion
with Him." [1] Harnack is far nearer the truth when
he observes that " the Historical Christ is the centre
(of his system) *not inasmuch as He is a teacher*—
though it is true that the rational [read quasi-
rationalist] theory sometimes comes into conflict
with the realistic theory of the Atonement—but
inasmuch as He is the God-Man." [2]

II

With St. Irenæus we may class a great Roman
Doctor who in some respect might be called his
disciple—St. Hippolytus. The mutilated fragments
of his works which remain and which might serve to
furnish arguments in favour of any hypothesis, allow
us, not indeed to reconstruct his system, but at least
to perceive its main lines.

In the first instance we find the current ideas concerning the atoning death. Salvation is connected
" with the cross and nails of our God." [3] Christ's death

[1] RITSCHL, *op. cit.* i. p. 7.

[2] HARNACK-CHOISY, *Précis*, p. 82, and *Dogmengeschichte*, i. pp. 515-
517.

[3] HIPPOLYT. *in Sanct. Pascha*, fragm. iv. ACHELIS ed. (Leipzig,
1897), p. 270.

is represented as an expiatory sacrifice : Christ is the Lamb of the true Pasch, slain for us,[1] and whose blood cleanses the world.[2] Our sins are the only real cause of His death ; Hippolytus touches on this penal aspect of Christ's death when he applies to the suffering Messias the words of *Psalm* lxviii. " *Quæ non rapui tunc exsolvebam*—*i.e.* I who had not sinned suffered death for Adam's sin."[3] The result was the blotting out and expiation of our sins. Christ nailed them with Him to the cross.[4] He is the high priest who, as the Baptist had said, takes away the sins of the world. Gabriel likewise had said of Him that He came to abolish iniquity and bring everlasting justice (*Dan.* ix. 24). This Christ did, for according to St. Paul He is our peace, reconciling all things and destroying the decree which was against us, nailing it to the cross, that He might blot out our iniquities and atone for our sins.[5]

Few Fathers have speculated more than Hippolytus on the mystical value of the Incarnation. " The eternal Word became man among men to restore Adam in Himself "[6]—an idea very similar, as Harnack points out,[7] to St. Irenæus's " recapitulation " theory. " He became man, man in his entirety, to save fallen man and to give immortality to those who would believe in Him."[8] Elsewhere Hippolytus

---

[1] *In Elcanam et Annam*, fragm. iv. *Ibid.* p. 122.

[2] *In Genes.* xxiv. *Ibid.* p. 60.

[3] *Adv. Iudæos*, ii. and iii. *P.G.* x. ; 789.

[4] *In Gen.* vii. *Loc. cit.* p. 54.

[5] *In Dan.* iv. 21. Bonwetsch ed., p. 268.

[6] Ἀναπλάσσων δι' ἑαυτοῦ τὸν Ἀδάμ. *De Christo et Antichr.* 26. Achelis ed., p. 19. *Cp. in Dan.* iv. 11 ; p. 214.

[7] *Dogmengesch*, 1, p. 560, note 1.

[8] *Contr. hær. Nœti*, 17. *P.G.* x. 825-828. *Cp. ibid.* 18. δι' ἡμᾶς γέγονεν καθ' ἡμᾶς.

distinctly hints that this benefit was secured by the Incarnation itself. " He wishes to make us all sons of God. . . . The Word of God, which was without flesh, took a holy flesh in the womb of a holy virgin in order to unite our mortal body to His power, to combine the incorruptible with the corruptible, the weak with the strong, and thus save man who was lost."[1]

" But if man is immortal, then he is God."[2] Even this consequence does not shock Hippolytus, and in the latter pages of the *Philosophumena* he presses the deification theory till it borders on paradox. We are not gods by nature. " The Creator was not mistaken, what He wished to make was not a god, nor an angel, but simply a man. Had He wished to make a god, He might have done so after the example of the Logos." But though we are not gods, by nature we may become such conditionally on obeying His precepts. The just will have " an immortal and incorruptible body similar to the soul itself. After having on earth served the King of Heaven thou shalt become a partaker in God and co-heir with Christ; thou shalt not be subject to concupiscence, to passions, or to bodily ailments ; *for thou hast become God.* Thou wert a man, and thou didst suffer as such; but God has promised to give thee the privileges of His Godhead because thou art deified and engendered unto immortality." We owe all these benefits to Christ. He it was that cleansed man from his sins and made of him a new creature. " If thou obeyest

---

[1] *De Christo et Antichr.* 3 and 4 ; pp. 6-7. ὅπως συγκεράσας τὸ θνητὸν ἡμῶν σῶμα τῇ ἑαυτοῦ δυνάμει, καὶ μίξας τῷ ἀφθάρτῳ τὸ φθαρτὸν καὶ τὸ ἀσθενὲς τῷ ἰσχυρῷ, σώσῃ.

[2] *Serm. in Theoph.* 8. *Ibid.* p. 262. εἰ ἀθάνατος . . . ὁ ἄνθρωπος, ἔσται καὶ Θεός. Though the authenticity of this sermon is denied by certain critics, it is upheld by the majority. In any case, this sentence gives in a handy form a view which was certainly current.

His precepts, if thou dost carefully imitate Him, thou shalt be honoured even as He. *God has power enough to make thee God for His own glory.*"[1] It would be difficult to push logic any further and to succeed better in running to death a theory which in itself was perfectly correct.

In another text we find an excellent summary of St. Hippolytus's views on the Atonement. "The first man, made from the dust, had been lost, death held him fast in its chains. He who came to snatch him from hell, He who came down from heaven to lead back the fallen, He who became the preacher to the dead, the atonement for sins, and the resurrection of the buried, was the eternal Logos. He came to the help of vanquished man, making Himself like unto him; in a virgin's womb He assumed the manhood of the first Adam, He who was a spirit comes to save earthly man, He, the Living One, comes to save him who had died through disobedience; coming from heaven, He recalled fallen mankind to its higher destiny; He, the Free, wills by His own obedience to restore a slave to freedom. He transforms into a diamond, man who had fallen into dust and become the prey of the serpent; He shows this Man hanging on the cross, mastering him who had vanquished Him; in the wood was His victory."[2] In spite of the confusion apparent in this summary the predominance of the "recapitulation" idea is very noticeable.

---

[1] *Philosoph.* x. 33-34.—*P.G.* xvi. *ter*; col. 3450-4. ἔσῃ ὁμιλητὴς θεοῦ καὶ συγκληρονόμος Χριστοῦ. . . . Γέγονας γὰρ θεός . . . ὅτι ἐθεοποιήθης, ἀθάνατος γεννηθείς. . . . Οὐ γὰρ πτωχεύει Θεὸς καὶ σὲ θεὸν ποιήσας εἰς δόξαν αὐτοῦ.

[2] *In cant. magn.* fragm. ii.; ACHELIS edition, p. 83. οὗτος ἦν ὁ τοῦ νενικημένου ἀνθρώπου γεγενημένος βοηθός, κατ᾽ αὐτὸν ὅμοιος αὐτῷ, πρωτότοκος λόγος τὸν πρωτόπλαστον Ἀδὰμ ἐν τῇ παρθένῳ ἐπισκεπτόμενος.

In fine, Hippolytus and Irenæus were both carried away by their system, which led them to consider the Atonement in the light of a deification of our nature, and consequently to insist rather too exclusively on the Incarnation. Nevertheless, they were kept back from going too far astray by the Scriptural teaching concerning Christ's salutary death. We shall have occasion to see how, even much later, the traditional realism tended to counterbalance the excessive speculativeness of the Greek mind ; it is not surprising that good, though unexperienced, theologians were not always able to prevent themselves from inclining too much to one side.[1]

III

Now that we have seen how speculative theories contrived to enfeeble the realism of the cross even amongst the most illustrious exponents of Western theology, we should hardly expect to learn that it was otherwise in that hot-bed of idealistic interpretation yclept the school of Alexandria. Nevertheless, the texts are there to show that it is the unexpected which is true. We do not indeed mean to assert that all the Alexandrine Doctors agreed in their theories respecting the doctrine of the Atonement ; in fact, the very first one of them whom we shall have to consider holds a curious mixture of dissimilar views, but from the beginning we find that they are realistically inclined and realism finally became characteristic of their school.

[1] Later on we find the "recapitulation" idea in St. Methodius of Olympus. "So far does he go that he appears entirely to identify Christ with the person of the first Adam." TIXERONT, *Hist. des Dogmes* (Paris, 1905), i. p. 422. *Cp.* METHOD. *Convivium*, iii. 4-5. *P.G.* xviii. ; col. 65-68. *Cp.* 8 ; col. 73.

Were we to judge Clement of Alexandria by a part only of his work, we might be tempted to believe that his views are at the antipodes of the traditional doctrine. We find him constantly speaking of incorruptibility as the supreme good and, strange to say, he derives it not from the Incarnation, but from the mere knowledge of the Logos and of His doctrine, from the true Gnosis. The Word is " our Saviour " in the sense that He is the " life-giving and peace-bringing spring which floods the earth."[1] A few lines farther down Clement, describing the manner of the Atonement, fails to ascribe it at all clearly to Christ's death.[2] " Man, who was happy and free in the earthly paradise, had yielded to pleasure, and offended God. He had become a captive in the bonds of sin. To deliver him the Saviour took on Him flesh, and with it vanquished the serpent and led death captive, and what is even more wonderful, He declared free the man who had been led astray by sin and entangled by corruption. How wonderful that a God should die and that man should rise again."

In other texts we can perceive even better how purely rational was Clement's Christianity. Speaking of Isaias's text : " The Lord delivered him for our sins," Clement merely adds : " To correct and punish them."[3] Against the useless sacrifices of the olden Law he can only set the sacrifice of the heart, which alone is pleasing to God.[4] Commenting on St. John's words : *Sanguis Christi mundat nos* (1 *Jn.* i. 7) he twice

---

[1] CLEM. ALEX. *Protrep.* x.   *P.G.* viii. ; 228.

[2] *Ibid.* xi. ; col. 228 f.

[3] *Pædag.* i. 8.   *P.G.* viii. 332.

[4] *Ibid.* iii. 12 ; col. 669.   Cp. *Strom.* ii. 18 ; col. 1017.   v. 14.   *P.G.* ix. 177.   *Ibid.* vii. 3 ; col. 417.   vii. 6 ; col. 444.

repeats that the blood of Christ is His teaching[1]; the same interpretation is found also in the *Pædagogus*. We do indeed find it stated in this work that we are united to Christ " by His blood, which redeems us," but this statement, qualified as it is by symbolic considerations, can scarcely be made to yield a meaning agreeable to tradition.[2]

But elsewhere Clement clearly tells us that Christ's blood is twofold: " There is the spiritual blood by which we have been anointed, and *the carnal blood by which we have been redeemed* "[3] from corruption. Jesus Christ is at one and the same time our High Priest and our Victim. " He is the wholly precious and perfect sacrifice offered for us."[4] It was for us that He gave Himself, to give us life and to cleanse even His enemies. Following in His footsteps, the Apostles too suffered for their Churches, and every true Christian should be ready to drink if needs be the chalice for the Church.[5] Such are the texts which we find in Clement's greater works and from which we gather that, though Christ's sufferings were not alien to our author's mind, yet that he dwelt on them comparatively little.

But the short moral tract, entitled *Quis dives salvetur*, tells a completely different tale. Right at the beginning we are told that Christ's death is the cause of our Salvation. " Had the law of Moses

---

[1] *Fragm. in* 1 *Ioan.*   P.G. ix. 735.

[2] *Pæd.* i. 6.   P.G. viii. ; 293, 300, 305, 308.

[3] σαρκικὸν [αἷμα] ᾧ τῆς φθορᾶς λελυτρώμεθα.   *Pædag.* ii. 2.   P.G. viii. 409.

[4] Ὁλοκάρπωμα ὑπὲρ ἡμῶν καὶ ἄπορον θῦμα ὁ Χριστός.   *Strom.* v. 11. P.G. ix. ; col. 108.   *Cp. ibid.* 10 ; col. 101.

[5] Παθεῖν ἠθέλησεν ἵνα τῷ πάθει ζήσωμεν αὐτοῦ.   *Strom.* iv. 7.   P.G. viii. ; col. 1256. . . . διὰ τὴν τῶν ἀπίστων ἀποκάθαρσιν.   *Ibid.* 9 ; col. 1284-1285.

sufficed to give life, it would have been vain for the
Saviour Himself to have come and suffered on our
account." [1] Farther on, Clement not only states that
Christ died for us, and by His death obtained for us
a whole treasury of virtues,[2] but elsewhere in the
same book he describes the expiatory character of
Christ's death in terms clearer than any we have
found so far, and, in fact, than we shall find even later.

" I regenerated thee," says Christ to the Christian
soul, " whom the world had brought forth to die ; I
delivered, healed, and redeemed thee. . . . I am thy
nurse . . . and thy master. . . . On thy behalf I
fought with death, and thus expiated the *death, thou
didst owe for thy sins* "(τὸν σὸν ἐξέτισα θάνατον, ὅν ὤφειλες
ἐπὶ τοῖς προημαρτημένοις).[3] Here the writer lays stress
on the substitutional character of the Atonement ;
farther on, he insists on the generosity of the self-
sacrifice it involved. " God was our Father by His
Divine nature ; He became our mother by His love
for us. . . . His eternal Son, the fruit of His love,
like Him is Love. That is why He came down,
became man, and willingly underwent our misfortunes. . . . Before offering Himself and giving
Himself for our redemption, He left us this new
testament : I leave you my love. What then is this
love ? It was what prompted Him to give His soul,
which is priceless above all else."[4] Lastly, Clement
tells the well-known tale of how St. John threw himself at the feet of one of his disciples who had become
a robber ; these are the words with which he tells us
the old man addressed the sinner : " Have pity on me,

---

[1] *Quis dives salv.* 8.   P.G. ix. ; 612.

[2] *Ibid.* 33 *f*; col. 640.   [3] *Ibid.* 23 ; col. 628.

[4] *Ibid.* 37 ; col. 641.   ὑπὲρ ἡμῶν ἑκάστου καθῆκε τὴν ψυχὴν, τὴν
ἀνταξίαν τῶν ὅλων.

my son ; fear not ; thou canst still hope for Salvation.
I shall answer for thee to Christ ; and if needs be I
shall willingly *suffer the death thou deservest, as Christ
suffered for us.* I shall give my life in exchange for
thine."[1]

It is not for us to seek to reconcile the two aspects
of the great Alexandrine philosopher's doctrine ; in
fact, this would not be an easy matter. It is enough
for us to point out that in spite of the intellectualist
moralism manifest in one part of his work, Clement,
either led by some hidden logic or by a fortunate in-
consequence, applies to Christ's death the traditional
principles of expiation and substitution, and, in fact,
comes very near using the very terms of vicarious
Satisfaction.

IV

Following in Clement's footsteps, Origen too describes the work of the Word made flesh as that of
the Divine Master who brings us perfect truth and
reopens for us the way to immortality. As was to be
expected, Ritschl knows no other side of his doctrine.[2]
On the other hand, Harnack with his riper knowledge
of the Patristic writers admits that "the atoning
work of the Logos is complex," and that an all-important position is given to "the death of Christ on
the cross, the salutary results of which Origen describes with an abundance of detail lacking in any
previous theologian."[3]

---

[1] *Quis dives salv.* 42 ; col. 649. Ἐγὼ Χριστῷ δώσω λόγον ὑπὲρ σοῦ·
ἂν δέῃ, τὸν σὸν θάνατον ἑκὼν ὑπομενῶ, ὡς ὁ Κύριος τὸν ὑπὲρ ἡμῶν·
ὑπὲρ σοῦ τὴν ψυχὴν ἀντιδώσω τὴν ἐμήν.

[2] *Op. cit.* i. p. 6.

[3] *Dogmengesch.* i. p. 635, note 1. *Cp.* HARNACK-CHOISY, *Précis,*
p. 106 *f.*

Whatever may have been Origen's theory on original sin, there can be no doubt that according to him all men are sinners and that they were unable to save themselves [1] and that salvation came only through God's mercy.

"Christ, when in the form of God, saw that by one man's fault death reigned over all the nations; He did not forget the creature of His hands. . . . It seemed to Him nothing to be equal to God and one with His Father so long as death consumed His handiwork. Hence He put off His Divine majesty and took the form of a servant, becoming man. In this guise the devil, who then reigned over men, was able to tempt though not indeed to vanquish Him. But Christ suffered the common death (not that of sin) that, like death, deliverance too should come through one man, and that there where sin had abounded grace might be spread abroad." [2] In all this Christ was following the bent of His love, offering Himself in sacrific for men who had nowise merited it. [3] But in so doing He was also obeying the will of His Father: "Christ humbled Himself; He ate and drank with sinners, He offered His feet to the tears of the repentant harlot, He put off His Divine majesty and put on the form of a servant; He so emptied Himself as to vouchsafe to die for sinners. In all this He was performing, not His own will, but rather that of His father who delivered Him for sinners. For the Father is good and the Son is the likeness of His goodness, and for this reason did He grant this benefit to the world to reconcile it unto Himself in Christ, even that world which had become

[1] ORIGEN in *Rom.* iii. 7. *P.G.* xiv. 946. *Cp. ibid.* v. 1, 1005 *f.*
[2] *Ibid.* v. 2, col. 1022.
[3] *In Matth. Series,* 135. *P.G.* xiii. 1786.

His enemy through sin."[1] Yet all this was done
by Christ freely. Especially when arguing against
Celsus, Origen is fond of insisting on the beauty of
this free and generous act of self-denial,[2] which he can
only compare to that of the pagan heroes casting
themselves into the jaws of death for their country's
sake. " Christ suffered willingly for the human race,
His death being like that of so many pagans who
offered themselves to save their country from plague
or famine or other calamities. *It would seem that
for mysterious reasons it had been established that the
death of a just man, freely accepted, should expel the
demons which vex the land."* Thus Christ's death was
not a mere example urging us to deny ourselves, but
also a source of immense benefits.[3] Nor does Origen
confine himself to such general considerations ; we
shall find him later on putting the same comparison
to a different doctrinal use.

It was not sufficient to deliver men from the outward yoke of the devil, they had also to be cleansed
from their sins, justified, and made friends of God ; it
was for this that Christ suffered.[4] " He came to
blot out the sins of the world, and He did so by His
death, of this no believer in Christ is ignorant."[5]
Hence so much does Christ's death depend on sin
that, " had there been no sin, Christ would not
have died."[6] But by His death it is destroyed.

---

[1] *In Ioan.* vi. 37. *P.G.* xiv. 300. *Cp. In Matth.* 75. *P.G.* xiii. ;
1720, and *Contr. Cels.* i. 69. *P.G.* xi. ; 789.

[2] *Contr. Cels.* ii. 11. *P.G.* xi. 816 ; ii. 24, col. 844 ; iii. 32, col.
961 ; viii. 43, col. 1581.

[3] *Ibid.* i. 31, col. 717-720. *Cp.* i. 61 ; ii. 16 *f*, 23, 34 ; iii. 17 ; vii.
17, 57.

[4] *Ibid.* iv. 19, col. 1052.

[5] *In. Num. Hom.* x. 3. *P.G.* xii. 638.

[6] *In Ioan.* i. 22. *P.G.* xiv. 57. οὔτ' ἂν ἀπέθανεν οὐκ οὔσης ἁμαρτίας.

It is destroyed, in the first instance, because Christ by a divinely decreed substitution takes on Him its penalty. Basing himself on Scriptural texts, Origen frequently describes Christ's death as a penal satisfaction.

Thus to prove to Celsus that His death had been foretold he quotes *Isaias* liii., and whilst establishing its Messianic meaning against the Jews, he himself applies it to Christ. " Men who until then had been subject to sin were to be healed by the Saviour's Passion . . . we were healed by His sufferings."[1] Elsewhere the same prophecy leads Origen to say that Christ on the cross bore our sins—*i.e.* underwent their penalty.[2]

" He bared His back to the scourges and gave His cheeks to be buffeted, nor did He recoil before being spat upon ; we it was who had deserved these outrages ; He delivered us by Himself suffering for us. He did not die to withdraw us from death, but that we might not have to die for ourselves. He allowed Himself to be buffeted for us that we who had deserved such handling might not suffer this for our sins, but that suffering all things for justice sake we might receive them all with joy."[3]

Origen also has recourse to the classical texts of St. Paul. " He who was blessed for ever was made a curse for us, but because He was blessedness itself, He abolished, destroyed, and blotted out the human curse."[4] " Christ knew not sin, but God made Him to be sin for us, so much so that we can no longer say of

---

[1] *Contr. Cels.* i. 54 *f.* *P.G.* xi ; 760 *f.*
[2] *In Levit.* i. 3.—*P.G.* xii. 408. *In Matth.* xii. 80. *P.G.* xiii. 1048. *In Rom.* vi. 7.—*P.G.* xiv. 1074.
[3] *In Matth. Series*, 113. *P.G.* xiii. ; 1761.
[4] *Ibid.* 125, col. 1776.

Him as of God : *Tenebræ in eo non sunt ullæ* (1 *Jn.* i. 5).
Zacharias depicts Him in sordid clothes, which signify
sin. He took on Him the sins of the believing
people in such a way as to be able to apply to Himself the words of the Psalm : *Longe a salute mea verba
delictorum meorum. Delicta mea a te non sunt abscon-
dita.* In saying this we are not wanting in respect
to Christ. For as the Father alone has immortality,
so, because our Lord through love vouchsafed to die
for us, it is the Father alone who can say : There is
no darkness in me. On the contrary, Christ in His
love for us took on Him our darkness, to destroy our
death by His power and chase away our darkness." [1]

Finally, in a remarkable passage Origen combines
these texts into one whole. [2] He first explains that
He who died is not the Eternal Word, who on account
of His Divinity stands above death, "but He who
died for the people ; He it was, the purest of all
creatures, who took away our sins and our infirmities.
He was able to take on Him all the sins of the world,
to abolish and wipe them out, because He had committed no sin, because no guile had been found on
His lips and because He knew not sin. This, I think,
is why St. Paul said : ' Him that knew no sin, for us
he hath made sin ' (2 *Cor.* v. 21). . . . In other
words, our Lord, who had committed no sin, took ours
on Him ; I might even say that, even more so than
His Apostles, He became a castaway." Here we
again find instanced the sacrifice of the heathen heroes

---

[1] *In Ioan.* ii. 21.—*P.G.* xiv. col. 160. διὰ τὸ ἀναλαβεῖν αὐτὸν τὰ τοῦ
λαοῦ τῶν πιστευόντων εἰς αὐτὸν ἁμαρτήματα.

[2] *In Ioan.* xxviii. 14.—*P.G.* xiv. col. 720-721. τῷ μηδὲν αὐτὸν
ἡμαρτηκότα τὰς πάντων ἁμαρτίας ἀνειληφέναι . . ., μόνου Ἰησοῦ τὸ πάντων
τῆς ἁμαρτίας φορτίον . . . ἀναλαβεῖν εἰς ἑαυτόν καὶ βαστάσαι τῇ μεγάλῃ
αὐτοῦ ἰσχύϊ δεδυνημένου . . . οὗτός γε τὰς ἁμαρτίας ἡμῶν ἔλαβε . . . καὶ
ἡ ὀφειλομένη ἡμῖν . . . κόλασις ἐπ' αὐτὸν γεγένηται.

L

to which a slight allusion had been made in the treatise against Celsus. We meet this comparison again and again,[1] but nowhere more eloquently expressed than in the following :—

"The Greeks narrate in their histories that certain heroes sacrificed themselves to ward off afflictions from their country. Whether the fact be true is not for us to say. But, what has never been related in any history, is that one suffered death for the whole world and that the whole world was cleansed by this sacrifice, whereas without such a sacrifice it must perforce have perished. Christ only could receive on the cross the burden of the sins of all; to carry this burden nothing short of His Divine might was required." The author then proceeds to apply to Christ the saying of Isaias: "He took on Him our sins and was smitten for our iniquities . . . the punishment awaiting us fell on Him instead . . . we are healed by the sufferings of His cross. His Father delivered Him . . . for our misdeeds, He was led to the slaughter for the sins of the people. . . ."

Hence Christ underwent for us the penalty of our sins, and He alone was capable of bearing it. We are told that the substitution was necessary, but were we to ask why, we should receive no answer. It never occurred to Origen to advert to the exigences of Divine Justice. In other words, Origen has not probed the mystery to the bottom, he has not succeeded in getting below the surface, but at any rate what he does he does well.

Nor does Origen confine himself to dealing with the penal character of Christ's death ; he also speaks of it as an expiation; we may have noticed this in

---

[1] *Cp. In Ioan.* vi. 36 ; *ibid.* col. 293 *f.—In Rom.* iv. 11 ; *ibid.* col. 1000.

some of the texts already cited. Christ's death is a sacrifice which destroys sin and reconciles us with God. " Christ offered Himself as a sacrifice to God in an odour of sweetness."[1] " He is the High Priest who appeased God for us and reconciled us to Him."[2] " He is the Lamb who takes away the sins of the world and cleanses us all by His death."[3] Origen seems to have a special fondness for this figure of the Lamb; certainly he uses none more frequently, and on one occasion it is apparent that he has at least some suspicion of the real mystery of the Sacrifice. " Christ is the Lamb *that was slain and which became, agreeably to certain occult laws, the cleansing of the whole world* for which, on account of the Father's love for man, He willed to suffer death."[4] " He is a propitiation for our sins, and not for ours alone, but for those of the whole world. . . . He annulled the decree that was against us . . . that not the slightest trace might remain of sins committed."[5]

Especially in his commentary on the epistle to the Romans, Origen by thus bringing together the texts of St. Paul and St. John is able to compose quite a little theology of Reconciliation. After having proved that Christ is our redemption, he continues : " But what is still more remarkable is that He is our propitiation by His blood—*i.e.* by offering His body He has made God propitious to us. . . . For God is just, and as such He cannot justify the unjust;

---

[1] *In Lev. Hom.* i. 2. *P.G.* xii. 408.

[2] *Ibid. Hom.* ix. 10 ; col. 523.

[3] *In Ioan.* i. 37. *P.G.* xiv. 85. *Cp. ibid.* xxviii. 20 ; col. 737, and *Contr. Cels.* ii. 10 ; viii. 43.

[4] *In Ioan.* vi. 35. *P.G.* xiv. 292. καθάρσιον γεγένηται κατά τινας ἀπορρήτους λόγους, τοῦ ὅλου κόσμου.

[5] *Ibid.* 37 ; col. 296.

wherefore He gives us a propitiator that by faith in
Him those might be justified who could not justify
themselves." Origen then proceeds to apply in
detail to Christ the symbolism of the propitiatory;
he recalls the Mosaic rite of propitiation by blood, and
adds : "Christ is both priest and victim ; priest as it
is apparent from the Psalms and from the epistle to
the Hebrews ; victim as St. John attests when he says
'Behold the Lamb of God who taketh away the sins
of the world.' Inasmuch as He is a victim He is
our propitiation, for by the shedding of His blood He
secures the forgiveness of sins. . . . If He did not
really forgive sins the propitiation would not be real."
To prevent anyone thinking that this doctrine is a
fond invention of St. Paul's, Origen quotes St. John,
who seems to him to enhance the mystery by declaring that Christ expiated not only the sins of the
faithful but those of the whole world.[1] Farther on,
Origen again returns to the same point : "All the
Scriptures bear witness that Christ was a sin-offering
and that He offered Himself for the cleansing of sin."
He proves this by the well-known texts of St. Paul
and concludes : "By this victim of His flesh offered
up for sin, He condemned sin—i.e. destroyed it and
put it to flight."[2]

He also reminds us that, according to St. Paul,
"when we were enemies we were reconciled with God
by the death of his Son," and resumes : "What a
shame, after such a reconciliation, after that the
enmity between God and man has been removed not
by a word of the sinner but by the blood of the
Mediator, for man to fall again into sin and again
offend Him whom only the blood of God was able to

[1] *In Rom.* iii. 8. *P.G.* xiv. 946-951.
[2] *Ibid.* vi. 12 ; col. 1095.

reconcile to us." The better to explain this atoning power of Christ's blood Origen appeals to the epistle to the Ephesians, and then explains, in somewhat ambiguous words, how "Christ's death killed the enmity between God and us," and how, since this enmity is in reality nothing but sin, "He, by His death, killed sin." He then continues : "After having discovered to us the secrets of this mystery—*i.e.* of Reconciliation through the death of Christ—Paul gives us its reasons and explains how that we were enemies of God and why this Reconciliation demanded the death of the Son of God." [1]

If we were enemies of God this was because of sin, which since Adam had ruled over men. The second question, the more important of the two, is scarcely answered adequately in the pages which follow, but elsewhere Origen gives it an answer which forms his most important contribution to the theology of the Atonement. We refer to his 24th Homily on the book of Numbers.

Origen here makes it clear that the sacrifices of the Olden Law were a figure of the Sacrifice of Christ, but that Christ's Sacrifice was alone in securing forgiveness of sins to the whole world. Christ reconciled God with man ; He is the innocent and pure victim, like unto the lamb, who soothes the anger of God. Such are the facts ; the underlying reason is this : So long as sins exist there must be victims for these sins. Had there been no sin the Son of God would not have become incarnate. "But sin entered into the world. Now *sin demands expiation, and expiation can only be by means of a victim.* Hence it was necessary to seek a victim for sin." But all the legal victims were imperfect and temporary. "*Christ alone could*

[1] *In Rom.* iv. 12 ; v. 1 ; col. 1002 *ff.*

blot out the sins of all." There was diversity of victims only until the coming of the perfect Victim who was to take away the sins of the world. But now that the great Victim has come, " all other victims have ceased because this Victim alone was sufficient for the salvation of the whole earth." [1]

Here we find the elements of an explanation, after-wards to become common, of the Atonement, by means of the Old Testament sacrifices. But Origen does not tell us why sin requires expiation nor how this is effected by the Saviour's death. We may even notice that the propitiatory character of the Sacrifice, being considered as independent of its penal character, remains as it were suspended between earth and sky. Origen following the lead of *Hebrews* has much to say of sacrifices and victims, but he has failed to explore the moral truths which these words cover. At any rate his efforts to reduce the scattered data into a system, however imperfect, was praise-worthy, nor was it a small thing to have given to the world a summary which for long after was sufficient to satisfy the needs of Christian thought.

The Greek Fathers of the third century thus seem to us to stand in two groups. Irenæus represents the speculative school in which Christ's death, though it does not altogether disappear, tends to retire into the shade ; on the other hand, Origen whose exegetical bent made him to be more realistically inclined, gives

---

[1] *In Num. Hom.* xxiv. 1.—*P.G.* xii. ; col. 755-759. " Quoniam peccatum introiit in hunc mundum, peccati autem necessitas pro-pitiationem requirit et propitiatio non fit nisi per hostiam, necesse fuit provideri hostiam pro peccato. . . . Sed . . . unus est agnus qui totius mundi potuit auferre peccatum ; et ideo cessaverunt ceteræ hostiæ, quia talis fuit hæc hostia ut una sola sufficeret pro totius mundi salute."

us the ordinary doctrine of Atonement by Christ's death, and moreover anticipates the later synthesis. We shall now see how these two currents persisted and presided over the development of Greek theology in the fourth century.

CHAPTER IX

THE SPECULATIVE SYNTHESIS

ST. ATHANASIUS—ST. GREGORY OF NYSSA

So far, even in the works of those great pioneers, Irenæus and Origen, we have found only scattered fragments which can scarcely be dignified by the name of a system. They only touch on the Atonement problem incidentally when considering other matters; not until the fourth century will anyone broach the question of the Atonement for its own sake. St. Athanasius and St. Gregory of Nyssa are superior to their predecessors in this respect, that they had on this question a system of well-defined though not always quite coherent ideas, which they both succeeded in marshalling in something like logical order; in other words, they wrote real treatises on the Atonement. These two treatises, in spite of certain noteworthy disagreements, agree in this, that they both express the specifically Greek doctrine. All things said, these earliest attempts at a combination are presided over by the Greek spirit of speculation; this is our reason for taking them together.

I

We find the doctrine of St. Athanasius in the first chapters of his *De Incarnatione Verbi*,[1] and it can be

---

[1] ATHAN. *De Incarn. Verbi. P.G.* xxv. 95-140. Ritschl himself

reduced to these three fundamental points: The reasons of the Atonement, the Person and the work of the Saviour.

God created man, like all other things, from nothing by His Word; but seeing that he was weak and mortal He was struck with pity, and by grace elevated man above his nature. This grace by giving man the likeness of God, and as it were a shadow of the Word of God, allowed of his being happy and of his living in Paradise the life of the saints (ch. iii.). But man sinned and fell back into his native corruption, and death, which had been a part of the law under which he was created, was rendered yet worse by the weight of the Divine displeasure. Death had extended its frontiers, and the whole human race was doomed (ch. iv., v.).

But God could not allow a creature to perish which had once partaken of the Divine Word. It was not worthy of His goodness to allow His eternal plans to be frustrated by the negligence of men and the craft of the devil. It would have been a proof of weakness to allow men to perish in His sight; it would have been better not to have created them at all (ch. vi.). Farther on, St. Athanasius explains himself by using a comparison. A king does not forsake a city which he has built; he defends it as his own against its foes; still less does he allow his subjects to desert it; he considers himself in duty bound to prevent such a contingency, and takes every means to hinder it. God likewise could not forsake man; in this His Divine Honour was involved (διὰ τὸ ἀπρεπὲς καὶ ἀνάξιον εἶναι τοῦτο τῆς τοῦ Θεοῦ ἀγαθότητος.

remarks that this work was published before the beginning of the Arian struggle and that its authenticity cannot be questioned. *Op. cit.* i. p. 8.

ch. x. and xiii.).[1]   What then was He do ?   He could not but give effect to the decree of death which He had passed ; His sovereign truthfulness demanded the carrying out of the penalty.   Of course He might have demanded penance, but apart from the fact that this would have impaired His veracity, no penance could change the course of nature.[2]   Moreover our author elsewhere says : " A creature can in nowise save a creature."[3]   To effect this restoration of grace it was necessary to employ the very Word of God. He alone who had created all could restore all, and at the same time safeguard God's rights (ch. vii.).[4]

Consequently the Word became flesh ; He took a body that He might subject it to death instead of us, and thus restore to us life and incorruptibility (ch. viii.).   Farther on, St. Athanasius lays stress on the necessity of the Saviour's human nature.   " It was quite fit that the Word should put on a body to restore everlasting life to our own body. . . . Straw is by nature combustible, keep away the fire from it and it will not be burnt.   But straw it remains, and, as such, it fears fire, which is ever able to consume it. But surround it with asbestos—a body which seems to resist fire — and then it is safe and no longer dreads fire, thanks to this incombustible dress.   Thus is it with the body and with death.   Had death been destroyed merely by an act of the Divine Will, the body would have remained mortal and corruptible according to the nature proper to all bodies.   To

---

[1] There are, however, other texts which allow us to infer that there was here no real necessity but only a question of fitness.

[2] Οὔτε ἡ μετάνοια ἀπὸ τῶν κατὰ φύσιν ἀνακαλεῖται, ἀλλὰ μόνον παύει τῶν ἁμαρτημάτων.   Cp. Cont. Ar. Or. iv. 68 69.   P.G. xxvi.; 291-5.

[3] Epist. ad Adelph. 8.—P.G. xxvi. ; col. 1082.   Cp. Cont. Arian. Or. iv. 6 ; ibid. col. 478.

[4] Cp. 13, also Orat. ii. 14.   P.G. xxvi. 178.

prevent this the bodiless Word of God put on a body, and thus the body no longer fears death on account of the sheath of life which surrounds it."[1]   Elsewhere we find the same principle still more energetically insisted on. "Just as we should not be delivered from sin and the curse if the flesh taken up by the Logos were not human flesh, so likewise man would not be deified were He who became incarnate not the true and real Logos of the Father."[2]

Hence the greater part of our salvation is accomplished by the very fact of the Incarnation ; we now meet as it were a secondary work, which is set side by side, rather than connected, with the previous. "The Word took a body in order to die for all. . . . He therefore offered His body to death as a most pure victim. *He payed the debt due to death, and God's rights were secured.* But at the same time He restored to men, to whom He had likened Himself by taking their nature, the privileges of immortality" (ch. ix.). Athanasius again returns to the point : "Death was necessary to pay the debt of all, and in this is the twofold wonder, that the death of all of us took place in the Saviour's body and that death was destroyed because of the Word which dwelt in that body." Hence the sentence of death passed on us is annulled. "Corruption has no longer any terrors for man because of the Word which dwelt among them in a like body. Just as if a great king comes to a city and takes up his abode in one of its houses, not only is the city honoured, but no enemy or robber dares attack it, the very presence of the king being a safeguard. So is it with the King of Heaven.

---

[1] Ch. xliv. *P.G.* xxv. 175.

[2] *Orat.* ii. 70 ; col. 296. *Cp. Orat.* iii. 33 ; col. 394 & *Ep. ad Adelph.* 5 ; *ibid.* col. 1078.

Once He had come unto the regions of mankind and dwelt in a body like unto ours, an end was made to all the attacks of man's enemy, and corruption is destroyed."[1]

This then was the principal reason why Christ came; but there was another—viz. to restore to man the knowledge of God. Men were made to know God; to help them to do this they had the works of nature, and moreover God had sent His prophets. In spite of all this men went astray from God, so far as to render Divine worship to creatures. God's honour demanded that such disorder should be repaired, and the Word alone, the eternal image of His Father, was able to do so. He therefore made Himself man to instruct and enlighten men, and this is why He did not will to die at once (ch. xi.-xvi.). The Word thus gained a twofold result : He destroyed death and made us anew according to His image. Our present death is not the death of the guilty who suffer for their sin, but the pledge of a better life, of which He gave us the promise and furnished us an example. (Ch. xxi. *Cp.* xiii.).

Athanasius goes on to prove by mystical reasonings how fit were the circumstances of our Saviour's death (ch. xxii.), and he concludes by saying that Christ achieved His victory by raising His body to life, and by thus giving us a pledge of our own resurrection. Death is evidently vanquished, for the Christians, even children and women, despise it and look to it fearlessly. Death was nailed to Christ's cross as to a pillory, and the Christian who chances to pass by, strong in his faith in Christ Jesus, exclaims mockingly : " O Death where is thy victory ? O Death where is thy

---

[1] This comparison is again found in almost the same language in the *Sermo maior de fide*, 6. *P.G.* xxvi. 1267.

sting ? ” (1 *Cor.* xv. 55).   Death has therefore been killed by the life, death, and resurrection of the Saviour.[1]

II

We can see that in this book two ideas are adduced to explain Salvation and the Saviour's work : the idea of immortality or of the supernatural reformation of our nature, and the idea of an expiation of our death.   By consulting the other writings of Athanasius we shall find that it is the former idea which has the first place in his mind.

By sin man had lost that incorruptible and Divine life for which he had been created.   Christ came to restore it to him, and this is the greatest benefit He confers.   “ He became man to make us to be gods in Him.”   This phrase frequently recurs in the works of St. Athanasius.[2]   This deification involves, so far as our soul is concerned, a better knowledge of God, an inward renewal of our being by which we are made children of the Heavenly Father in the image of His eternal Son, surely an unspeakably great dignity, but one which we owe entirely to God's grace, and which does not make us cease to be menials by nature.[3]   Our body too thereby regains its immortality, and this even in this life through hope in the resurrection.

To make this deification possible the Incarnation was necessary, so necessary that it finally appears

---

[1] Μετὰ τὴν ἐπιδημίαν τοῦ Σωτῆρος καὶ τὸν τοῦ σώματος αὐτοῦ θάνατον καὶ τὴν ἀνάστασιν (ch. xxix.).

[2] *Ep. ad. Adelph.* 6.   *P.G.* xxvi. 1078.   *Cp. De Incarn. Verbi et contr. Arian.* 3, col. 990.   *De Incarn. Verbi*, 54.

[3] *Contr. Arian. Orat.* ii. 51 ; *ibid.* col. 254.   *Orat.* iii. 23-25 ; col. 371-376.   *De Inc. Verbi et contr. Arian.* 8 ; col. 995.

sufficient in itself. This was the reason which led Ritschl to ascribe the invention, and Harnack the elaboration of that theory of physical Redemption peculiar to Greek theology, to St. Athanasius.[1]

We have already seen how according to Athanasius the Redeemer must have two natures, Divine and human, for our own nature to be transformed and deified. He also lays so much stress on this union that· he almost seems to say that by the mere bringing into physical contact in Christ of the Divine and the human our Salvation was effected. Just as the king's presence is sufficient to honour and protect a city, so we are saved by the mere presence of the Word amongst us. " Because the Word of God, the eternal Son of the Father, clothed Himself with flesh and became man, we are delivered."[2] " Human nature and the Divine are linked together in Christ, and thereby our Salvation is established."[3] Our flesh is no longer earthly, now that it has been touched by the Word,[4] which became flesh for us. " By the very fact that the Saviour became man really and truly, the whole man was saved."[5] " The Saviour's presence in the flesh works our redemption and the Salvation of every creature."[6] Of course, in these texts Athanasius does not pretend to express the whole reason of Salvation, he merely demands a perfect union between the human and the Divine, a *conditio sine qua non* of Christ's work. But when we

---

[1] RITSCHL, *op. cit.* i. p. 10 *f.* HARNACK, *Dogmeng.* ii. pp. 157 and 159. *Précis,* p. 170 *f.*

[2] *Contr. Arian. Orat.* ii. 60. *P.G.* xxvi. 290.

[3] *Ibid.* 70, col. 296.

[4] *Orat.* iii. 33, col. 305 λογωθείσης τῆς σαρκὸς διὰ τὸν τοῦ Θεοῦ λόγον.

[5] *Ep. ad Epict.* 7. *P.G.* xxvi. 1062.

[6] *Ep. ad Adelphium,* 6 ; *ibid.* col. 1079.

find Athanasius labouring this point again and again, and when we consider it in connection with the Saint's theology as a whole, it is difficult not to think that St. Athanasius was guilty of a confusion and mistook a mere condition for the efficient cause.

The benefit of Salvation which is concentrated and summed up in the very fact of the Incarnation is expanded in the Saviour's life. He willed to load Himself with all our misfortunes—τὰ ἡμῶν, a general expression of which St. Athanasius is fond—that He might relieve us of them. "All our sufferings were laid on Him who could not suffer, and He destroyed them."[1] "He destroyed death by death and all human weaknesses by His human actions ; our fear also He destroyed by His fear and made men no longer to dread death."[2] "He took our poor, vile nature to give it some of His wealth ; His death made us to be impassible ; His tears are our joy, His burial is our resurrection, His baptism is our sanctification, His humbling Himself is our raising up, and His ignominy is our glory."[3] For, having become our Mediator, He offers to God all our weakness and wretchedness, giving us the good things He Himself had received.[4] "The Divine flesh because it was united with the Word was the first to be saved and delivered, afterwards we also were saved, being as it were in body one with Him (ὡς σύσσωμοι)."[5] Thus does Christ's whole life become the cause as well as the type and living realisation of our salvation.

---

[1] Orat. iii. 34 ; col. 395. ὡς εἰς τὸν ἀπαθῆ μεταβάντων αὐτῶν τῶν παθῶν καὶ ἀπηλειμμένων.

[2] Ibid. 57, col. 445.

[3] De Inc. Verb. et contr. Arian. 5. P.G. xxvi. 991.

[4] Orat. iv. 6, col. 475.

[5] Orat. ii. 61 ; ibid. col. 278.

Nor have well-informed Catholic writers neglected this side of the doctrine of St. Athanasius. "Athanasius," says M. Le Bachelet, "lays special stress on an aspect of the Atonement suggested by St. John and developed by Irenæus and the Asiatic school—i.e. the physical aspect. . . . But this aspect is by no means the only one known to him."[1]

In effect, the Saviour's death retains a place of importance in the plan of Salvation.[2] St. Athanasius explicitly states that the Saviour came "to suffer death for our sakes." Not only do His sufferings in general console us, it was also through His death that we obtained immortality ($\delta\iota\grave{\alpha}$ $\tau o\hat{v}$ $\theta\alpha\nu\acute{\alpha}\tau o\upsilon$ $\mathring{\eta}$ $\mathring{\alpha}\theta\alpha\nu\alpha\sigma\acute{\iota}\alpha$).[3] In fact, our salvation would not have been possible except by the cross[4]; though Christ came to restore man, He first of all paid our debt for us ($\mathring{\alpha}\nu\theta$ ' $\mathring{\eta}\mu\hat{\omega}\nu$ $\tau\grave{\eta}\nu$ $\mathring{o}\phi\epsilon\iota\lambda\grave{\eta}\nu$ $\mathring{\alpha}\pi o\delta\iota\delta o\grave{\upsilon}\varsigma$).[5] For each one of us was subject to that law of death which God had enacted against sin. This decree could not but be carried out; Christ abrogated it by dying in our stead. As Christ stood for the whole of mankind, we may truly say that all died with Him ($\mathring{\omega}\varsigma$ $\pi\acute{\alpha}\nu\tau\omega\nu$ $\mathring{\alpha}\pi\alpha\theta\alpha\nu\acute{o}\nu\tau\omega\nu$ $\mathring{\epsilon}\nu$ $\alpha\mathring{\upsilon}\tau\hat{\omega}$)[6]; henceforth death is our ruler no longer, for it has already obtained all it can claim. Here we find as clear as possible the substitutional idea, and as we have seen this idea lies at the very foundation of the *De In-*

---

[1] LE BACHELET in VACANT. *Dict de théol. cath.* art. *Athanase* ; col. 2169.

[2] This is acknowledged by HARNACK, *Dogmeng.* ii. p. 158 *f*, note 2. *Cp.* p. 172.

[3] *Cp. Orat.* ii. 55, col. 262. *Omnia mihi trad.* 2, col. 211. *De Inc. Verbi,* 54. *Cp. Orat.* iii. 58, col. 446.

[4] *De Inc. Verbi,* 26, col. 140. $\mu\grave{\eta}$ $\mathring{\alpha}\lambda\lambda\omega\varsigma$ $\mathring{\alpha}\lambda\lambda\grave{\alpha}$ $\delta\iota\grave{\alpha}$ $\tauο\hat{\upsilon}$ $\sigma\tau\alpha\upsilon\rho o\hat{\upsilon}$ $\mathring{\epsilon}\delta\epsilon\iota$ $\gamma\epsilon\nu\acute{\epsilon}\sigma\theta\alpha\iota$ $\tau\grave{\eta}\nu$ $\sigma\omega\tau\eta\rho\acute{\iota}\alpha\nu$.

[5] *Orat.* ii. 66, col. 287. *Cp. ibid.* 69, col. 295.

[6] *De Inc. Verbi,* 9, col. 111.

carnatione Verbi. Here, for the first time, we find this idea to the fore, and expressed not indeed by ἀντί,[1] but by ἀντίψυχον, which in its substantival meaning, though hardly to be translated, is as significant as could be wished.[2] At times we could almost fancy that we are reading a contemporary handbook of theology.

But when it comes to explaining the wherefore of this inexorable decree of death, which is so inflexible that in default of the guilty it must take its course on a substitute, St. Athanasius instead of seeking it in God's Justice never succeeds in getting beyond the Divine Veracity; God has sentenced sin to death, and His word cannot fail to come to pass, nor can His threat have been launched in vain. Athanasius seeks no further reason to account for this seeming obstinacy; in other words, he scarcely touches on the real problem, and His answer to it, if it be an answer at all, is but a superficial one.

Side by side with this explanation, which is peculiar to him, Athanasius also puts the traditional ideas, but without in any way attempting to co-ordinate them. Christ became our ransom[3]; He offered Himself to God as a sacrifice[4] and thereby redeemed us from our sins and washed us in His blood.[5] On account of sin the earth was cursed and Heaven was wroth; Christ came to destroy this curse,[6] and He did this

---

[1] A word we find used in IRENÆUS, *Adv. Hær.* V. i. 1. *P.G.* vii. 1121.

[2] *De Inc. Verbi,* 9; col. 111. τὸ σωματικὸν ὄργανον προσάγων ἀντίψυχον ὑπὲρ πάντων, ἐπλήρου τὸ ὀφειλόμενον.

[3] *Sermo maior de fide,* 26.—*P.G.* xxvi.; col. 1279.

[4] *De Inc. Verbi,* 6-10, 20, etc.

[5] *Serm. maior de fide,* 36; col. 1290. *Epist. ad Ep.* 4; *ibid.* col. 1058. *Or.* ii. 7; *ibid.* col. 162.

[6] *Omnia mihi tradita sunt,* 2.—*P.G.* xxv. col. 210 and 211.

M

by Himself becoming a curse for our sakes.[1] Following St. Peter, Athanasius also teaches that Christ bore our weaknesses and sins; that He not only healed them but actually bore them. This is a burden which weighs Him down.[2] Elsewhere he quotes Isaias to show that in Christ's sufferings we are healed, that His shame is our glory, and that He was chastised for our peace.[3] Lastly, combining these divers data, he says : "He was not made a curse, or sin, rather He took our curse, and He carried our sins and bore them in His body on the cross." [4]

These texts show that St. Athanasius was acquainted with the traditional realism under all its forms ; but as we already know, his attention was riveted elsewhere ; he preferred to dwell on the destruction of death and the restoration of men to their place as children of God ; in other words, he considered the positive rather than the negative side of the Atonement. Though he did not altogether neglect to consider the metaphysical inordinateness of sin, he dwelt rather on its practical consequences, the result being to make his system somewhat indefinite, not to say incoherent. From the point whence Athanasius viewed the question, the Saviour's death is only a phase of His Atoning mission, and possibly not even the principal ; this is why our Doctor has little to say of it, and when he does allude to it, is content with passing and superficial explanations.

---

[1] *Ep. ad Epict.* 8 ; col. 1063. τὴν ὑπὲρ ἡμῶν ἀνεδέξατο κατάραν. Cp. *Orat.* iii. 33 ; col. 395.

[2] φέρει, βαστάζει. *Orat.* iii. 31 ; col. 390.

[3] *De Inc. Verbi et contr. Arian.* 5. *P.G.* xxvi 991

[4] *Orat.* ii. 47 ; *ibid.* col. 247.

III

With St. Athanasius it is customary to class St.
Gregory of Nyssa. The latter in his *Great Catechesis*[1]
gives us a complete and systematic account of his
views on Salvation; it is a rather dry philosophical
exposal, with none of the easy, simple charm characteristic of Athanasius; nevertheless, save for this
difference of form, the system of both Fathers is the
same, though it is true that in Gregory's hands it
tends to assume more scholastic precision and consistency.

God created man through love, to partake of the
Divine goods; He adorned him with life, reason,
wisdom, and, in a word, with all the good things
which belong to God. Of these goods immortality
is the greatest, and in it man must also have shared.
To sum up, man was made to the image of God, and
this through God's liberality (ch. v.). But man fell
into sin, and the result was the downfall of mankind
unto death, error, and vice (ch. viii.).

God, who had foreseen the fall, had already
chosen the means to effect a restoration. He alone,
who had created man, could restore him, hence the
Incarnation of which Gregory gives us his theory
(ch. ix.-xiv.). He then goes on to ask himself the
cause of it, and replies that it can be nothing else
than God's love for men. " Our nature was sick and
sought a remedy, it had fallen and sought to be lifted
up, it was dead and sought resurrection. We had
lost possession of the good and it had to be restored to
us, we were in darkness and light had to be brought
us, we were captives and awaited a Redeemer, we

---

[1] GREG. NYSS. *Oratio catechetica magna*. *P.G.* xlv. 9-106.

were prisoners and desired a helper, we were slaves and hoped for a liberator. Was not this sufficient to move God even to descend to our poor human nature ? " (ch. xiv.).

But could not God have saved man by His Will ? " He who created the world by His Will, who drew it out of nothingness by one act of His Power, why should He not by a fiat of His Divine Will have snatched man from his enemy and restored him to his former condition ? But no, He prefers to proceed by other means ; He assumes bodily nature, and having entered life by way of birth He was made subject to the law of growth, He died and in His own body gave us the first-fruits of the resurrection ; just as if He could not, whilst remaining in the majesty of His glory, have saved man by a single command and avoided the round-about process which we attribute to Him " (ch. xv.). The objection thus frankly stated is answered with no less precision.

Our author first of all points out that human nature, apart from sin, is not an evil thing, and it was thus that the Saviour assumed it. Moreover, and here we see the great benefit conferred by the Incarnation, the eternal Word put on our nature to make real in Himself and to make permanent for ever the union of the two parts of our being, soul and body, which were tending to separate. The Incarnation according to our Doctor's matter-of-fact language glues together (καθάπερ τινὶ κόλλῃ) the broken fragments of human nature. Just as death entered by one man, so also the resurrection came through one, for the Saviour's resurrection is the life-giving principle of the whole of mankind.[1] In this is the mystery of our

---

[1] Οἶον ἀπό τινος ἀρχῆς εἰς πᾶσαν τὴν ἀνθρωπίνην φύσιν ... ἡ τοῦ διακριθέντος ἕνωσις διαβαίνει.

Salvation, that the Saviour should have willed to suffer death—*i.e.* allowed His soul to be separated from His body according to the natural course of things and that He again united them by His resurrection. Having taken on Him the divided elements of our nature He became the principle of their union [1] (ch. xvi.). Hence our death is merely a passing trial, of which the object is to disentangle our nature of its grosser elements. Gregory had already explained his meaning: " As a skilful potter when foreign matter has filled his vessel, breaks it and makes it anew, so does God rend our body by death to make it anew by the glorious resurrection " (ch. viii.).

Lest some should not be satisfied with this reply, St. Gregory proves the fitness of the Incarnation by other considerations (ch. xvii.-xxi.) amongst them by his theory of the devil's rights (ch. xxi.-xxiv.) of which more anon. But he ends by returning to his old thesis; God united Himself to our nature to make it divine (κατεμίχθη πρὸς τὸ ἡμέτερον ἵνα τῇ πρὸς τὸ θεῖον ἐπιμιξίᾳ γίνηται θεῖον). In escaping from the prisons of death He brought us with Him to life everlasting (ch. xxv.).[2] After having refuted some unimportant objections (ch. xxvii.-xxxi.) he again gives the same reason to justify Christ's death. If He died, it was because He wished to recall us to life, for He did not rise again alone, He restored to life the whole of mankind (ὅλον συναναστήσας τὸν ἄνθρωπον). For just as the members of our body are mutually dependent, so also, as if the whole of mankind were

---

[1] ἐν ἑαυτῷ μὲν στήσας διαιρουμένην τῷ θανάτῳ τὴν φύσιν, αὐτὸς δὲ γενόμενος ἀρχὴ τῆς τῶν διῃρημένων ἐνώσεως. *Ibid.* 16 ; col. 52.

[2] Ἡ γὰρ ἐκείνου ἀπὸ τοῦ θανάτου ἐπάνοδος ἀρχὴ τῷ θνητῷ γένει τῆς εἰς τὴν ἀθάνατον ζωὴν ἐπανόδου γίγνεται. *Ibid.* 25 ; col 68.

one being, the resurrection of one of its members involves the resurrection of the others (καθάπερ τινὸς ὄντος ζώου πάσης τῆς φύσεως. Ch. xxxii.).

But why the shameful death of the cross? St. Gregory sees in it a profound mystical reason. Are not the four arms of the cross stretching out from a common centre a figure of Christ, who unites all things in Himself? This is what St. Paul was alluding to when he spoke of the breadth and length and height and depth (*Eph.* iii. 18) of God's plans.[1]

We have now seen how Christ by His Incarnation and Resurrection has restored human nature; but for this benefit to be applied in detail to the individual, certain conditions must be fulfilled. The first is that he be united to the Word by baptism, which likens us unto Christ's death; from the font man emerges born again, dead to sin, and immortal (ch. xxxvi.). But this immortality will only be perfect in the future life, for which we must prepare here below by putting our body in touch with Life in the Holy Eucharist, and by preparing our soul by means of faith and good works (ch. xxxvii., xl.).

IV

From what we have said it is clear that the *Great Catechesis* is a synthetic work in which the author has grouped all dogmatic truth and all moral duties round the main idea of Salvation. From it we gather, even more clearly than from St. Athanasius, that the whole question of Salvation may be reduced to the idea of immortality. To this we had been

---

[1] To this subtle allegorism St. Gregory holds strongly. We find it again at least twice in his works. *Cp. Contr. Eunomium*, v. *P.G.* xlv. 695. *In Christi Resurrectionem. Orat.* i. *P.G.* xlvi. 622-626.

destined; we had lost it by sin, and the eternal Word came to restore it to us. It is clear too that Gregory conceives of this restoration after an entirely physical fashion, and, except that his expression is rather barbarous, we quite agree with Harnack when he says that "Gregory made of the whole system a rigorous physico-pharmacological process,"[1] which means that our human nature is deified by the very fact of its union with the Word in the Incarnation, and that this deification is perfected at the Resurrection. In all these acts what was sanctified by the Word is not so much individual humanity as mankind in general.

Must we say of this doctrine, as Ritschl ironically does, that it is "mystical aud consequently incomprehensible?"[2] Or if we wish to understand it, must we have recourse to some "idea of a universal man" borrowed from the Platonic philosophy? Harnack, unwilling to forsake his master Ritschl, would take this line.[3] As for ourselves, we think that Gregory's system may be sufficiently explained by the supernatural solidarity which he believes to exist between Christ, the head of mankind, and us, who are its members; in this way the Saviour can easily be considered as the representative and type of mankind in general without its being necessary for Him to have had in Himself any concentrated essence of humanity. For this reason it does not seem to us that Gregory's doctrine contains any of that unconscious pantheism which Harnack fancies he can discern in it.[4]

---

[1] HARNACK-CHOISY, *Précis*, p. 172.

[2] RITSCHL, *op. cit.* i. p. 13.

[3] RITSCHL, *ibid.* HARNACK, *Dogmengeschichte*, ii. p. 164.

[4] *Dogmeng. ibid.* p. 162; p. 166 *f. Cp.* in French trans. p. 172 *f.*

But if these reproaches seem to us undeserved, there can be no manner of doubt that Gregory's whole system was conceived of independently of Christ's atoning death, and this in itself is serious enough. What saves us is the Incarnation, and above all the Resurrection; in the *Great Catechesis* we find scarcely anything else hinted at as necessary; the most we do find is a passing reference here and there to the Saviour's death, such as " He saved man by experiencing death " (ch. xvii.). In no other work has mystical speculation succeeded so well in expelling the older realism. To find traces of the idea of an atoning death we must go to Gregory's other works, in which, if we only search diligently, we shall find all we want.

In St. Gregory, as in St. Athanasius, and in similar words, we find expressed the idea of substitution. " Christ is our Redeemer because He gave Himself a ransom for us. Henceforward we no longer belong to ourselves, we are the property of Him who bought us at the price of His life, and we must not live save for Him." [1] " After having made Himself the ransom of our death, He broke the bonds of death by His own Resurrection." [2] Elsewhere we find similar ideas expressed under the figure of the ancient sacrifice. Christ is the Paschal Lamb slain for us; He offered Himself as a victim for us.[3] A great portion of the sermon *De Occursu Domini* is on this theme; he shows that bloody sacrifices of the Old Law

[1] *De perf. Christiani forma.*—*P.G.* xlvi. ; col. 261-262. ἑαυτὸν δόντα λύτρον ὑπὲρ ἡμῶν . . ., ζῆν τῷ κτησαμένῳ ἡμᾶς διὰ τοῦ τῆς ζωῆς ἀνταλλάγματος.

[2] *Cont. Eunom.* v.—*P.G.* xlv. ; col. 693. ἀντάλλαγμα τοῦ ἡμετέρου θανάτου γενόμενος.

[3] *De perf. Chr. forma, loc. cit.* col. 264. ἑαυτὸν ἐνήνεγκε προσφορὰν καὶ θυσίαν ὑπὲρ ἡμῶν.

were only defective figures of the sacrifice of Christ, which alone was holy, efficacious, and final. For "Christ is the holy, innocent, spotless, and sinless Priest who offered Himself to God *in the name and in the stead of mankind.* . . . Thereby He became the ransom of many, or rather the ransom of all nations."[1]

This sacrifice was likewise expiatory. In the words of St. Paul, Gregory reminds us that Christ is our propitiation in His blood,[2] and in those of *Hebrews* that He offered Himself once, at the end of time, to blot out sin[3]; from which Gregory infers that by this death the whole world was cleansed,[4] and that "Christ became man, destroyed our enemy sin, and reconciled us to the Father."[5] Gregory, elsewhere arguing against the Arians, explains that he does not ascribe sufferings to the Divine nature of the Word. It is by His human nature that He is our Priest, for "with His own blood He presented the priestly expiation for our sins . . . He sacrificed His own body for the world's sin . . . He humbled Himself in the form of a servant and offered Himself in sacrifice for us."[6] "He who knew no sin made Himself to be sin to take away the sin of the world."[7] So far as we can find, St. Gregory nowhere explains the wherefore of this expiation, but we can see at a glance that according to him this idea is inseparable from the idea of sacrifice.

---

[1] *De Occursu Domini.—P.G.* xlvi.; col. 1161-1164. σωματικῶς προσενηνέχθαι γιγνώσκομεν ἀντὶ τῆς ἀνθρωπότητος.

[2] *De perf. Christ. form. loc. cit.*

[3] *De Occ. Domini, loc. cit.* col. 1157.

[4] Τὸ τοῦ κόσμου καθάρσιον λύτρον; *ibid.* col. 1168.

[5] *Ibid.* col. 1173. Χριστὸς ἐνηνθρώπησε καὶ τὴν πολεμοποιὸν ἁμαρτίαν ἐξηφάνισεν, καὶ τῷ Πατρὶ ἡμᾶς κατήλλαξεν.

[6] *Cont. Eunom.* vi. *P.G.* xlv. 717. τὸν τῷ ἰδίῳ αἵματι περὶ ἁμαρτιῶν ἡμῶν ἱερατικῶς ἱλεωσάμενον, κτλ.   [7] *Ibid.* col. 729.

This expiation was rendered not only by the Saviour's bodily sufferings during His Passion, but also by the inward feelings experienced by His soul; this we may see from the following passage :—" The Highest humbled Himself in becoming united to our humble nature; having taken the form of a servant and become one with it, He made His own all the misfortunes of the servant. Just as, on account of the inter-dependence of the members of our body, anything happening even to the tip of a finger causes the whole body to suffer with the part hurt, so the Word of God by becoming one with our nature made our misfortunes His, and, as Isaias says, bore our infirmities and carried our sufferings, and was wounded for us that we might be healed by His sufferings. . . . This was done that sin might be destroyed in the same way as it had come ; as death had entered the world by the disobedience of a man, so it was expelled by the obedience of another man. *This is why He became obedient even unto death that He might heal by His obedience the sin of disobedience* and destroy by His resurrection death, which had entered the world through disobedience." [1]

All these various ideas are found together in the following text :—" Was He not good who for thy sake took the form of a servant, who instead of the joy which was His, expiated the sufferings of thy sin, who gave Himself in exchange for thy death and who willed to make Himself a curse and sin for us ? " [2]

---

[1] *Antirrheticus adv. Apollinarem, ibid.* col. 1165. οἰκειοῦται τὰ ἡμέτερα πάθη . . ., τὴν ὑπὲρ ἡμῶν ὑποστὰς πληγὴν, ἵνα τῷ μώλωπι αὐτοῦ ἡμεῖς ἰαθῶμεν.

[2] *Cont. Eunom.* xi. ; col. 860. τὰ παθήματα τῆς σῆς ἁμαρτίας ἀναμαξάμενος, καὶ δοὺς ἑαυτὸν ἀντάλλαγμα τοῦ σοῦ θανάτου, καὶ ὑπὲρ ἡμῶν κατάρα καὶ ἁμαρτία γενόμενος.

In yet another passage we find an admirable summary of the whole economy of the Atonement. " God the Father created man, and by His Providence provided for his needs; does not the very name of God stand for Providence? But the devil by trickery sowed among us the tares of rebellion; our nature had not retained the impress of the *character* of the Father, but it had received the shameful stamp of sin. . . . For which reason mankind had been disinherited by the Father, who seemed no longer to have any care for it. Then did God, like the good Father He was, leave in heaven His spotless flock, and urged by His love of man go in search of the stray sheep—*i.e.* of mankind. . . . As our soul by turning aside from God was incapable of ever returning to heaven, He who knew no sin made Himself sin for our sake and delivered us from our curse by taking it on Himself. We had by sinning put an enmity between ourselves and God; He took it on Himself and put it to death, according to the teaching of the Apostle, for the enmity was sin. In a word, by making Himself what we are He drew the human race nigh unto God." [1]

It is noticeable that whilst we here find the same theme as in the *Great Catechesis*, yet Salvation is here clearly ascribed to the atoning death of the Son of God. Hence as in the doctrine of Athanasius, so in that of Gregory we find two parts. Whereas the speculative conception of the Atonement is the view explicitly embraced in their special treatises on the subject, the realistic conception is apparent here and there in scattered texts. In other words, their syn-

---

[1] *Cont. Eunom.* xii.; col. 888-889. τῆς κατάρας ἡμᾶς ἐλευθεροῖ, τὴν ἡμετέραν κατάραν οἰκειωσάμενος καὶ τὴν ἔχθραν ἡμῶν τὴν διὰ τῆς ἁμαρτίας πρὸς τὸν Θεὸν γεγενημένην ἀναλαβών, κτλ.

thesis was premature and badly constructed, as it failed to comprise all the traditional elements. But we must also admit that the idea of an Atonement by the cross occupies no higher place in their mind than in their system, and though they were not entirely ignorant of it, it failed to rivet their attention.

CHAPTER X

THE REALISTIC SYNTHESIS—EUSEBIUS OF CÆSAREA —ST. CYRIL OF JERUSALEM

READING modern historians of dogma we might be led to believe that Greek theology and Greek literature came to a close at the epoch which we have now reached. St. Athanasius and St. Gregory of Nyssa receive the honour of special dissertations, in which their system is exposed, explained, and appreciated, whereas the very names of their successors are scarcely recorded. These two Fathers are considered to represent so well the Greek school that they, as it were, absorb all the others. Harnack, who is good enough to mention a few more names and quote a few texts in an appendix,[1] sees, however, no reason for altering the main lines of his historical *aperçu*, from which it would appear that without exception there prevailed among all the Greek Fathers the idea of a rehabilitation of human nature by the life-giving action of the incarnate Word, and that they attached but little importance to the Atonement by death. We have laid due stress on the important position occupied by this speculative conception of Salvation, but we have not failed, as some of our opponents have, to point out that this conception never totally ousted the traditional realism. But our task is not yet finished; as yet we have seen only one side of the question. It is now our duty

[1] *Dogmeng.* ii. pp. 173-176.

to see how Eusebius of Cæsarea and St. Cyril of
Jerusalem continued in the lines of Origen's realism.
Though their works do not contain a system they do
comprise an assemblage of ideas sufficiently coherent
to act as a counterpoise against the speculative synthesis of Athanasius and Gregory of Nyssa.

<h2 style="text-align:center">I</h2>

By combining different passages of his *Demonstratio
Evangelica* we may form some idea of Eusebius's
doctrine.

At the commencement of the fourth book [1] the
author tells us that after having, in the previous
book, dealt with the Saviour's human nature he will
now enter deeper into the mystery by means of a
more learned and profounder theology (c. i.). He
does this by explaining the Divine plans of Salvation
and the cause of the Incarnation of the Son of God.

God enlightens and directs all by His Word, just
as the sun enlightens the whole earth (c. vi.). This
is why He placed man, the reasonable being and the
image of His Word, at the head of all creatures, en-
dowing him also with freedom. But men abused
their freedom and did evil (c. vii.). Ever since that
time the devil has established over them his kingdom
and divided its control among his infernal satellites ;
hence the ignorance which has spread its pall over
mankind, bringing idolatry, impurity, and all other
crimes in its train (c. ix.-x.).

Such was man's condition ; nor was any angel able
to bring relief. Then the Word, urged by God's love
of men and unwilling to allow His own cherished
mankind to perish, decided to interfere. He came

---

[1] EUSEB. CÆSAR. *Demonstr. Evangel.* iv. 1-14. *P.G.* xxii. 249-289.

to save, not Israel alone, but all men, to whom He makes the Father to be known, and loved, and to whom He promises forgiveness of sins. He preached by word and example ; He cast out devils, raised the dead, healed afflictions both of body and soul ; He changed hearts and led men to life everlasting. He is the Sun of Justice, He is the physician of souls, He is the sovereign Priest, the mediator between God and man, who alone can propitiate God (c. x.). And now that His sacred manhood is in heaven at the right hand of God, He emboldens us to expect a share with Him in His blessed immortality (c. xiv.).

But this general description of our Saviour's work does not seem sufficient to our author, and he proceeds to enumerate didactically the reasons which prompted the Incarnation of the Word. " The reason is not one but many—first, that the kingdom of the Logos may be established over the living and dead ; *secondly, to cleanse our sins by allowing Himself to be struck and by becoming a curse for us* ; *thirdly, to offer Himself in sacrifice to God for the whole world* [1] ; fourthly, to destroy the reign of the devil ; fifthly, to ensure to His disciples everlasting life with God." This classification of the ends of the Incarnation is logically far from perfect, but the second and third reasons alleged by Eusebius have to do with the expiation of our sins, and elsewhere we shall find our author enlarging on the same subject.

Eusebius holds a certain theory concerning the olden sacrifices. He points out clearly enough their divine origin, he reminds us that they prefigured the death of our Saviour, and he shows that a certain

[1] ὅπως τὰς ἡμετέρας ἀπομάξοιτο ἁμαρτίας, ὑπὲρ ἡμῶν τρωθεὶς καὶ γενόμενος ὑπὲρ ἡμῶν κατάρα . . ., ὡς ἂν ἱερεῖον Θεοῦ καὶ μεγάλη θυσία ὑπὲρ τοῦ σύμπαντος κόσμου προσαχθείη . . . Θεῷ. *Dem. Evang.* 12 ; col. 284.

mysterious substitution is essential to them.[1] Differently from the Greeks, who it appears were content with unbloody sacrifices, the Bible shows us that from the very beginning the patriarchs were inspired to offer bloody sacrifices. As they were holy men, God revealed to them the need of a special and higher worship to wipe out their sins. Hence knowing of nothing *more precious than their soul, they offered in its stead the lives of animals.*[2] This same substitutional character becomes more noticeable in the Mosaic legislation. " I have given you the blood of victims that you may make an atonement with it . . . and that the blood may be for an expiation of the soul " (*Leviticus* xvii. 11). Eusebius points out that we here find a real case of substitution ; " the Scripture clearly says that in the stead of the human soul it is the blood of sacrificed animals which expiates sin."[3] This character is seen from the very ritual used in the sacrifice ; he who offered it had to lay his hand on the victim's head, to show that he was substituting it for himself. Thus the victim's life was literally *an exchange for the soul of the sinner* (ἀντίψυχα τῆς αὐτῶν ψυχῆς). In this there is nothing shocking, for the soul of beasts is not rational. As they come nearest to man, no fitter victims could be found until the coming of the great Victim, who cleansed the world, and of which these sacrifices were a figure.

The prophets too had foretold that Christ would

---

[1] EUSEB. CÆSAR. *Demonstr. Evangel.* i. 10 ; col. 84-85.

[2] ἀντὶ ταύτης τέως τὴν διὰ τῶν ἀλόγων ζώων προσῆγον θυσίαν, τῆς σφῶν ψυχῆς ἀντίψυχα προσκομίζοντες . . ., ψυχὴν ἀντὶ ψυχῆς ἀναφέροντες . . ., λύτρα τῆς ἑαυτῶν ζωῆς καὶ ἀντίψυχα τῆς οἰκείας φύσεως. *Ibid.*

[3] Σαφῶς γὰρ ἀντὶ τῆς ἀνθρωπίνης ψυχῆς τὸ τῶν σφαγιαζομένων ζώων αἷμά φησιν ἐξιλάσκεσθαι. *Ibid.*

be slain for the human race. Eusebius quotes Isaias, Jeremias, and lastly John the Baptist, who ended the prophetic series by actually pointing out the Lamb of God who takes away the sins of the world. Then our author, led away by the grandeur of the subject, describes in high-flown language the sacrifice of the Lamb : τὸ μέγα καὶ τίμιον λύτρον . . . τὸ τοῦ παντὸς κόσμου καθάρσιον, πάντων ἀνθρώπων ἀντίψυχον, τὸ πάσης κηλίδος καὶ ἁμαρτίας καθαρὸν ἱερεῖον, ὁ ἀμνὸς τοῦ Θεοῦ, τὸ θεοφιλὲς καὶ ἀγνὸν πρόβατον, τὸ προφητευόμενον ἀρνίον.

Throughout two pages, Eusebius goes on describing thus poetically how Christ became "a curse and sin for us," and how " *God laid on Him our sins*," and how He " *caused to fall on Him the penalty due to our misdeeds.*" [1]

This doctrine of substitution, which is here only touched on, is dealt with professedly in the tenth book. Here Eusebius begins by observing that all that is said concerning the Saviour's Passion and death is to be understood of His human nature alone. Through this nature it was, that He offered Himself as a victim to His Father, for He is indeed the Lamb foretold by the prophets which must be slain for the other lambs, His brethren, and for the whole human flock.[2] Eusebius then goes on to apply to our Saviour the words of the Psalmist : *Sana animam meam quia peccavi tibi* (*Ps.* xl. 5), which he explains as follows [3] :—If Christ can speak thus, this is because He has taken on Him our sins (τὰς ἡμετέρας εἰς ἑαυτὸν κοινοποιεῖ . . . ἁμαρτίας) according to the saying of Isaias (liii. 4-6). He therefore made

---

[1] EUSEB. CÆSAR. *Demonstr. Evangel.* col. 88-89. τούτῳ τε ἐπιγράψας τὰς πάντων ἡμῶν ἁμαρτίας . . . πάσας τε αὐτῷ δι᾽ ἡμᾶς τὰς ἡμῖν ἐπηρτημένας τιμωρίας ἐπιθείς.

[2] *Ibid.* x. *præf.* col. 716 *f.*   [3] *Ibid.* x. 1, col. 724 *f.*

N

Himself, and God also made Him, Him the Innocent, a curse, and sin, that He might be the living exchange for our sin (ἀντίψυχον ὑπὲρ πάντων ἡμῶν), and that we might be justified in Him. In His love He went so far as to take our sins to His account.

But how was this substitution effected? Eusebius answers with St. Paul (1 *Cor.* xii. 26) that we form but a single body with Christ. Just as in our body one member cannot suffer without all suffering, so also is it with the spiritual body. The members were sinning and suffering; Christ by means of the nature which He shares with us took on Him our misfortunes according to the laws of solidarity and physical sympathy (κατὰ τοὺς τῆς συμπαθείας λόγους); He suffers, like us and for us (πάντων ἡμῶν ὑπεραλγεῖ καὶ ὑπερπονεῖ). But what is more, He was chastised for us; the torment which He suffered had been earned, not by Him, but by us on account of our many faults; He thus became the cause of the forgiveness of our sins by accepting death for us, by taking on Him the punishments and insults and bruises which were due to us, by calling down on Himself the curse which was meant for us, until He verily became a curse for our sake.[1] Does not this show that Christ is nothing else than a substitute of our souls? (τί γὰρ ἄλλο ἢ ἀντίψυχον ;)

A little farther on Eusebius again enforces this same doctrine, depicting Christ as dyed with our

[1] ὑπὲρ ἡμῶν κολασθείς, καὶ τιμωρίαν ὑποσχών, ἣν αὐτὸς μὲν οὐκ ὤφειλεν, ἀλλ' ἡμεῖς τοῦ πλήθους ἕνεκεν τῶν πεπλημμελημένων, ἡμῖν αἴτιος τῆς τῶν ἁμαρτημάτων ἀρέσεως κατέστη, ἅτε τὸν ὑπὲρ ἡμῶν ἀναδεξάμενος θάνατον, μάστιγάς τε καὶ ὕβρεις καὶ ἀτιμίας ἡμῖν ἐποφειλομένας εἰς αὐτὸν μεταθείς, καὶ τὴν ἡμῖν προστετιμημένην κατάραν ἐφ' ἑαυτὸν ἑλκύσας. . . . EUSEB. CÆSAR. *Demonstr. Evangel.* col. 724-5. Ritschl, who quotes this text of Eusebius when speaking of the Latin Fathers, seems to consider it as quite exceptional, *op. cit.* i. p. 15.

sins and crucified in our stead.[1]   In his other works likewise we find similar sayings.[2]

Teaching very like to that of Eusebius will also be found in the works of one of his best-known contemporaries—Theodore, Bishop of Heraclea.   In one of the few extant fragments of his commentary on Isaias, he expresses himself as follows :—" As men's wickedness was at its height and had led them to commit all kinds of iniquity, the chastisement and penalty were at hand.   But the death which was due to us was willingly received by the Son of God, who had come into the world, who had performed all justice, and had fallen into no sin.   He thereby changed our chastisement into peace and good-will ; for He indeed suffers wounds and tortures, whilst we by faith appropriate to ourselves His sufferings, dying with Him by grace, in order to be saved."[3]

From all these texts, which under their differences are all alike, we gather the same doctrine, which we may appropriately sum up in the words of Eusebius himself.   " Christ was the victim delivered to death in the stead of the human race,"[4] who thereby " cleansed the world from its sins."[5]

---

[1] τὰς ἡμετέρας ἁμαρτίας ἀναμαξάμενος ἐσταυρώθη, ὃ ἐχρῆν ἡμᾶς τοὺς πρὶν ἀσεβεῖς παθεῖν, ἀντίψυχον ἡμῶν καὶ ἀντίλυτρον γεγενημένος. EUSEB. CÆSAR, Demonstr. Evangel. x. 8 ; col. 768.

[2] Cp. in Psalm. xxi.—P.G. xxiii.; col. 204.   Psal. lxviii.; ibid. col. 723, 731, 735.   In Isaiam, liii.—P.G. xxiv.; col. 457

[3] THEODOR. HERACL. In Isaiam, liii. 5.—P.G. xviii.; col. 1356. τιμωρία καὶ κόλασις ἐπήρτητο, ἥντινα δίκην χρεωστουμένην ἡμῖν ὁ μονογενὴς τοῦ Θεοῦ Λόγος . . . ἑκοντὶ δέχεται, ἵν᾽ ἡμῖν μεταβάλῃ τὴν κόλασιν εἰς εἰρήνην τε καὶ εὐμένειαν. . . . Cp. ibid. 10; col. 1357.   τὰ ἡμῖν χρεωστούμενα παθήματα αὐτὸς ἀναδεξάμενος ᾠκειώσατο. . . .

[4] EUSEB. Serm. de Theophania, 3.   P.G. xxiv. 613 and 616. ἱερεῖον ἦν ἀντίψυχον τοῦ κοινοῦ γένους παραδιδόμενον.

[5] De solem. paschali, i.   Ibid. col. 696.   καθαρσίου δίκην τοῦ παντὸς ἀφεῖλε κόσμου τὴν ἁμαρτίαν.

Hence the two ideas of penal substitution and of expiatory sacrifice, which in Origen we found disconnected, are found combined in Eusebius, who in consequence is able to give the outlines of the legal theory of penal expiation. Later on, scholasticism will press deeper into the problem, and will seek in the rights of Divine justice the reason of this substitution ; but even in the fourth century the doctrinal edifice was already built. No doubt this idea of the Atonement is not the only one, nor is it the most profound—this we have already admitted—but remembering that this theory, doubtless on account of its very simplicity, was long to remain a favourite, it is well to bear in mind that we find it already expressed by Eusebius with a precision which modern theologians have seldom reached and possibly never surpassed.

II

Should the systematised theology of Eusebius have tired the reader, and should he wish for something simpler, for some popular exposition of faith which may stand for the current teaching of the Church's pastors to their flocks, he has only to open the *Catecheses* of St. Cyril of Jerusalem.

St. Cyril in his fourth *Catechesis*, in which he summarises the doctrines of Christianity, in two sentences tells us what is the Church's belief concerning the mystery of the Atonement. " It was on account of our sins that the Son of God came down from heaven . . . it was for our sins that He was crucified " ; and again : " It was not for His own but for our sins that He died."[1] This twofold and yet

[1] CYRIL. HIER. *Catech.* iv. 9 & 10.—*P.G.* xxxiii. ; col. 465 and

identical object of the Incarnation and Passion is enlarged upon in the two following *Catecheses*.

Our Salvation depends on Christ's manhood. Against certain heretics Cyril affirms that if Christ's human nature is not real we are not saved. Christ is therefore God-made-man, not God only, or man only, or man-made-God, but truly God-made-man, the eternal Son of God clothed in our manhood. Our Salvation was the reason which prompted this condescendence. Cyril likewise reminds us of the condition of the first man, the lord of creation, the image of God, and the finest production of God's hands. He lived happily in paradise, from which, however, he was driven by the malicious stratagem of the Evil One. After this, sin was multiplied in the world—even the Jews, the chosen race, did not succeed in escaping it. The whole of mankind was covered with the incurable sore produced by it. Men could not help themselves, and God, who alone could, was struck with pity for the race, and sent His Son to save us. Such is the chief reason of the Incarnation, which it takes Cyril the greater part of his twelfth *Catechesis* to describe.[1]

For our Salvation the Saviour's death was also needed, and Cyril speaks of it in words similar to those he had used of the Incarnation. "If the cross were only an appearance, our Salvation too would be unreal."[2] From this we can see the importance he attaches to the mystery of the Passion. Hence the thirteenth *Catechesis* starts on an oratorical note. All Christ's actions are the glory of the Church, but

---

468-469.   διὰ τὰς ἁμαρτίας ἡμῶν ἐξ οὐρανῶν κατῆλθεν ἐπὶ τῆς γῆς . . ., ἐσταυρώθη ὑπὲρ τῶν ἁμαρτιῶν ἡμῶν ἀληθῶς.

[1] *Catech.* xii. 1-8 ; *ibid.* col. 728 *ff.*

[2] *Catech.* xiii. 4 ; col. 776.   *Cp. ibid.* 37 ; col. 816 *f.*

the glory of glories is the cross. Christ cured the man born blind, He raised Lazarus, and delivered the woman held captive by Satan. But these miracles were of no use to the sinners of the whole world; it is the cross which brings to all, light and redemption and deliverance from sin (c. i.). Nor is this universal efficaciousness at all surprising: it was not the death of a man, but the death of the only Son of God.[1] If the sin of one brought death into the world, much more will life reign by the justice of one. If Phineas would appease God by sacrificing a guilty man, will not Christ, who offers Himself as a ransom, appease God's wrath against men?[2] (c. ii.). And if the blood of victims cleansed sins, how much more the blood of the Son of God? (c. iii.). For He did not die for Himself, being innocent; it was for our sins that He willingly yielded up His life (c. iii.-vi.; c. xxi.-xxiii.). All this Cyril proves or illustrates by recourse to the prophecies and figures of the Old Testament (c. vii.-xviii.; xx.-xxi.; xxiii.-xxxii.).

In these passages the idea of penal expiation appears at least once: " He was crucified that His humanity having been nailed to the cross, *that same humanity which bore the sins of the world,* sin might die with it and we might rise again unto justice."[3] We should perhaps compare with this passage a text from a previous discourse in which he speaks of

[1] Καὶ μὴ θαυμάσῃς εἰ κόσμος ὅλος ἐλυτρώθη · οὐ γὰρ ἦν ἄνθρωπος ψιλὸς, ἀλλὰ Υἱὸς Θεοῦ μονογενὴς ὁ ὑπεραποθνήσκων. *Cat.* xiii. 2; col. 773.

[2] Ἰησοῦς, οὐκ ἄλλον ἀνελὼν, ἀλλ' ἑαυτὸν ἀντίλυτρον παραδοὺς, ἆρα τὴν ὀργὴν οὐ λύει. *Ibid.*

[3] Ἵνα τῆς ἀνθρωπότητος τῷ ξύλῳ προσπαγείσης, τῆς βασταζούσης τῶν ἀνθρώπων τὰ ἁμαρτήματα . . . συναποθάνῃ μὲν ἡ ἁμαρτία. . . . *Ibid.* 28; col. 805.

Christ as "dying, loaded with the sins of the whole world."[1]

By His death Christ reconciled heaven with earth; it was to hint at this that He willed during His Passion to reconcile Herod and Pilate (c. xiv.); but above all, and St. Cyril seems unable to state this too often, our sins were destroyed (c. xvii. and xxxii.). He also depicts Christ as the second Adam, who repairs the fault of the first. This comparison, which, to begin with, he makes in the words of St. Paul, he soon pushes even further than the Apostle: "Adam lost us by the tree; by the tree too, Christ has saved us" (c. ii.); and utilising the prevalent allegorism, he seeks to compare the two, even in the minutest details (c. xviii.-xix.).[2]

These different points of view are combined by St. Cyril at the end of his *Catechesis*. "By the blood of His cross He reconciled heaven and earth. We were enemies of God through sin, and God had sentenced the sinner to death. Hence of two things one: either God would be true to His word and put us to death, or else, moved by mercy, He would annul His sentence. But consider God's wisdom; He reconciled the carrying out of His sentence with the needs of His love. Christ took our sins in His body on the cross that we, dying by His death to sin, might live in justice."[3] In this we have an idea fundamentally that of Athanasius; but St. Cyril continues: "He who died for us was no little thing, He was not a victim devoid of

---

[1] *Cat.* iii. 12; *ibid.* col. 444. ἀναλαβὼν τας οἰκουμενικὰς ἁμαρτίας.

[2] For instance, he considers that the wound in Christs's side— which reminds him that Eve had been taken from Adam's side— was inflicted as an expiation for women. *Ibid.* 21; col. 800.

[3] Ἀλλὰ βλέπε Θεοῦ σοφίαν· ἐτήρησεν καὶ τῇ ἀποφάσει τὴν ἀλήθειαν, καὶ τῇ φιλανθρωπίᾳ τὴν ἐνέργειαν. Ἀνέλαβε Χριστὸς τὰς ἁμαρτίας ἐν τῷ σώματι. . . .

reason, nor a common man, no, nor merely an angel, but God-made-man. The iniquity of sinners was less than the justice of Him who died for us, we have not committed sin equal in magnitude to the justice of Him, who for us delivered up His soul."[1] Minus the technical terms, we here find the first theological statement of the infinite superabundance of the Satisfaction made by the God-man.

From all this we may see that St. Cyril, in spite of the disorder apparent in his homilies, clearly sums up the whole of the Saviour's work in His death. This death was the last end of the Incarnation, this too it is which obtains for us the pardon of our sins. Whence comes, and what is the explanation of, this supernatural efficaciousness? St. Cyril hardly tells us; he rather states the fact than studies its manner. Here and there he mentions the ideas of ransom and sacrifice; occasionally he alludes to the idea of penal expiation. These were well-known ideas and formulæ, but St. Cyril was the means of introducing into them a new element. More than anyone else he laid stress on the fact that Christ offered Himself to die, freely and through love; and he adds that His dignity as Son of God gives an infinite price to His sacrifice. In a word, it seems that according to St. Cyril the mystery of the Atonement ultimately resides in the soul and in the very Person of the Redeemer. This idea could easily have proved fruitful, but St. Cyril, either because he did not advert to its inner meaning, or because the nature of his catechetical work prevented him from entering into theological speculations, most probably for both reasons, was content to make

---

[1] Οὐ τοσαύτη ἦν τῶν ἁμαρτωλῶν ἡ ἀνομία ὅση τοῦ ὑπεραποθνήσκοντος ἡ δικαιοσύνη · οὐ τοσοῦτον ἡμάρτομεν, ὅσον ἐδικαιοπράγησεν ὁ τὴν ψυχὴν ὑπὲρ ἡμῶν τεθεικώς. . . . *Ibid.* 33, col. 813.

once or twice a passing statement of his idea without attempting, as Eusebius had done for the idea of penal satisfaction, to weave it into the centre of a system.   At any rate Cyril's idea is of value, not only because it is original, but especially because, of all the answers so far given to the Atonement-question, his is the deepest.

However, whatever differences exist between Cyril and Eusebius, their ideas are at the bottom quite the same, though in one they are cast into systematic form and are consequently narrowed, whilst in the other they are diffuse and as a consequence broader and more supple.   However much their theology may be lacking the qualities of penetration and consistency, both agree in making our Salvation to depend on Christ's death, because by it, and by it alone, we receive forgiveness and reconciliation.

CHAPTER XI

THE FURTHER PROGRESS OF REALISM—ST. BASIL, ST. GREGORY NAZIANZEN, ST. JOHN CHRYSOSTOM

WHAT we have already said will, we think, be sufficient to demolish the hastily constructed syntheses which some historians, to gratify their fondness for system, have built up, utterly regardless of facts. We now know that Greek theology, in spite of an undeniable tendency to speculation, was by no means so simple as some imagine, and that at the time when the speculative element was at the heyday of its triumph, the traditional realism, of which the lines had been laid down by Origen, had accredited exponents in the persons of Eusebius and Cyril. Having thus reassured ourselves as to the orthodoxy of earlier Greek thought, we may now pass to the consideration of the later Fathers. The fact that our adversaries, well aware of the attitude of these Fathers, have nothing—or practically nothing—to say of them,[1] may well give us courage. We shall be less prudent, we shall examine, with all the attention they deserve, the writings of the great Doctors of the fourth century, and we shall see that, though the speculative element retains its rightful place, it is far from absorbing the other element. Side by side with it we shall find the older realism, which has now become the predominant partner, and which by that inward logic which makes every true idea to prove

---

[1] *Cp.* HARNACK, *Dogmeng.* ii. p. 174 *f.*

and state itself ever more clearly, is growing steadily stronger and enlarging its sphere.

I

St. Basil devoted most of his efforts and works to stamping out the last embers of the Arian quarrel, hence it was only incidentally that he touched at all on the doctrine of the Atonement.

According to the usual tradition of the Greek Fathers, St. Basil believed the general end of the Incarnation to be the supernatural transformation or deification of our nature. " It was for us that He became mortal, that He might deliver us from our mortality and make us partakers in heavenly life." [1] He consequently contends for the real and physical union of the Word with our nature. " If the Lord's coming was not in the flesh, then the Redeemer gave death no ransom for us, nor did He by His power break the rule of death. For if the nature held in thrall by death were other than the nature assumed by Christ, then death would not have ceased its rule, the sufferings of His Divine flesh would not have been to our profit, He would not have slain sin in His flesh, we should not have been restored to life in Christ—we who had died in Adam—what had fallen would not have been raised, what had been broken would not have been mended, what had been far from God would not again have been made nigh unto Him." [2] Likewise our Saviour must be God also. " We cannot give what we have not; hence if the Son is a creature and a servant, He cannot deliver

[1] BASIL, *Ep.* viii. 5. *P.G.* xxxii. 256.
[2] *Epist.* cclxi. 2 ; *ibid.* col. 969.

others." [1] But as in reality Christ is both God and man, in His person " He deified the human race." [2]

St. Basil does not confine himself to such general considerations, in which Salvation is identified with exemption from death. He also speaks of the expiation of sin, and he is fully aware of the salutary worth of Christ's death. He looks on it as a sacrifice : " The Son of God gave life to the world when He offered Himself to God as a victim for our sins." [3] Again, combining Isaias with St. Paul, he deals with the penally expiatory side of Christ's death. " He took on Him our weaknesses and carried our misfortunes ; He was bruised for us to heal us by His wounds ; He delivered us from the curse by becoming a curse for us ; He underwent for us a shameful death in order to lead us into life everlasting." [4]

But by far the most important passage occurs in St. Basil's commentary on *Psalm* xlviii., where he examines the conditions of our Salvation and concludes by showing that they could not have been fulfilled save by God. " Far from man being able to redeem his brethren, he is unable even to appease God for his own sins " ; the reason being precisely that he is himself a sinner. " Moses did not deliver his people from sin, he was unable even to offer an expiation to God for himself when he was in sin. *Hence it is not from a man that we must expect this expiation, but from one who surpasses our nature,*

---

[1] *Adv. Eunomium*, iv. 2. *P.G.* xxix. ; col. 692.

[2] In the summary of faith attributed to St. Basil. *P.G.* xxx. 834.

[3] *In Psalm.* xxviii. 5. *P.G.* xxix. 296. With this we may compare (though its authenticity is not above suspicion—Bardenhewer, ii. p 76) tho commentary on *Isaias* i. 24. *P.G.* xxx. 165. *Cp.* 169.

[4] *Regulæ fusius tractatæ, Interrogatio*, ii. 4. *P.G.* xxxi. 916.

from Jesus Christ the God-man, who alone can offer God a sufficient expiation for all of us."[1]

At the same time Basil also enlarges on the redemption-metaphor. He reminds us that by sin we fell into the bondage of Satan, and that every captive in order to be set free requires a ransom. Now, nobody can buy out his brethren or himself, for the buyer must be better placed than the prisoner. Hence we need a Redeemer who surpasses our nature. "Such a single ransom sufficient for all men (ἀντάξιον) was found in the blood of Christ which was shed for us."[2]

Hence on either hand the conclusion is the same. Christ alone could save us; He who, having no sin, stood in no need of making expiation for Himself nor of redeeming His own soul. Hence He in His kindness came down to our level, redeemed us and made expiation for us, and not for us alone, but for the whole world. The writer ends by praising, in the words of *Hebrews*, the greatness and the holiness of the Priest whom God has given us.

St. Basil's examination of sin is not as penetrating as we could wish, but however superficial, his consideration of the current metaphors leads him to infer that man was unable to redeem himself and that he needed for his Redeemer a God-man. Hence Basil does not merely state and describe the atoning work

---

[1] *In Psalm.* xlviii. 3-4.—*P.G.* xxix.; col. 437-440, οὐδὲ ὅλως ἄνθρωπος ἐξουσίαν ἔχει πρὸς Θεόν, ὡς καὶ ἐξιλᾶσθαι περὶ ἡμαρτηκότος, ἐπεὶ καὶ αὐτὸς ἁμαρτίας ὑπόδικος . . . Ζήτει . . . τὸν ὑπερβαίνοντά σου τὴν φύσιν· μήτε ἄνθρωπον ψιλόν, ἀλλ' ἄνθρωπον Θεὸν Ἰησοῦν Χριστόν, ὃς καὶ μόνος δύναται δοῦναι ἐξίλασμα τῷ Θεῷ ὑπὲρ πάντων ἡμῶν.

[2] Ἀλλ' εὑρέθη ἐν ὁμοῦ πάντων ἀνθρώπων ἀντάξιον, ὃ ἐδόθη εἰς τιμὴν λυτρώσεως τῆς ψυχῆς ἡμῶν, τὸ ἅγιον καὶ πολυτίμητον αἷμα τοῦ Κυρίου. Cp. *ibid.* 8, col. 452 & *Psalm.* lxi. 3; col. 475.

of Christ, he also seeks its wherefore, and by investigating its cause he perceived the better its true character. We have indeed found Basil's idea before, but this is the first time that we find it dealt with explicitly and as it were advanced as a thesis. Here then we see a step forward in the path of reflection and in the way which will lead to still greater things in the theology of the future.

II

It is more difficult to unify the doctrine of St. Gregory Nazianzen, for in the first instance it exists only in fragments scattered throughout his works, whilst in the second its parts can only with difficulty be placed in order. We find, however, in abundant detail the different aspects under which we have already seen the work and death of the Redeemer portrayed by other Fathers.

St. Gregory on several occasions lays it down generally that Christ died for us to save us, as the good shepherd gives his life for his sheep.[1] Elsewhere we are told that He is our ransom, for He bought the world at a great price, that of His own precious blood.[2] "He delivers us from the power of sin *by giving Himself in our stead as a ransom which cleanses the whole world.*"[3]

His death is also viewed as a sacrifice, a voluntary but true sacrifice, in fact the only true sacrifice,

---

[1] GREG. NAZ. *Orat.* i. 4-6. *P.G.* xxxv. 397-400. *Cp. Orat.* iv. 78 ; *ibid.* 604.

[2] λυτρὸν ὑπὲρ ἡμῶν καὶ ἀντάλλαγμα. *Orat.* i. 5 ; col. 400. *Cp. Orat.* xxix. 20. *P.G.* xxxvi. 101.

[3] *Orat.* xxx. 20 ; *ibid.* col. 132. λύτρον ἑαυτὸν ἀντιδιδοὺς ἡμῶν τῆς οἰκουμένης καθάρσιον.

and one which was pre-figured by the rites of the Old Testament.[1] And Gregory waxes very wroth with Julian the Apostate: "Wouldst thou rise up with thy sacrifices against the sacrifice of Christ ? with the blood of thy victims *against that blood which has cleansed the world ?*"[2]

If our Saviour willed to die, He did so freely and generously in order to expiate our sins. "He made Himself man for us, He took the form of a servant, He was led to death for our sins. . . . And He did all this, whereas he could, as God, have saved us by a simple act of His Will."[3] Farther on Gregory points to the mystery of substitution which is involved in this death. "Just as He became a curse, and sin for my Salvation, He made Himself into a second Adam in the stead of the old; *He took unto Himself and made His own our rebellion, as the head of the whole body.* On the cross it was not He who was forsaken; He occupied our own position; we it was who were abandoned and despised; He saved us by His sufferings, *for He made our sins His own.*"[4] To express how much Christ became like to us in becoming all things to all, Gregory finds in the Greek language no words sufficiently strong, and he therefore coins two new ones: "*He became sin itself and the curse itself*" (αὐτοαμαρτία καὶ αὐτοκατάρα).[5] How could it be otherwise than that our sin should be

---

[1] ἑκούσιον θυσίαν. *Orat.* i. 7. *P.G.* xxxv. 400. θυσίαν οἰκειοτάτην. *Orat.* vi. 4; *ibid.* col. 728.

[2] Κατὰ τῆς Χριστοῦ θυσίας . . . κατὰ τοῦ τὸν κόσμον καθήραντος αἵματος. *Orat.* iv. 68; *ibid.* col. 589.

[3] *Orat.* xix. 13; *ibid.* col. 1060.

[4] Τὸ . . . ἀνυπότακτον ἑαυτοῦ ποιεῖται, ὡς κεφαλὴ τοῦ παντὸς σώματος . . . ἐν ἑαυτῷ . . . δὲ τυποῖ τὸ ἡμέτερον, . . . τὸ πλημμελὲς οἰκειούμενος. *Orat.* xxx. 5. *P.G.* xxxvi. 108 *f.*

[5] *Orat.* xxxvii. 1; *ibid.* col. 1060.

destroyed by such an expiation? " The Saviour took it with Him on the cross, there to put it to death [1]; He was crucified, but at the same time He crucified our sin." [2]

But quite apart from this supernatural efficaciousness of Christ's death, St. Gregory sees a salutary meaning in the whole work of the Incarnate Word, and he thereby comes into line with the majority of the other Greek Fathers. As Salvation consists in a reformation and restoration of our nature, our Saviour accomplished this work by physically uniting Himself with our humanity by His Incarnation. " He carries us bodily in Himself with all that is in us; He is the leaven mixed with our paste in order to transform it entirely." [3] " He became wholly man without ceasing to be God, thinking of man who was wholly bruised by sin, in order that He might destroy the whole condemnation and save the whole of man; in a word, He became as much man as we are, that we might become God through Him." [4] Christ having thus become a perfect man and a new Adam, owed it to Himself to retrace the steps of the first Adam. St. Gregory does not fail to see this atoning parallelism even in the tiniest details. Not only did the Word take a soul, thinking of that one which had disobeyed the law of God, and a flesh to remind Him of the one that fell into sin, but even the apparently most insignificant incidents

---

[1] Ἐπὶ τὸν σταυρὸν ἀναβάντα καὶ συναγαγόντα τὴν ἐμὴν ἁμαρτίαν τεθνηξομένην. *Orat.* iv. 78.—*P.G.* xxxv.; col. 604.

[2] σταυρούμενον καὶ συσταυροῦντα τὴν ἐμὴν ἁμαρτίαν. *Orat.* xxxviii. 16.—*P.G.* xxxvi. col. 329.

[3] *Orat.* xxx. 6.—*P.G.* xxxvi.; col. 109. Cp. *ibid.* 21; col. 131. *Orat.* xxxviii. 4; *ibid.* col. 315.

[4] *Orat.* xl. 45; *ibid.* col. 424. τοσοῦτον ἄνθρωπον διὰ σὲ, ὅσον σὺ γίνῃ δι' ἐκεῖνον θεός.

of the Passion occurred in order to make amends for our fall.[1]

St. Gregory concludes by saying that "He is struck and wounded, but He heals every ailment and weakness. He is raised and nailed to the wood, but He brings us back to the Tree of Life. . . . He dies, but He gives life and destroys death."[2] Lastly, His ultimate aim was our deification, which will be accomplished in life everlasting.[3]

Gregory's great Paschal sermon may serve as a fair epitome of his views.[4] In striking language he there discourses on the Divine nature, the creation of the angels and of the world, and especially that of man, the finest work in the universe (c. iii., vii.). Man was endowed with freedom, but when tried he fell (c. viii.). After having essayed several means of Salvation but without result, God decided to intervene by Himself becoming incarnate. "He takes on Himself flesh for the sake of our flesh, He assumes a rational soul for the sake of our soul, and, to cleanse our nature by means of a similar nature, He becomes man in all things save in sin. . . . He took our flesh to save His image and to make our flesh immortal " (c. ix.).

Then Gregory enters on the Paschal mystery. He reminds us that the old Law was the figure of the new, and though He distrusts that allegorism which seeks to explain every detail, He, nevertheless, will en-

[1] *Orat.* ii. 23-25.—*P.G.* xxxv.; col. 434. *Cp. Orat.* xxxiii. 9. —*P.G.* xxxvi.; col. 225.

[2] ἀποθνήσκει, ζωοποιεῖ δὲ καὶ καταλύει τῷ θανάτῳ τὸν θάνατον. *Orat.* xxix. 20; *ibid.* col. 101.

[3] ἕως ἂν ἐμὲ ποιήσῃ Θεόν. *Orat.* xxx. 14; *ibid.* col. 121. *Cp. Orat.* i. 5.—*P.G.* xxxv.; col. 398.

[4] *Orat.* xlv. *P.G.* xxxvi. 624-664. Several of the passages are repeated verbatim in *Orat.* xxxviii. 7-16; *ibid.* col. 317-330.

deavour to explain the Christian Pasch by means of the Jewish (c. ix.-xii.); for the Jewish sacrifices especially were the preparation and image of " that great Victim which was to cleanse not merely a portion of the world and for a time, but the whole world for ever." [1] The pious orator then proceeds to apply to Christ, in a long mystical commentary, the Mosaic rites of the Paschal Lamb. Of this it will be sufficient to retain the following :—Our Saviour is innocent and without blemish though He took on Him our sins and carried our infirmities [2] ; He was slain chiefly for sinners, and we must make our own, by reflection and Christian practices, the fruits of His Sacrifice ; each one must make his own the cleansing of the world [3] (c. xiii.-xxvi.). St. Gregory finishes up with a sharp rebuke to the hypocrites who consider this mission of Salvation as unworthy of the Word, as if we were to find fault with a physician for attending sick people—even though he should bring away with him some of their pestilential stench—when it is possible to cure them.

Whilst thus exhorting his people St. Gregory had made an important digression, to which we must now return.

" There is a matter, usually neglected, but which deserves serious consideration. To whom, and why, was that blood paid which was shed for us, that noble and precious blood of the Divine Priest and Victim ? " To begin with, he indignantly sets aside the theory that the Divine blood was given as a ransom to the

[1] Τὸ μέγα καὶ ἄθυτον ἱερεῖον . . . παντὸς τοῦ κόσμου καὶ διαιωνίζον καθάρσιον. *Orat.* xlv. 13 ; col. 640.

[2] Καὶ τὰς ἁμαρτίας ἡμῶν ἀνέλαβε καὶ τὰς νόσους ἐβάστασεν. *Ibid.* 13 ; col. 641.

[3] σὸν γενέσθω τὸ τοῦ κόσμου καθάρσιον. *Ibid.* 24 ; col. 656.

devil, a theory of which we shall speak farther on, and
he continues : " If it was to God the Father, we may
ask, Why ?   For it was not He who held us captive.
Moreover, how can we admit for a moment that the
Father should take pleasure in His Son's blood, the
more so as He refused Isaac when offered by his
father, and chose a ram to replace the human victim ?
*Hence it is clear that if the Father accepts His Son's
blood, it is not that He had asked for it, or needed
it, but on account of the economy of Salvation,* and
because it was necessary that man should be hallowed
by the manhood of the Saviour.   Thus God Himself
delivers us, after having put to flight the tyrant, and
leads us back to Himself by the mediation of His
Son, who did all this for His Father's glory, whose
will He ever obeys." [1]

Ritschl sees in this clause a proof that Gregory's
thought was similar to that of Athanasius.[2]   This is
perfectly true, but it is also true that Gregory goes
beyond St. Athanasius ; the Incarnation is indeed
necessary in the plan of Salvation, but not less so
the Passion.   St. Gregory does not explain here the
function of Christ's Passion, this he has done elsewhere, but he is anxious even here to prevent a
misunderstanding of the Passion ; he does not call
into question Christ's Sacrifice, but he carefully
waives any attempt to make the Father's will
appear cruel, and is most anxious that the Son's
death should be considered as free and at the same
time as an act of loving obedience, a double character
which, as we have seen, gives it all its merit.

St. Gregory sums up his discourse in a series of
antitheses, and concludes as follows [3] :—" *We stand*

---

[1] *Orat.* xlv. 22 ; col. 653.   [2] RITSCHL, *op. cit.* i. p. 16 *f.*
[3] Ἐδεήθημεν Θεοῦ σαρκουμένου καὶ νεκρουμένου.   *Ibid.* col. 661.

in need of the Incarnation and death of a God, in order to have life; we died with Him in order to be cleansed; we rose again together with Him because we also died together; we have been glorified together because we rose again together." Among all the miracles which occurred at our Saviour's death, the greatest is assuredly our Salvation. " A few drops of blood renewed the face of the earth; they were to men what rennet is to milk; they brought men together and caused them as it were to coagulate." Glory be then to the Word-made-Flesh (c. xxviii.-xxx.).

This discourse gives us a good insight into St. Gregory's doctrine. We see that in his teaching Greek speculation retains its rightful position but that the greatness of the benefits conferred by the Incarnation does not make him blind to the benefit which accrues to us from the Passion. Here we find the two ideas existing together, without indeed being as yet subordinated, but at the same time without clashing. "We stand in need of the Incarnation and of the death of a God." Such is Gregory's own summary of his views, and if he did not contribute anything original, he at least succeeded in enlarging and explaining considerably the common views.

III

In the writings of St. Epiphanius we have succeeded in finding only a few unimportant passages in which allusion is made to the Atonement. He describes Christ's death as a Sacrifice, a living and true one offered for the whole world, and in which Christ is at once Priest and Victim, and which is also the end of the temporary sacrificial dispensation of the Old Testament.[1] He also states that "Christ by His voluntary death took away the curse which had been drawn down by sin, and that He was the death of our death and the curse of our curse."[2] Less eloquently, but meaning the same, he elsewhere says: "Since Christ came to bear our sins on the wood on which He gave Himself for us, His blood has redeemed us and His body has blotted out our curse. His death destroyed that death which was the penalty of sin."[3]

It is also to St. Epiphanius that we owe that excellent formula used to express the general end of the Incarnation and the special object of the Passion. "No man could save us. For this reason the Lord took flesh of our flesh, and the Word became a man like unto us, that He might give us Salvation through His Godhead and suffer for us through His Manhood, destroying suffering by His Passion and slaying death by His death."[4]

We shall have to linger much longer over St. John Chrysostom. He, the commentator of St. Paul and the popular preacher, as might be expected blends in his sermons two forms of inspiration which are, unfortunately, seldom found together—familiar eloquence and good theology. His works show us in how living a form it was possible for a preacher to present to the faithful the elements of doctrine.

He starts by declaring the Incarnation to be a work of love and mercy. "He took our flesh solely through

---

[1] Epiph. *Adv. Hæreses, Hær.* lv. 4.—*P.G.* xli.; col. 980. *Cp. Hær.* xlii.; *ibid.* col. 792.

[2] *Hæres.* xlii. 8; *ibid.* col. 705.

[3] *Hær.* lxvi. 79.—*P.G.* xlii.; col. 153.

[4] *Ancoratus,* xciii.—*P.G.* xliii.; col. 185-188.

love to have pity on us; beyond this there was no reason for the Incarnation."[1] This Divine work has, however, two aspects, two principal parts, as he elsewhere says, to deliver us from evil and confer on us the goods which He alone was able to give.[2]

As to the positive part of this work, Chrysostom speaks like the rest of the Greek Fathers. "After having said that those who have received Christ are born of God, and are sons of God, the Evangelist gives us the reason and cause of this great honour. It is, in brief, that the Word became flesh, that the Master took the form of a servant. The Son of God became a son of man that the sons of men might become sons of God." This was the only means by which we could be saved. "For our nature had truly experienced an irremediable fall, and to be saved it needed this mighty hand. It could not have risen had not He who had made it in the beginning given it His hand."[3]

But it seems to us Chrysostom is less concerned with this specifically Greek idea than with the negative side of Christ's work.

Christ died for us, as the good shepherd gives his life for his sheep.[4] He died for each of us; nor would He have refused to die even for one.[5] He not only died for us, but because of us, for it was our sins which were the cause of His Passion.[6] Chrysostom elsewhere treats this truth as a veritable thesis, and proves it by numerous quotations from Scripture.

[1] Ioan. Chrysost. *In Hebr. Hom.* v. 1. *P.G.* lxiii. 47.
[2] *In Galat. Hom.* iv. 1. *P.G.* lxi. 657.
[3] *In Ioan. Hom.* xi. 1 and 2. *P.G.* lix. 79.
[4] *In Ioan. Hom.* lx. 1; *ibid.* col. 328.
[5] *In Gal. Hom.* ii. 8. *P.G.* lxi. 646.
[6] *In. Matth. Hom.* lxxxii. 1. *P.G.* lviii. 738. *Cp. ibid. Hom.* lxxxvii. 2, col. 771, and *in Rom. Hom.* ix. 1. *P.G.* lx. 467.

"There are many sayings in Scripture which predict that the Saviour was to die, and die for our sins." He quotes *Isaias* liii. 8, 6, 5, and to please those who were not content with the Old Testament, he also adduces JOHN i. 29 ; 2 *Cor.* v. 21 ; *Gal.* iii. 13. "There are also thousands of other texts which announce His death, and that He should die for our sins." [1]

To enter more into detail, by sin we had passed under the yoke of Satan ; Christ became our ransom and delivered us from it.[2] Sin is a stain on the soul ; Christ cleansed us by His Sacrifice. " It is the Lamb of God who takes away the sins of the world. . . . He offered but a single Sacrifice for sins, but He ceases not to cleanse us by that one Sacrifice." [3] Especially in his homily on *Hebrews* does Chrysostom enlarge on this idea. The sacrifices of the Old Law were insufficient, this was why they had to be con- stantly repeated ; but Christ sanctified us by a single Sacrifice.[4]

The especial evil of sin is that it makes us enemies of God ; Christ's death restores us to favour. " We were all of us under sentence ; we deserved execution. We were accused by the Law, and God had con- demned us. We were to die as in the days of the deluge, and virtually we were already dead. Christ snatched us from death by delivering Himself to death. The presence of Christ mollified the Divine wrath." [5] " He offered a Sacrifice which was able to

[1] *In* 1 *Cor. Hom.* xxxviii. 3.—*P.G.* lxi. ; col. 325.
[2] *In Matth. Hom.* lxv. 4.—*P.G.* lviii. ; col. 622.
[3] *In Ioan. Hom.* xviii. 2.—*P.G.* lix. ; col. 116.
[4] *In Hebr. Hom.* xv. 2.—*P.G.* lxiii. ; col. 119-120. *Cp. ibid. Hom.* xvii. 1-3; col. 129-131 ; *Hom.* xviii. 1 ; col. 135 & *Hom.* xiii. 3 ; col. 107.
[5] *In Gal.* ii. 8.—*P.G.* lxi. ; col. 646.

appease His Father,"[1] and this sacrifice effectively "reconciles us to God and God to us, for where there is sacrifice, there there is remission of sins."[2] By this sacrifice too we have been delivered from the future punishment.[3] "For we were all subject to sin and to its penalty; *Christ by His Passion abolished both the sin and the penalty.*"[4] Here we find the scholastic distinction between *culpa* and *pœna*.

The texts we have quoted contain only statements which we have met before. But Chrysostom goes further. He is not concerned merely with effects; he also seeks out the underlying reasons and endeavours to give some sort of an answer to the many questions raised by our Saviour's atoning death.

Why did Christ die? Because, on the one hand, we were all sinners, and, on the other, only the sinless can die for sinners[5]; the conclusion being that Christ alone could save us. "He is the only Priest who could deliver us from our sins; that is why He became man in order to offer a victim which might cleanse us. We were foes of God, and were condemned and dishonoured, and there was no one who could offer a sacrifice for us. Seeing us in this wretched state, He took pity on us, and did not give us a priest, but Himself became our Priest."[6] "The Saviour's death was necessary to save us."[7]

---

[1] *In Hebr.* xvii. 1.—*P.G.* lxiii.; col. 128.

[2] *Hom. I de Cruce et Latrone*, 1.—*P.G.* xlix.; col. 399. *Cp. ibid.* ii.; col. 407-408.

[3] *In Ioan. Hom.* lxv. 1.—*P.G.* lix.; col. 361.

[4] *Col. Hom.* vi. 3.—*P.G.* lxii.; col. 340. πάντες ἦμεν ὑφ' ἁμαρτίαν καὶ κόλασιν· αὐτὸς κολασθεὶς ἔλυσε καὶ τὴν ἁμαρτίαν καὶ τὴν κόλασιν.

[5] 1 *Cor. Hom.* xxxviii. 2. *P.G.* lvi. 394.

[6] *Hebr. Hom.* v. 1.—*P.G.* lxiii. 47.

[7] *Rom. Hom.* ix. 3. *P.G.* lx. 471. διὰ τοῦ θανάτου τοῦ Δεσπότου δεῖν σωθῆναι.

How does Christ's death save us? Chrysostom, of all the Fathers, is most explicit in stating the doctrine of substitution. We find it first of all stated in general terms. "God spared sinners and did not spare His Son."[1] On the contrary, "to pardon us He sacrificed His Son."[2] "For all the outrages which we heaped on Him in return for His benefits, He not only did not punish us, but gave us His Son. He made Him to be sin for us—that is, He allowed Him to be condemned as a sinner and die as one accursed. He made Him to be a sinner, and sin, who far from having committed sin, knew no guile." All this Chrysostom explains by a comparison. "A king seeing a robber about to receive his due, sends his beloved and only son to death *and lays on him not only the penalty but also the crime* (μετὰ τοῦ θανάτου καὶ τὴν αἰτίαν . . . μετήνεγκεν), and this he does to save the guilty one and to promote him afterwards to high dignity."[3] "*Men ought to have been punished, but God did not do so; they ought to have perished, but He gave His Son in their stead*" ('Απόλλυσθαι ἔμελλον · ἀλλ' ἀντ' ἐκείνων τὸν αὐτοῦ ἔδωκεν Υἱὸν).[4]

But our Doctor is far from forgetting that Christ's oblation was voluntary. "Let us suppose," he says, "that a man has been sentenced to death; if anyone offers to take his place he delivers the condemned from death. This is what Christ did for us."[5] He took on Him the outward legal curse of the cross to

---

[1] *Rom. Hom.* ix. 3. ὁ . . . τῶν ἐχθρῶν οὕτω φεισάμενος ὥστε μὴ φείσασθαι τοῦ Παιδός.

[2] *Eph. Hom.* xvii. 1. *P.G.* lxii. 116. ἵνα γάρ σοι συγγνῷ τὸν Υἱὸν ἔθυσε.

[3] 2 *Cor. Hom.* xi. 3-4.—*P.G.* lxi. col. 478-480.

[4] 1 *Tim. Hom.* vii. 3.—*P.G.* lxii.; col. 537.

[5] *Gal. Hom.* iii. 3.—*P.G.* lxi.; col. 652-653.

deliver us from the real curse due to our sins. "This does not mean that He was despoiled of His essential glory and really made into an accursed thing. Even the demons do not believe this, nor the most senseless of men, for such an idea is at once too stupid and too impious. What the Apostle means is not this, but that He took on Himself the curse which was on us, and thereby delivered us."[1] In a word, "He paid our debt for us" (τὴν ὀφειλομένην δίκην αὐτὸς ὑποστὰς διὰ τοῦ σταυροῦ).[2]

We may have noticed how, in describing this process of rigorous justice, Chrysostom never forgets the love which is its principle. To bring out the Father's love he is fond of quoting the text Proprio Filio non pepercit Deus (Rom. viii. 32). "St Paul's fervour leads him to use this hyperbole (μεθ' ὑπερβολῆς) to show God's love. How could God forsake us when He did not spare even His own Son, but delivered Him for us? Fancy His refusing to spare His own Son, but giving Him up for all, wretched, ungrateful men, His foes and blasphemers! How great is His love."[3] Another text of Romans serves Chrysostom as a theme to tell of the generosity of the Son. "If no one would die for a virtuous man, how great must be the Saviour's love to die for sinners and enemies. In this act I see two, three, in fact a whole crowd of benefits. He died for the wicked; He has reconciled, saved, justified us, and made us immortal sons and heirs of God. Had He merely died for us this would of itself

---

[1] In Ioan. Hom. xi. 2.—P.G. lix.; col. 79. τὴν καθ' ἡμῶν κατάραν δεξάμενος οὐκ ἀφίησιν ἡμᾶς ἐπαράτους εἶναι λοιπόν.

[2] Eph. Hom. v. 3. P.G. lxii. 40.

[3] Rom. Hom. xv. 2.—P.G. lx.; col. 543. Cp. Eph. Hom. i. 3.— P.G. lxii.; col. 14. Thess. Hom. ix. 4; ibid. col. 451. Hebr. hom. iv. 2.—P.G. lxiii.; col. 39.

be a signal mark of His love, but in dying He heaps such great gifts on such great sinners that His benefaction is beyond any hyperbole, and should bring to the faith even the most dull."[1]   St. John Chrysostom never tires repeating these texts, finding in them ample material for pathetic discourses, which, however, we have not room enough to quote.

Hence Christ's death was voluntary, and this was the reason why He foretold it to His disciples.[2]   But how can we reconcile this freedom with the necessity of the Divine command?   Chrysostom answers by denying the existence of any commandment properly so called; the texts which seem to hint at something of the kind are in reality merely speaking of the perfect agreement of the Father's and the Son's will.[3] The Atonement is really a work of both.   " *The Father planned it and the Son executed it in His blood.*"[4]

We are now able to see better the worth of this Sacrifice.   Such a Victim sufficed to save all men[5] for ever.[6]   For " Christ offered Himself for all and His death covered all our faults " (ἀντίρροπος).   If He did not take away and blot out the sins of all it was their fault.[7]   Our Redemption was not merely sufficient but superabundant.   " A creditor throws into prison a debtor who owes him ten pence, and not only the debtor, but his wife and children and slaves with him.

---

[1] *In Ioan. hom.* xxvi. 1-2.   *P.G.* lix.; col. 158-159. *Cp. Eph. hom.* xx. 2.—*P.G.* lxii.; col. 137 & *Tit.* vi. 1; *ibid.* col. 688.

[2] *In Matth. hom.* lxv. 1.—*P.G.* lviii.; col. 617.   *Cp. ibid.* lxxxiii. 2, col. 747.

[3] *In Ioan. hom.* lx. 2-3.—*P.G.* lix.; col. 330-1.

[4] *Rom. hom.* vii. 2.—*P.G.* lx.; col. 444.

[5] *Gal. hom.* ii. 8.—*P.G.* lxi.; col. 647.

[6] *Hebr. hom.* xvii. 3.—*P.G.* lxiii.; col. 131.

[7] *Ibid.* 2; col. 129: ἀντίρροπος γὰρ ἦν ὁ θάνατος . . . τῆς πάντων ἀπωλείας.

A third person enters the scene and gives the ten pence required, and over and above, ten thousand talents of gold. . . . After this, could the creditor have any more thought of the ten pence? So was it with us. Christ paid more that we owed, an ocean for a single drop." [1]

[1] *Rom. hom.* x. 2.—*P.G.* lx.; col. 477. *Cp. ibid.* 3; col. 479.

CHAPTER XII

THE SUM OF THE GREEK THEOLOGY—ST. CYRIL OF ALEXANDRIA, ST. JOHN DAMASCENE

GREEK theology has now almost reached the end of its term of prosperity. The time is fast approaching when this great Church, even before falling into schism, will feel creeping over it that decay which will soon numb for ever its once so subtle genius. Before, however, sinking into insignificance it will produce, in the person of St. Cyril of Alexandria, one of the greatest of its lights. The great defender of orthodoxy against the Nestorian heresy naturally devoted most of his efforts and his writings to solving the Christological problem. But the work of the Redeemer is so intimately connected with His person, and the Greek Fathers in particular had united so closely the two questions of the Incarnation and the Atonement, that one could not make progress without gain to the other. St. Cyril, in fact, so well sums up his predecessors, and has impressed their teaching with so personal a stamp, that his work really constitutes the final and best effort of Greek theology; those who came after were mere compilers, content to repeat what they had received without adding to it anything of their own.

I

It is no easy task to find one's way through the great and varied works of St. Cyril. The narratives of Genesis, the rites of Leviticus, the writings of St. John and of St. Paul, all furnish him with matter for reflection, and he has embodied his doctrinal views no less in his moral exhortations and in his letters than in his dogmatic and polemical tracts. It being physically impossible for us to follow St. Cyril step by step through all his works, we shall perforce have to be content with indicating those outlines of his system which appear to us to remain constant beneath the ever-varying details.

St. Cyril throughout represents the Atonement as a gratuitous work of God's mercy. Yet there is at least one passage in which he seems, like St. Athanasius, to admit in God a sort of obligation arising from His goodness. After having stated that God was moved to succour us out of pity for our misery, St. Cyril continues : " For it was necessary that God should come to our help, to bring to naught the devil's treachery, to transform our nature and to forge it anew for everlasting life. All men were plunged in sin, and prophets were losing their time and their pains. What then had God to do ? Leave man in the devil's hands with ruin staring him in the face ? But how then could He be called good, if, when He could save us without trouble, He paid no heed to us ? What object could He have in creating man if He was not to take pity on his unforeseen misfortunes ? "[1]

In any case, and whatever may have been His motive, God sent His Son. But what was the object of the Incarnation ? Certainly its primary object was to enlighten men, who were held by the demons in ignorance and idolatry.[2] It was to draw nearer to

[2] CYRIL. ALEXANDR : *Contra Iulian.* viii. *P.G.* lxxvi. 925.
[3] *Ibid.* vi. col. 794.

mankind; but it involved more than this, for even the Docetæ would concede this much. Its object was to renew and transform our nature. " Is it not clear that if the Son of Man made Himself like unto us—*i.e.* a perfect man—that He did so to deliver our earthly body from the corruption which had invaded it through sin, by becoming the same as us by means of the mystery of the hypostatic union " (τῇ καθ᾽ ἕνωσιν οἰκονομίᾳ καταβεβηκὼς εἰς ταυτότητα) " to make our human nature stronger than sin by making it His own and by, as it were, imparting to it some of His own immortality ? This is our reason for saying that the whole Logos was united to the entire man. . . . He thus became the root, and, as it were, the first-fruits of those who lead a new life." [1] Cyril elsewhere [2] speaks of the " second stock of the human race which brings us back to our early immortality."

Two Scripture texts which aptly convey St. Cyril's meaning—*Hebrews* ii. 14, which he understands as referring to the healing of our mortal body, and *Romans* viii. 3, which speaks of the deliverance of our sinful soul—occur, either in conjunction or separately, more than twenty times in his works [3]; but it is in his commentary on St. John that he gives us in didactic form the clearest possible expression of his views. [4]

---

[1] *De Inc. unigeniti.—P.G.* lxxv. ; col. 1212-1213.

[2] *Glaphyra in Genesim,* 1, 5.—*P.G.* lxix. ; col. 28. ῥίζαν ὥσπερ τοῦ γένους δευτέραν.

[3] *Cp. In Isaiam,* lib. v. t. i.—*P.G.* lxx. ; col. 1166. *Cp.* col. 1174. 1 *Cor.* xv. 12.—*P.G.* lxxiv. ; col. 897. *Hebr.* ii. 14 ; *ibid.* col. 964-5. *ibid.* xii. 2 ; col. 993. *Quod unus sit Christus.—P.G.* lxxv. ; col. 1306. *Cp.* col. 1336-1337. *Scholia de Inc.* xii. ; *ibid.* col. 1383-4. *De Inc. Dom.* x. ; *ibid.* col. 1430. *Adv. Nest.* v.—*P.G.* lxxvi ; col. 210. *De recta fide ad Theod.,* 19-20 ; *ibid.* col. 1160-1.

[4] *In Ioan.* lib. IX. (xiv. 20).—*P.G.* lxxiv. ; col. 272-282.

In order to refute those of his opponents who believed that Christ was only morally united to the Godhead, Cyril sets about defining the object of the Incarnation. " The Apostle," he says, " assigns one cause only to the Incarnation because it is the most true and general one : *Instaurare omnia in Christo—i.e.* to restore mankind to its primitive state. The two means of bringing about this restoration are dealt with elsewhere by the Apostle in well-known texts ; sin had to be condemned in the flesh and death destroyed by His death. St. John mentions a third—viz. to make us sons of God and regenerate us." Here then we have a clear statement of the conditions of the " restoration " and of the reasons of the Incarnation ; these we shall now consider in detail.

How did God condemn sin in the flesh ? By becoming incarnate ; He who was essentially incapable of sin, so raised up the flesh as to make it share in the Divine sinlessness. We must beware of fancying that He saved Himself alone ; on the contrary, He secured the same benefits to the whole human race, in Himself and through Himself, He being the first-fruits of mankind. From the first man we had inherited death and all the passions, likewise we are heirs of Christ who in a thousand different ways saves and sanctifies the flesh in Himself. St. Paul rightly said (1 *Cor.* xv. 49) : " As we have borne the image of the earthly, we shall bear also the image of the heavenly "—that is, we shall be exempt from passions and corruption. Hence He condemned sin, commanding the flesh to cease its rule and become comformable to God's will rather than to its own ; thus of our animal body He made a spiritual body. In all this Cyril is alluding mystically to the potency of Christ's precepts and example.

But He had also to deliver us from death. Man, who had been raised by God to a supernatural state, had by sin reverted to his pristine mortality. He could only be restored by again entering into connection with God. This is why the eternal Word took our flesh after a mysterious fashion, which He alone knows, in order to bring it back to its real life and to make it share, through Himself, in God the Father. For Christ unites in Himself two natures —the Divine nature which belongs to Him, and the human nature which He assumed at the Incarnation. Hence God is now our Father and we are His children, and partake of the Divine nature thanks to the Holy Ghost which is in us.

Here St. Cyril is so anxious to describe the wonderful benefit of our union with God that he seems to ascribe everything to the Incarnation and to forget our Saviour's death. But elsewhere he makes amends for this seeming negligence and tells us that it was by His death that Christ destroyed our death.[1] So much so in fact that, were it not for this blessed death, we might say that the Incarnation itself was of no avail.[2] St. Cyril elsewhere lays it down as a principle " that death had to be destroyed by death, and, with death, sin also and the kingdom of Satan. Hence it was necessary that Christ should die and for Him to die He had to put on mortal flesh." [3] " *Christ's death was as it were the root of life*, it destroyed corruption, abolished sin, and made an end of God's wrath." [4]

---

[1] Cp. especially *Glaphyr. in Genesim, loc. cit.   De Inc. unigeniti, loc. cit.   In Ioan.* lib. xi. 10 (xvii. 18 *f*).   *P.G.* lxxiv. 548.

[2] 1 *Cor.* xv. 12 ; *ibid.* col. 897.

[3] *De SS. Trinitate. Dialog.* v.—*P.G.* lxxv. ; col. 936 : καταργεῖσθαι θάνατον ἐν θανάτῳ Χριστοῦ.

[4] *In Hebr.* ii. 14.—*P.G.* lxxiv. ; col. 965 : ῥίζα γὰρ ὥσπερ ζωῆς ὁ Χριστοῦ θάνατος.

P

" God's will was to redeem the world by the cross and to restore all things through Christ and in Christ."[1] Or to quote a text which sums up all the others. " By shedding His blood for us, Christ destroyed death and corruption. . . . *Had He not died for us we should never have been saved and the cruel sovereignty of death would never have been abolished.*"[2]

This is why St. Cyril is so anxious to retain the union of the two natures in the Redeemer. But there is this difference between the earlier Fathers and St. Cyril; the former, when dealing with Gnostics and Docetæ, had to show that Christ had a human nature, or when contending with Arians and Apollinarists, they had to prove that this human nature was complete; but the latter, whose opponents were the Nestorians, had to lay most stress on Christ's Divine nature. If the Word of God is a creature, how then are we united to God and deified by our union with Him? How is Christ the mediator between God and man? He indeed unites Himself with us by the Incarnation, but how will He unite Himself to God? Again, how are we saved by Him if He is a mere creature? How are we justified? How was that curse of God's abolished : " Dust thou art and to dust thou shalt return " ?[3] " To say that it was not the Word of God who took flesh—that is, who consented to be born of a woman—is to upset the whole economy of Salvation. . . . For then the sovereignty of death is not at an end, sin is not destroyed, we are still under Adam's guilt nor have

---

[1] *Quod unus sit Christus.*—*P.G.* lxxv. ; col. 1345. διὰ τοῦ τιμίου σταυροῦ λύτρωσις καὶ ἀνακεφαλαίωσις. . . .

[2] *Glaphyr. in Exodum.* ii. 2.—*P.G.* lxix. ; col. 437.

[3] *Thesaurus de Trinitate. P.G.* lxxv. 284.

we been restored to a better condition."[1] "The Saviour's object was to die for us, and to do this in order to destroy death. *As the destruction of death was above the power of human nature it was necessary that the Word of God should take flesh.*"[2]

Thus we find St. Cyril constantly using the same argument against the Nestorians : If Christ is not God we are not saved. On the other hand, if it is true that we are saved—*i.e.* delivered from death and restored to a Divine life—then Christ was God. Underlying this dilemma there is always the fact of the Atonement, from which Cyril starts to prove the true doctrine of the Incarnation.

II

We have now seen how all-important is the position occupied by Christ's death in St. Cyril's conception of the mission of the Word ; it is an indispensable condition of our restoration. Judged in this light, it would seem that St. Cyril's synthesis should be classed with those of Athanasius and of Gregory of Nyssa. But St. Cyril does not rest content with the general statement we have heard him make ; again and again he reverts to Christ's death, ever endeavouring to enter more fully into its significance.

Thus we are told that Christ died for us ($\upsilon\pi\grave{\epsilon}\rho$ $\dot{\eta}\mu\hat{\omega}\nu$), and because of us ($\delta\iota'$ $\dot{\eta}\mu\hat{a}\varsigma$),[3] and that our sins were the reason of this undeserved death.[4]

---

[1] *Quod unus sit Christus.* P.G. lxxv. ; col. 1268 *f.*

[2] *Ad reginas de recta fide.* Oratio altera, 31. P.G. lxxvi. 1376.

[3] Cyril seems to be fond of bringing these two expressions into conjunction in order the better to show simultaneously the effect of this death and its cause. *Cp. Glaphyr. in Exod.* ii. 2. P.G. lxix. 424. *In Ioan.* iv. (vi. 51 *f*). P.G. lxxiii. 565 ; *ibid.* v. 1 ; col. 720 and x. (xv. 11). P.G. lxxiv. 377.

[4] *Heb.* ix. 12 ; *ibid.* col. 985, etc.

In the first instance Christ's death has the character of a sacrifice—of a spotless sacrifice—of which Christ is at once the Priest and the Victim ; a sacrifice of which all the legal offerings were but an imperfect figure, which the advent of the real sacrifice has abolished for ever. Ideas such as these fill Cyril's commentaries both of the Old Testament and of the epistle to the Hebrews.[1] He distinctly states that it was a sacrifice for sin and that it was more especially prefigured by the Paschal Lamb and the scapegoat.[2] So persuaded was Cyril of the sacrificial character of Christ's death that he embodies it as a doctrine in one of his anathemas against Nestorius, which afterwards received the sanction of the Council of Ephesus, " It was not for Himself that He offered His sacrifice —for He stood in no need of it—but rather for us." [3]

Hence Christ was verily our ransom, " *the exchange for all our lives* " (ἀντάλλαγμα τῆς ἁπάντων ζωῆς). In several passages Cyril affirms this as a fact,[4] but more frequently he goes further, and by using the adjective ἀντάξιος, implies that the ransom given was a good equivalent for all of us. This idea is not novel, and we have already seen that the same word had been used by Basil and Clement of Alexandria. St. Cyril, however, lays far more stress on it, and is constantly

---

[1] *Heb.* ii. 18, col. 969 ; iii. 1, col. 972 ; vii. 27, col. 975 ; ix. 12, col. 983 ; x. 14, col. 987 ; *cp. Glaphyr. in Exodum,* ii. 2. *P.G.* lxix. 440. *In Levit.* 2 ; *ibid.* col. 544, 549, 580. *In Num.* 2 ; *ibid.* col. 621, etc.

[2] *In Exod.* ii. ; *ibid.* col. 425 *f.* *In Levit. ibid.* col. 588 *f.* *Adv. Iul.* ix. *P.G.* lxxvi. 966 *f.*

[3] *Anath.* x. *P.G.* lxxvi. 310. *Cp.* 311, and *Contra Theodoret. ibid.* col. 443 and 451.

[4] *Cp. De Adorat. in spiritu et verit.* xv. *P.G.* lxviii. 972. *In Exod.* ii. *P.G.* lxix. 480. *Quod unus sit Christus.* *P.G.* lxxv. 1337. τῆς ἁπάντων ζωῆς ἀντίλυτρον.

using the word.[1] Here, for instance, is a text which expresses both the fact and its reason : " Christ, the only Son of God, redeemed us, not with perishable metals like gold or silver, but by giving His soul for us, by offering Himself to His Father as a blameless sacrifice, by giving His blood in exchange of all our lives. For He was of more worth than all, even than the whole of creation, because though a perfect man he remained the only Son of God." [2]

But sin is not merely a fault which must be blotted out, or a bondage which must be broken. These are but its results. Sin is moreover an offence against God.[3] Hence the ultimate effect of Christ's sacrifice is to reconcile us with God, to overthrow sin, which was as a wall or partition between us and Him, and to restore us to His friendship.[4]

In several passages Cyril combines all these results of our Saviour's death into one picture. " Christ, the true Paschal Lamb, was sacrificed for us to bring to naught the sovereignty of death and to buy at the price of His blood the whole earth. We have been bought, we no longer belong to ourselves. *For one who was of more worth than all, died for all* " (εἶς ὑπὲρ πάντων ἀπέθανεν ὁ πάντων ἀξιώτερος), " that henceforth we might live only for Him. Hence we all belong to Christ, who reconciled us to His Father by

---

[1] Cp. *Glaphyr. in Levit.*—P.G. lxix. ; col. 548 : δέδωκεν ἑαυτὸν ὑπὲρ πάντων εἶς, ὁ πάντων ἀντάξιος.—*De Inc. unigeniti.* P.G. lxxv. ; col. 1216. *De recta fide ad Theod.* 21.—P.G. lxxvi. ; col. 1164.

[2] *Epist. ad Maxim. Const.*—P.G. lxxvii. ; col. 152.

[3] Cp. *In Rom.* v. 3.—P.G. lxxiv. ; col. 784. *Ibid.* v. 18 ; col. 788.

[4] *In Ioan.* xi. (xvii. 18-19) ; *ibid.* col. 544. κόσμον αὐτῷ καταλλάσσων καὶ συνάγων εἰς φιλίαν. Cp. *De ador. in sp. et ver.* iii.—P.G. lxviii. ; col. 292. Cp. col. 297. *Adv. Nest.* v. 1.—P.G. lxxvi. ; col. 220.

suffering for us in the flesh, that He might cleanse us." [1]

Here the various ideas are not co-ordinated, but elsewhere Cyril clearly shows that in his estimation the most important benefit is the forgiveness of sins, which is the source of all the rest. "The spotless Lamb, pre-figured from of old, is now led to death as a sacrifice for all, to expel sin from the world, to slay our enemy, to destroy death by dying for all, taking off the ban which crushed us, and abolishing God's decree: 'Dust thou art, and to dust shalt thou return.'" Changing places with our first father He became a second Adam and the principle of a new life. "For one only Lamb died for all to save the whole flock, one died for all to bring all to God, one died for all to earn them all. . . . Whereas we were guilty of many crimes, and deservedly under sentence of death and corruption, the Father gave us His Son as a ransom, one for all, because in Him are all things and because He is better than all. He therefore died for all that we all might have life in Him. . . . For we were in Him who died and rose again for us. *And sin being destroyed, how can it be otherwise than that death, which is its result, is destroyed? The root being dead, how can the branches survive? Sin being dead, how could we henceforward die?*" [2]

This passage clearly shows that sin was the main obstacle to our Salvation, and that, consequently, the main result of Christ's death was its destruction. But how exactly was it destroyed? We have seen that Cyril frequently speaks of sacrifice, purification, expiation; but as a matter of fact he does not confine himself to such superficial ritualism; he wishes to

[1] *Quod unus sit Christus.* *P.G.* lxxv. 1356.
[2] *In Ioan.* ii. (i. 29). *P.G.* lxxiii. 192.

give something more than a mere verbal explanation of the supernatural efficacy of this Sacrifice and of the worth of this redemption.

III

The first explanation ventured on by Cyril invokes the idea of a penal substitution. He first makes use of it in his commentary on *Isaias* liii.

Our Doctor begins by reminding us that the ancient sacrifices were unable to wipe away sin. Accordingly, Christ came to offer the perfect Sacrifice of which we stood in such dire need. " By undergoing the death of the flesh He delivered all flesh from death and sin. For one died for all who also was worth more than all " (εἷς ὁ πάντων ἀνταξιώτερος). Leaving this idea Cyril continues : " It was not for His sins but for ours that He was wounded. We had disobeyed God and it was we who should have been chastised. *But the chastisement which was due to sinners fell on Him. God struck Him for our sins in order to absolve us from the penalty.*" But Christ's willing self-oblation keeps its place beside God's justice. " To destroy the world's sin, He took it on Himself and thus, dying for all, He, who was an equivalent for all " (εἷς ὑπὲρ πάντων ἀποθανὼν ὁ πάντων ἀντάξιος), " became useful to many." [1]

The same idea occurs elsewhere. " He who had never sinned, Him did God make sin—*i.e. made Him to suffer all what is due to the greatest of sinners.* Thus were we justified in Him, for one died for all, being Himself the due equivalent of all." [2] " We

---

[1] *In Isaiam*, liii.—*P.G.* lxx. ; col. 1174-1176. *Cp.* 1182 and 1189.

[2] 2 *Cor.*—*P.G.* lxxiv. ; col. 945, τὸν οὐδὲν ἡμαρτηκότα πώποτε παρεσκεύασε παθεῖν τὸ τῶν σφόδρα φιλαμαρτημόνων.

deserved a punishment for our sins; He who had never committed sin, but who had walked in all righteousness, *received the punishment of sinners* and destroyed by His cross the ancient ban." [1] "Christ alone died for all because He was the rightful equivalent of all, and He gave His soul in exchange for ours. Thus did He put a stop to the devil's pretensions and silenced the voice of sin crying for our punishment." He then goes on to explain his meaning: "Since sin had reigned on earth . . . we had all of us incurred the pain of death. For the penalty for infringing the Law of God and the Will of the Lord is death. But the Creator took pity on our fallen nature and the Lord God became man . . . to undergo the death which threatened us on account of our sin. He thereby destroyed sin and put an end to Satan's claims, *for in Christ we have paid the penalties due to our sins.*" Cyril concludes: "Christ having suffered for us how could God any longer demand the penalty of our sins ?" [2]

Hence, if our sins have been blotted out, this was because Christ put Himself in our place to bear their penalty. But, as we have already seen, Christ is, according to St. Cyril, not an ordinary substitute: He is a real equivalent (ἀντάξιος) for all sinners. Christ is this on account of His Divine nature, which takes on itself the voluntary sacrifices of His Divine Manhood. "*One had to die for all who might be the equivalent of the life of all.* We must not fancy that the Apostles' death had for its object to destroy death and cor-

---

[1] *De Inc. Domini*, 27.—*P.G.* lxxv.; col. 1465, αὐτὸς . . . τὴν τῶν ἁμαρτωλῶν κατεδέξατο τιμωρίαν.

[2] *De adorat. in sp. et ver.* iii.—*P.G.* lxviii.; col. 293-297. ὡς ἐκτετικότων ἡμῶν ἐν αὐτῷ τῷ Χριστῷ τῶν εἰς ἁμαρτίαν αἰτιαμάτων τὰς δίκας.

ruption, for they too, like us, were delivered from death, having a like nature with us.   Hence He, the first and the only Son of the living Father, had to lay down His life as a ransom for the life of all."[1]   "It was not for Himself that Christ offered Himself in sacrifice, but for the sins of the world ; for no common man was required, to offer a sacrifice able to quicken the whole world."[2]   "It was no common man that God gave us as a Mediator, no not even an adopted son, nor one merely in close union with God, but the Word—who is consubstantial with the Father and above all creatures—that He might be the equivalent of our life."[3]   We can already see how much these views would avail Cyril in his contention with Nestorius.   The traditional data of the Atonement is the foundation on which he bases the real Godhead of the Redeemer.

"If Christ was only a common man, how could His death have saved the world?   The death of the many just men of old, of Abraham, Jacob and Moses, were of no use to us; but Christ's death saved us. Hence if the death of one sufficed for all, this one must have been, by His Divine nature, superior to all" (ἤρκεσε γὰρ εἷς ὑπὲρ πάντων ἀποθανὼν ὁ πάντων ἀξιώτερος, ὅτι καὶ φύσει Θεός . . .)[4]

Farther on St. Cyril quotes all the New Testament texts which describe the Atonement as the result of Christ's death, and shows how each of these texts points to the same conclusion.   Christ was our pro-pitiation in His blood—and not otherwise.   Hence

---

[1] *In Ioan.* xi (xviii. 7-9).   *P.G.* lxxiv. 585.
[2] *In Hebr.* iii. ; *ibid.* col. 972.
[3] *Quod unus sit Christus.   P.G.* lxxv. 1341.
[4] *De recta fide ad reginas,* 7.   *P.G.* lxxvi. 1208.   *Cp. ibid.* col. 1252.

the Word of God must have become man. Christ
is our redemption and sanctification, therefore He is
God. Christ redeems us at the price of His blood.
Were He a mere man how could this redemption be
an equivalent? But if He is really God then we
understand that the exchange is more than sufficient
(ἀξιόχρεως ἡ λύτρωσις). Christ became a curse and
thereby delivered us from our curse ; hence His
death was not that of a common man. Only the
Passion of the Word-made-Flesh could redeem the
world. Christ's death cleanses us ; but how could
the blood of a man justify us ? As all admit, Christ's
death saved the whole world ; how could it have done
so had He not been God ? He is able to redeem all
because He is above all. Many Prophets died, and
yet we do not say of them that they died for our sins,
nor that their death brought us any nearer to God ;
this was done by Christ alone ; hence it was not as
man, but as God Incarnate that He delivered His
body in exchange for the life of all.[1]

In the text we shall now give, this idea of a Divine
equivalent is combined with the idea of a penal
expiation. "Christ redeemed us from the law by
becoming a curse for us. As the Law cursed those
who had committed wrong, He who knew no sin,
by an unjust sentence, underwent the chastisement
which was deserved by those who were under the
ban of the Law. Thus He who was the equivalent
of all, by dying for us, absolved us from the crime
of disobedience, and in His blood redeemed the whole
world. Had He been but a man, He could not
have been the adequate ransom of all. But if He
is God Incarnate, suffering in the flesh which He
willed to assume, then all Creation is as naught in

[1] *P.G.* lxxvi. ; col. 1289-1297.

comparison with Him, and His death, once incurred, suffices to redeem the world."[1] In Cyril's epistle to Valerian we again find the same reasoning. "How could one die for all, and be the equivalent of all, were His sufferings those of a common man ? *But if it was God who suffered in human nature, then we can say, and say rightly, that the death of this one is equivalent to the life of all, for it will then not be the death of a man like us, but of God Incarnate.*"[2]

We have given more texts than were quite necessary for our demonstration ; in fact we have possibly quoted too many ; but we were anxious to show how important the idea seemed to St. Cyril. At any rate there can be no doubt that according to the great Alexandrian Doctor our redemption is a result at once of the Redeemer's sufferings, which are the penalty of our sins endured in our stead, and of the person of the Redeemer, to whom the sufferings owe all their merit ; in other words Cyril of Alexandria unites the twofold fact discanted on separately by Eusebius of Cæsarea and Cyril of Jerusalem. If we seek the underlying reason of this Divine plan we soon see that it could not be otherwise. If God claimed a sacrifice commensurate with the grievousness of sin, a ransom equivalent to all sinners, then the Son of God alone was able to give both one and the other. In all this Cyril is simply driving home the great truth, already perceived by Basil, of the relative necessity of the Incarnation. Baur had rightly said : " The only point wanting to a total conception of satisfaction was that all should be ascribed to God and to Divine Justice. This is just

---

[1] *De recta fide ad reginas. Oratio altera*, 7. *P.G.* lxxvi. 1344.
[2] *Ep. ad Valerianum. P.G.* lxxvii. 264.

what was missing in the older theories." [1] We also said that the Fathers seldom explored sin beneath its surface, and that they think more of its results than of its essential disorder. But though their conclusions were not as profound as we might have wished, they were not different from those of a later and more perfect theology. St. Cyril in the matter of investigation did not excel his predecessors, but to him we owe the synthesis of their teachings ; this combination, and the vigorous and exact language in which it is expressed, gives Cyril's doctrine its strength and also its appearance of being new.

In conclusion we must add that Cyril does not leave, as it were, in two separate compartments the two ideas of Salvation which we have pointed out in his works : the Saviour's uniting Himself to our nature in the Incarnation, and His death for us—the speculative and the realistic aspects of the Atonement. The attentive reader will have already noticed several texts in which the two ideas seem to be beginning to fall into line, but in this respect by far the most important passage is the following :—" I die for all [it is Christ who is speaking] to quicken all, and my flesh I give as a ransom for all flesh. Death will die by my death and fallen mankind will rise again with me. For this reason it was that I became like unto you." There then follows the well-known text of *Hebrews* ii. 14. Death, and the devil who was its sovereign, could not be destroyed save by Christ, He who is above all, offering Himself as a redemption for all. He therefore offered Himself to God as a spotless sacrifice. As the blood of the legal victims was not sufficient to expiate sin, *Christ Himself came to suffer after a fashion the penalty of all.* He was crucified

[1] Quoted by DöERHOLT, *op. cit.* p. 123.

for all and in the stead of all, that one being dead
for all we all might have life in Him. According to
His own words (JOHN xvii. 19), He offered Himself
a victim for us ; He delivered His body for the life
of all, and He Himself again engrafted life on us.
This is the fact, and Cyril, to explain its manner, tells
us that the Word of God who quickens all by uniting
Himself to the flesh, made it to share in the benefit
peculiar to Himself—*i.e.* in life—and made it a
principle of life such as He Himself is. This is
why Christ's body enlivens all those who partake
of it, and expels death and destroys corruption.[1]

This text shows us how the strictest " realism "
can keep its place side by side with the broadest
"speculation." The Incarnation is, in the Divine plans,
the general principle ; Christ's death is the particular
means ; or in other words the Incarnation is the
indispensable condition, whilst Christ's death is the
efficient cause of our Salvation. Hence we have here
a combination in one harmonious whole of the two
tendencies of Greek thought—the speculative and
the realistic. On this matter too, Cyril's strong
mind was able to grasp all the elements of the Greek
theology, and put a term to its indecision.

IV

The Greek Fathers who follow St. Cyril are less
remarkable for their ingenuity. However we must
pause a while to see their views, were it only to find
out how much they preserved of the teaching of
their predecessors.

In the writings of St. Proclus, Bishop of Constanti-
nople, we find a few texts bearing on our subject.

---

[1] *In Ioan.* iv. (vi. 52). *P.G.* lxxiii. 564 *f.*

" Having become man, without sin, He delivered human nature from sin by the cross ; His tomb was the end of death."[1] " The Passion was the world's expiation ; His death was a spring of immortality."[2] " He was the true Paschal Lamb offering Himself willingly to God to obtain for us in His blood the forgiveness of our sins."[3] We even find an allusion to the penal expiation afforded by Christ's death : " By becoming man He saved those like unto Him ; by dying, as man, for all, He paid the debt of sin."[4] But in this writer we find a much more interesting text in which he establishes with an exactness we seldom meet elsewhere, the relative necessity of the Atonement by the God-man.

" In consequence of sin the human race had contracted many debts which it was unable to repay. For we had all shared in Adam's sin, and hence were all of us slaves of the devil, who proudly displayed his credit-bill and claimed us as his prey. Hence of two things one ; either the death-sentence would be carried out on all, because all had sinned, or else a compensation rigorously equivalent to the debt would have to be furnished. But no man could save us, for every man is a subject of sin ; nor could an angel do so, not being able to furnish so great a ransom. The only alternative was that God, who is sinless, should die for sinners." Hence, in His Goodness, God became man, to die as man and to redeem us as God. " His worth was not only enough, but immeasurably more than enough for the crowd of guilty " (οὐκ ἀντιταλαν-

---

[1] Procl. Const. *Orat.* ii. 2.—*P.G.* lxv. ; 693.

[2] *Orat.* xi, 4, col, 785.

[3] *Orat.* xiv. 2 ; *ibid.* col. 796-797. *Cp. ibid.* 3 ; col. 800.

[4] *Epist.* iv. 7. *Ibid.* col. 861. ἐκτίσας τῆς ἁμαρτίας τὸ χρέος τῷ ὑπὲρ ἁπάντων ἀποθανεῖν.

τεύουσαν μόνον ἔχων τὴν ἀξίαν . . ., ἀλλὰ καὶ . . . ὑπερέχουσαν).
For He is God, and as such has God's Holiness and
mercy and all-powerful intercession. No man has
anything like this. Whence we obtain some idea
of His Goodness : "Being willingly condemned He
destroyed that death which was due to His executioners and changed the crime of His murderers into
the Salvation of sinners." Our Salvation was beyond
the power of man—Proclus is not afraid of repeating
this too often—for every man stood in need of a
Saviour. Hence we were in a hopeless state when
God Himself took pity on us. "He gave His blood
as a ransom for us, and delivered His virginal flesh in
exchange for ours. He thus snatched the world from
the curse of the Law and destroyed death by His
death." Our Saviour was therefore neither a simple
man nor God only, but God-made-Man. "For He
came to save us and for this He had to die. Now
how can these two things agree? *A common man
could not save us, God as such could not suffer. Then
God Himself became man ; what He was, saves us ;
what He became, suffers."* [1]

Among the ancient theologians it would be difficult
to find a finer attempt to explain God's plan of Salvation than in this eloquent page which seems, as it were,
to anticipate the dialectics of St. Anselm.

Another contemporary of St. Cyril's, Theodoret,
Bishop of Cyr, in his commentaries, describes Christ's
work in the customary way. His death was a ransom,
or rather "a kind of ransom," a correction of the
traditional saying which Theodoret twice makes.[2]
Above all, this death was a Sacrifice, a voluntary

---

[1] *De laudibus S. Mariæ. Orat.* i. 5-9, col. 685-689.
[2] THEODORET CYR. *in Rom.* iii. 24. *P.G.* lxxxii. 84. 1 *Tim.* ii.
6 ; *ibid.* col. 800.

and spontaneous one made to expiate our faults,[1] and to reconcile us to God.[2] This reconciliation presupposes that Christ paid our debt (Χριστοῦ τὸ ὑμέτερον ἀποδεδωκότος χρέος).[3] This idea pervades the commentary on *Isaias* liii. : "We ought to have died for our sins, but He died for us; to save us from the curse of the Law He became a curse. *We had earned a chastisement for our sins; He, the guiltless, underwent this chastisement in our lieu.* . . . Through sin we had become God's enemies, and to be restored to peace we had to be chastised; but He took on Him this chastisement and gave us peace. . . . In a word, *He took on Him the penalty due to sinners.*" [4]

Theodoret elsewhere gives us his theology of the Atonement in systematic form.[5] Christ foretold His Passion and accepted it willingly. He was indeed crucified, not because He bore the penalty of His sins but because He was paying the debt of our nature. Mankind had in effect contracted a debt by transgressing the Law of its Creator, and this debt it was unable to pay. Then did God with great wisdom see to its payment. Instead of money He assumed the members of human nature and, by a dispensation at once just and wise, he paid the debt and freed mankind. Theodoret proves his thesis by quotations from Isaias and St. Paul, for "the former predicts the Passion and the latter expounds the prediction." From afar Isaias saw the sufferings of the Messias and perceived their cause. Those who saw Him hanging

---

[1] *Dan.* ix. 24. *P.G.* lxxxi. 1472. *Cp. ibid.* 27, col. 1482.

[2] *Rom.* v. 8. *P.G.* lxxxii. 98. *Cp. Eph.* ii. 14; *ibid.* col. 524.

[3] *Coloss.* i. 20, col. 600 *f.*

[4] *In Isaiam*, liii. 4-12. *P.G.* lxxxi.; col. 441-444.

[5] *De Providentia, Sermo* x. *P.G.* lxxxiii.; col. 753-758. οὐχ ἁμαρτημάτων δίκας τίνων . . ., ἀλλὰ τῆς ἡμετέρας φύσεως ἐκτίνων τὸ χρέος.

on the cross fancied that it was for His many sins
that He was punished, but the Holy Ghost teaches
us by the prophet that it was for our sins that He was
wounded, and that He bore the chastisement of our
peace and that we have been healed by His sufferings.
For when we as sinners were enemies of God we had
richly deserved a penalty and a chastisement, but
these our Saviour underwent for us and thus restored
us to peace with God. . . . Thus did the blessed
Isaias describe to us His wholesome suffering, and at
the same time reveal to us its cause. In his turn the
divine St. Paul also tells us that He became a curse
for us, thus showing us that Christ the guiltless made
Himself a debtor in our stead. We indeed were
overwhelmed with debts and had in consequence been
reduced to slavery ; He delivered us by buying us at
the price of His blood. For which reason He also
chose to die on the cross that by this curse He might
take away the curse with which we were burdened.

In Procopius of Gaza we find a like realistic conception of events. "We should have pointed out
that He is the Saviour of our souls, who also bears
our sins and suffers for us. For it was for us that He
suffered that He might deliver us from the chastisement which was due to our sins." The expositor, in
St. Cyril's language, points out that He was the
equivalent of all (ὁ πάντων ἀνταξιώτερος). "*The chastisement which we deserved He underwent, in order to
reconcile us to God.* He endured the blows meant
for us and by His wounds we are healed. If we ask
why He who had done no sin should undergo death,
the Father answers : 'It was the sins of my people
which led Him to death' ; for the Father had indeed
delivered Him as a ransom for our souls (αὐτὸν ὑπὲρ
ἡμῶν ἀντίψυχον ὥσπερ παρέδωκεν). We must not how-

Q

ever imagine that He died by any necessity; His death was a willing one. He took on Himself the chastisement which should have fallen on us (τὰ ἡμῖν χρεωστούμενα πάθη αὐτὸς ἀναδεξάμενος οἰκειώσατο), and thus He died for us in order to absolve the world of sin."[1]

As we have already said, in these writers there is scarcely anything new to be found; in fact, a little more penetration and variety of expression would have been welcome; but one thing admits of no doubt, and that is that they unanimously connect Salvation with the death of Christ, who sacrificed Himself, and thus paid our debts for us. The constant repetition of such sayings proves that there was a long-standing tradition in the Greek Church favouring the realistic conception of Salvation.

V

In the eighth century the Greek Church was to produce the last of her Fathers and the first of her scholastic theologians—St. John Damascene, who was to sum up her doctrine and systematise its elements and thus transmit them, duly grouped and classified, to the West and to the Middle Ages.

What is most noticeable is the fact that the Atonement has no separate place in his system, a fact which shows that the Greek Church had not evolved any definitive theory on the matter, or in other words that the theology of this dogma was not yet built. If, however, we combine the various allusions and partial explanations made by our author we shall find all those doctrinal elements with which we are already familiar.

---

[1] Procop. Gaz. *In Isaiam,* liii. *P.G.* lxxxvii. (*pars secunda*), col. 2521-2532.

First of all we find the speculativeness which we have learnt to expect from writers of the Greek school. St. John Damascene describes the plan of Salvation as follows :—Man, ever since his first sin, had been deprived of grace, shut out of paradise, and subject to death. To save us it was necessary to destroy death, which was ravaging mankind like a wild beast, and to do this the Redeemer had to be exempt from sin, and consequently from death also. It was also necessary to restore and strengthen our nature by teaching it the way of virtue. For this did the Son of God come down from His throne to save us by making Himself like unto us.[1] Our author lays frequent emphasis on this necessary identity between our Saviour's nature and our own, and he repeats St. Gregory Nazianzen's principle ὅλον ὅλος ἀνέλαβέ με καὶ ὅλος ὅλῳ ἡνώθη, ἵνα ὅλῳ τὴν σωτηρίαν χαρίσηται.[2]

Farther on St. John Damascene exposes similar views, but with more abundance of detail. " Man by sinning had lost God's gifts. The Saviour came to share our nature, to restore in Himself and through Himself the image of God, to teach us by His example the path of virtue, to deliver us from corruption and give us life by becoming the principle of our resurrection, to repair the useless broken vessel of our nature, to deliver us from the tyranny of the devil by calling us to the knowledge of God."[3] Elsewhere in the same sense he says : " In the bowels of His mercy He became man, and in all things like unto us save in sin. As we had not preserved His

---

[1] IOAN. DAMASC. *De orth. fid.* iii. 1.—*P.G.* xciv. ; col. 981-984. τῷ ὁμοίῳ τὸν ὅμοιον ἀνεσώσατο.

[2] *Ibid.* iii. 6 ; col. 1005. *Cp.* iii. 18 ; col. 1072.

[3] *Ibid.* iv. 4 ; col. 1007.

image, He Himself came to unite Himself to our poor nature, to purify us, to make us incorruptible and again sharers in his Godhead. . . . This is why *by His Incarnation, His Baptism, His Passion and His Resurrection, He delivered mankind from the sin of its first parent, from death also and corruption,* and became the principle of our resurrection and the perfect model of our life."[1]

In the above passage all our Saviour's actions are placed on the same level, but our author elsewhere lays due emphasis on Christ's death. "If Christ died, this was not for Himself, for He was sinless, but for us; He offered Himself to God as a victim for us. For it was against God that we had sinned, and it was to Him therefore that the price of our redemption had to be paid, before the ban which was on us could be removed."

In another passage St. John Damascene had expressed even more clearly the idea of substitution. "If Christ was called a curse, this was for us, *because He was playing our part* (τὸ ἡμέτερον ἀναδεχόμενος πρόσωπον), as would he who through kindness would put himself in another's stead to pay debts which he had not contracted."[2] "Hence it was by this precious death, and by it alone, that death was destroyed, the sin of our first parents obliterated, Hell despoiled of its prey, whilst we again were able to find resurrection and the way to Heaven."[3]

All these different views receive still ampler statement in St. John Damascene's commentary on St. Paul. "We were foes of God and under sentence of death, and there was none who could offer sacrifice

[1] IOAN. DAMASC. *De orth. fid.* iv. 13; col. 1136 *f.*
[2] *Ibid.* iii. 25 and 27; col. 1093 and 1095 *f.*
[3] *Ibid.* iv. 11; col. 1130.

for us. But Christ took pity on us and gave us no other high priest, but Himself assumed this office to expiate His people's sins."[1] "His death delivers us from sin and snatches us from our doom, and justifies us, loading us also with gifts."[2] Especially does it unite us to God, taking away for ever the enmity which was set between us—viz. sin.[3]

If Christ's death produces all this good result then this must be because it is a real expiation. Our author reminds us of the universally admitted principle of law, that every sinner must be punished, and he adds "that we have been delivered from our punishment only through the Atonement of Christ, whom God made the expiatory victim of our sins."[4] For according to the prophecy of Isaias, God delivered His Son for the sins of the world.[5] "Not only did He allow Him to die for sinners; He made Him die, and He made Him to be sin, who knew no sin."[6] "*Men should have been punished for their misdeeds, but in their stead*" (ἀντ᾽ ἐκείνων) "*He delivered His own Son*"[7] But, all the same, Christ offered Himself of His own will. "He came to take on Himself our sins and to die."[8] And by His willing death He delivered us from the curse and from death; and our author concludes by repeating the fine comparison already used by Chrysostom. "When a man has been condemned to death, if another offers himself to take his place, he thereby delivers him from death; this is exactly what Christ did for us."[9]

If the reader still seeks a synthetic view of all the

---

[1] *Hebr.* ii. 17. *P.G.* xcv.; col. 941.
[2] *Rom.* vi. 17-21; col. 479-482. *Cp.* viii.; col. 500.
[3] *Eph.* ii. 16; col. 833 and *Col.* i. 20; col. 889.
[4] *Rom.* iii. 23; col. 464-465.   [5] 1 *Cor.* xv. 3; col. 690.
[6] 2 *Cor.* v. 22.; col. 736-7.   [7] 1 *Tim.* ii. 2; col. 1004.
[8] *Hebr.* ix. 15; col. 972.   [9] *Gal.* iii. 13; col. 796.

conditions of Salvation, he will find it in the passage in which St. John Damascene sums up his view with almost scholastic exactness. "God's greatest favour towards us was to have taken and sanctified us in Himself, in such a way that we have become His body, and have Him for our head. *The cause of this favour was God's goodness, and the means by which it was obtained was the Atonement by Christ's blood.*" [1]

We have now completed our study of the Greek theology on the Atonement. Were the statements ventured on by certain writers true, we should have found it full of a speculation centred round the Incarnation; but we now know what to think of such rash statements. We have seen that the historians in question lay inordinate stress on those texts which are favourable to them, and slur over those which are in contradiction to their preconceived views. Such a manner of proceeding is a sufficient condemnation of their cause. On the other hand, our impartial investigation has shown us the existence of two currents —one of them speculative, considering Salvation as a supernatural restoration of mankind to an immortal and Divine life; the other realistic, considering Salvation as the effect rather of the expiation of our sins by Christ's death. These two currents proceeded side by side, at first indeed somewhat confusedly, but at no time did one completely absorb the other, and, in the event, it was the more realistic current which gained the day. Of all the Greek Fathers we may say what has been said of St. John Damascene, that, according to them, "the death on the cross, though not indeed the only, was the culminating, event of the work of the Atonement." [2]

---

[1] *Eph.* i. 1, col. 821.

[2] SCHWANE, *History of Dogma.* French trans. by DEGERT (Paris, 1903), ii. p. 628.

PART THE THIRD

THE ATONEMENT AMONG THE LATIN FATHERS

CHAPTER XIII

THE EARLIEST WITNESSES : TERTULLIAN, ST. CYPRIAN

THE opposition between the Greek and Latin minds has ever been a favourite theme of a certain class of writers. Virgil had already acknowledged the former's right to claim all the charms of eloquence and art, whilst to the latter he allowed the less brilliant though more precious gift of governing. We are told that Christianity furnished a new food to the tendencies of the two races. Undoubtedly, speaking generally, this is true ; the East provided the theologians, whilst Church organisation was mainly the work of the West. But though no subject is better fitted to be fruitfully discussed, no subject, especially if the parallel be pressed, is more apt to lead us astray into the by-paths of superficial rhetoric. By exaggerating the light and shade we can only succeed in falsifying the picture.

After having reduced the Greek theology on the Atonement to a mere speculative idealism, we shall not be surprised to hear that our adversaries, in order to make the contrast more striking, would have us believe that the Latin theology on the same matter never rose above the level of a merely practical

247

moralism. Historians of dogma have not failed to be misled by this false rhythm. Among the Greeks they find nothing save vague mystico-philosophical speculations, whilst among the Latins everything seems to them to be reducible to legal quantity ; such is the view which has Harnack's approval. The learned historian points out that, by the Latins, God was conceived of as "the Judge," whose commandments are "the Law." Him every Christian must obey by acknowledging His rights. Should a Christian come to offend God he must at once appease him and make satisfaction by a series of penitential works, of which the worth is calculated on a tariff, and which begin to acquire merit as soon as they exceed the amount of the debt. All this is worked out from a strictly legal point of view, for God weighs minutely the quantity of penance. Harnack elsewhere compares the God of the Latins to a "powerful king" whose first care is to see to His rights.[1]

We are asked to believe that it was Tertullian who was mainly responsible for the introduction into Latin theology of legal ideas and terms. This Harnack seeks to establish in a few pages of terrific learning.[2] We have no intention to discuss this question now, but we may observe that it would be well not to be misled by the metaphors used by the subtle African lawyer, and that if it be true that several legal expressions have obtained a footing in our Church-language, and are still in use in our theological vocabulary, they are used, not to hide, but rather to express, moral truths. It is only wilfully that their real meaning can be misunderstood.

[1] Harnack, *Dogmeng.* ii. p. 175 *f.* and iii. p. 14 *f.*
[2] *Ibid.* iii. p. 16, note 1—a note which overflows its page and invades a large portion of pages 17 and 18.

What however is of interest to us is the fact that
these legal principles were applied to the Atonement
of Christ, whose work was looked upon as a Sacrifice
intended to appease God's anger. We are told that
this conception, which was scarcely known to the
Greeks, became familiar to the Westerns; whence
it came about that the Atonement was considered as
more especially a work of the Saviour's humanity, a
conception which allowed of the strict application of
the substitutionary view, and impelled theologians to
make calculations as to the exact worth of this expiation.[1] Harnack elsewhere repeats that though "the
Incarnation was still presupposed, it was Christ's
death which in the West became the *punctum saliens.*
Even before St. Augustine it had been looked at
under all its aspects: as a Sacrifice, as a reconciliation,
as a ransom, as a penal substitution. But St. Ambrose was the first to see in it a relationship with sin
conceived of as a debt."[2]

We need not point out one by one the numberless
inaccuracies which disfigure the pages of Harnack's
otherwise invaluable work. They all result from the
historian's neglect of a large portion, if not indeed
of the larger portion, of Greek theology, and from
the fact that he has only considered the speculative
syntheses of Athanasius and of St. Gregory of Nyssa.
By thus sifting the facts it is, of course, an easy
matter to evolve general ideas and to build them
into fine systems and ingenious antitheses. But
against all such proceedings reality sooner or later
gets its revenge, and it would not be difficult to show
that Harnack thereby fell into some most unfortunate

---

[1] HARNACK, *Dogmeng.* ii. pp. 177-180. *Cp.* HARNACK-CHOISY,
Précis, p. 174. The origin of all this is RITSCHL, *op. cit.* i. p. 15 *f.*
[2] *Ibid.* iii. p. 50 *f.*

blunders.[1] We have already seen that the Greeks too, considered our Saviour's death as the greatest event of His Atoning work and that they, in consequence, connected Salvation with His human nature which had been infinitely raised by its union with the Godhead. With regard to the ideas of ransom, expiatory sacrifice, penal substitution and reconciliation with God, they occur so constantly in the works of the Eastern Fathers that our only fear is that some of our readers may have found their recurrence somewhat tedious.

This must not, however, be taken to mean that the Latin character did not contribute something of its own peculiarity to theology in general and to the theology of the Atonement in particular. We shall have occasion to see that the Latins, who were less prone than the Greeks to speculation, really understood the question better, and, with the exactitude peculiar to their race and language, embodied their conclusion in precise, and sometimes in really legal, formulæ. But these slight differences do not amount to the radical contrast which some think they can establish. On the contrary, we shall see that, among the Latin Fathers, as among the Greeks, the fundamental doctrine was the same, and that it likewise was cast in the same mould of traditional metaphors, and that it issued in nothing profounder than had already been reached by the Greeks.

---

[1] For instance he finds in the Latins the first mention of any true substitution, and instances as exceedingly bold St. Ambrose's dictum. "*Quia peccata nostra suscepit, peccatum dictus est.*" *Op. cit.* ii. p. 178, note 2. We cannot, however, bring ourselves to see anything very bold in a statement which we have already found in every Greek Father from Origen down to St. John Damascene. The many other texts with which Harnack enriches his notes, will, if verified, lead to similar negative results.

I

Having cleared the ground, we have now to consider in detail the doctrine of the Latin Fathers concerning the Atonement. The earliest among these, Tertullian and St. Cyprian, whose influence was so great on Latin theology, will be perceived to be wanting in explicitness; if we recollect that they were contemporaries of Irenæus and Origen, then their teaching will seem to us all the cruder. But we must bear in mind that we are at the very starting-point of the Latin theology, and that if it be true that doctrines, like living beings, follow a law of gradual progress, nobody need be pained to find amongst its beginners merely the outlines of the doctrine which will be developed in the future.

In Tertullian we find for the first time the word satisfaction, which will later on occupy so important a place in Latin theology, and which will finally be used as the technical expression most suited to express the mystery of the Atonement. But Tertullian, who borrows it from the vocabulary of Roman Law, uses it merely to express that repairing of personal sins by means of which we re-enter into communion with God. This satisfaction must consist not in prayer alone, but in good works—such as fasting, almsgiving and other penances which the sinner voluntarily imposes on himself in order to obtain forgiveness for his sins.[1]

This kind of satisfaction re-establishes harmony between God and the penitent sinner: but this idea was never applied by Tertullian to Christ's mediation.

[1] Cp. *De patientia*, xiii. *De oratione*, 23. *De pœnitentia*, 5, 7, 8. *De pudicitia*, 13. *De cultu fem.* i. 1. *De Ieiunio*, 3, etc.

In fact, the language he occasionally uses would seem to exclude such an application. Thus he speaks of the forgiveness which God had decided to grant to fallen mankind, but without a word about, or even an allusion to the Saviour's atoning work.[1] But elsewhere he tells us, not only that Christ died for us, but also that He came only to do so (*mori missus*)[2]; and, in yet another passage, that Christ's death was a necessary item in the Divine plan of Salvation: "*Quia nec mors nostra dissolvi posset nisi Domini passione, nec vita restitui sine resurrectione ipsius.*"[3]

To ensure the reality of this wholesome death, Tertullian warmly defends against the Docetæ the reality of the Saviour's flesh: "*Si phantasma fuit Christus, nec habuit ullam substantiam corporis quod pro nostris corporibus dependeret.*" As the Apostle tells us that we have been bought at a great price, Christ must have had wherewith to buy us; for God's plan was to redeem our sinful flesh by a similar flesh and make our salvation, thus secured, the finest work of his omnipotence: "*Ob hoc missum Filium in similitudinem carnis peccati, ut peccati carnem simili subtantia redimeret.*"[4] In fact, God had even established a touching parallel: "That which had perished by the wood, in Adam, was to be re-established by the wood, thanks to Christ."[5]

Hence, to deny Christ's flesh is to deny the Passion

---

[1] *Cp. De pœnitentia,* 2 and 4.

[2] *De carne Christi,* 6. *Cp. De pat. 3*: "Taceo quod figitur: *ad hoc enim venerat.*"

[3] *De baptismo,* 11. As Harnack observes, in Tertullian's works the texts to this effect are "numberless." *Op. cit.* i. p. 567, note 2.

[4] *Adv. Marcionem,* v. 7, and *ibid.* v. 14.

[5] Ut quod perierat olim per lignum in Adam, id restitueretur per lignum Christi." *Adv. Iudæos,* 13. *Cp. De resur. carnis,* 48.

and overthrow all God's works, amongst which the cross holds the uppermost place, and indeed is, in a sense, the whole of Christianity.

"Si mendacium deprehenditur Christi caro . . . nec passiones Christi fidem merebuntur. Eversum est igitur totum Dei opus. *Totum Christiani nominis et pondus et fructus, mors Christi negatur,* quam tam impresse Apostolus demandat, utique veram, summum eam Euangelii fundamentum constituens, et salutis nostræ, et prædicationis suæ" (1 *Cor.* xv. 3).[1]

Evidently this death was not our Saviour's due ; it was the result of our sins : " *Propter tuum (Eva) meritum, id est mortem, etiam Filius Dei mori debuit."* [2] Hence this death has the character of a Sacrifice : " *Hunc oportebat pro omnibus gentibus fieri sacrificium. . . . Ipse etiam effectus hostia per omnia pro omnibus nobis."* [3] This sacrifice was the result of Christ's willing self-devotion (*se tradidit pro peccatis nostris*),[4] but, at the same time it was also due to the Father's supreme Will (*Christi in victimam concessi a Patre*).[5] By the death on the cross this Sacrifice also received the character of a curse : " *Pro nobis factus est maledictio. . . . non maledicimus illum, sed maledictum legis referimus."* [6]

It is easy to see that all these are just the reflections concerning Christ's death, its cause and its character, which a cursory inspection of the Scriptures would suggest.

Tertullian also tells us of its effects, for the blood of Christ was far more effective even than that of the

---

[1] *Adv. Marc.* iii. 8.
[2] *De cultu fem.* i. 1.   Cp. *De pudicitia,* 18.
[3] *Adv. Iud.* 13 & 14.   Cp. 10.
[4] *Adv. Gnos. Scap.* 7.
[5] *Adv. Marc.* iii. 18.   Cp. *Adv. Prax.* 30.
[6] *Ibid.* 29.   Cp. *Adv. Marc.* v. 3.

Paschal Lamb ; to it the Saviour owes His glory and we our Salvation.[1]

To describe this Salvation Tertullian makes use of the word redemption, meaning thereby principally the forgiveness of sins. To show Christians how shameful it would be to buy their freedom at the price of money, he reminds them that they have been redeemed by the blood of God, and then sums up the various characters possessed by Christ's death.

" Ut autem redimas hominem tuum nummis, quem sanguine suo redemit Christus, quam indignum Deo et dispositione eius, qui Filio suo non pepercit pro te, ut fieret maledictum pro nobis, quia maledictus qui pependit in ligno ; qui tamquam ovis ad victimam ductus est . . . et inter iniquos deputatus est, et traditus est in mortem, mortem autem crucis : *totum hoc ut nos a peccatis lucraretur.*" [2]

By Christ's Passion our corrupt flesh was cleansed from its stains,[3] and each of us individually shares this purification at his baptism, which draws all its efficaciousness from the blood and Passion of our Saviour.[4] Yet another effect of Christ's death was the destruction of our own death, and as we have already seen, Tertullian is of opinion that this could have been effected only by the Saviour's Passion. He returns to this same idea, with no greater explicitness, but using words which hint at, if indeed they do not express, the idea of substitution : " *Quis alienam mortem sua solvit nisi solus Dei Filius ? Ad hoc enim venerat ut ipse, a delicto purus, et omnino sanctus pro peccatoribus obiret.*" [5] Tertullian elsewhere, re-

---

[1] Cp. *Adv. Marc.* iv. 10, v. 7, *De baptismo*, 16.   "Venerat ut aqua tingueretur, sanguine glorificaretur, perinde nos faceret aqua vocatos, sanguine electos."

[2] *De fuga in persecut.* 12.

[3] *De Pudic.* 6.

[4] Cp. *De Bapt.* 11 ; and *Adv. Iud.* 13.

[5] *De Pudic.* 22.

peating what St. Paul had said before, speaks of our Reconciliation : "We had offended God ; by His blood He restored us to the grace we had lost."[1]

Such are the data which we have succeeded in finding in Tertullian.[2] By his statement of the cause, character, and results of Christ's death, Tertullian shows that it was to this death and to it alone that he ascribed Salvation. But as we have seen our author is chary about venturing on an explanation, and scarcely dares to utter more than is contained in the letter of Scripture.

II

Even more frequently than Tertullian, St. Cyprian uses the words *satisfacere, satisfactio* ; and his works show that in his time these terms had already established themselves in the official vocabulary of the Church as the best expressions of those penitential works by which the sinner appeases God and obtains forgiveness for his sins.[3]

Harnack even says twice that Cyprian applied the expression "*satisfacere Deo*" to Christ Himself.[4] Unfortunately he gives no reference, and we have been unable to find the text to which he alludes ; we must also add that we scarcely think it probable that Cyprian could have used so exact a formula, see-

---

[1] *Adv. Marc.* v. 17 and 19 : "Creatori redigit in gratiam cuius amiseramus offensam."

[2] *Cp.* D'ALÈS, *La Théologie de Tertullien* (Paris, 1905), p. 199 *f.*

[3] CYPRIAN, *De opere et eleemos,* 5 (HARTEL's ed.), i. p. 376 : "Remedia propitiando Deo ipsius verbis data sunt : operationibus iustis Deo satisfieri, misericordiæ meritis peccata purgari." *Cp. De lapsis, passim. Ad Demetr.* 25, *Epist.* xi. 2 ; xxx. 3 ; xliii. 3 and 7 ; lv., etc.

[4] HARNACK, *Dogmengeschichte,* i. p. 568 in the note, and ii. p. 177.

ing the exceeding meagre character of his doctrine concerning Christ's death.

According to St. Cyprian, Christ is not only our model and our Master, He is also the Mediator between God and us; the necessary Mediator, in fact, for we cannot reach the Father save through His Son Jesus Christ.[1]

His mission was to raise up and give new life to our nature: " *Quem vivificandis et reparandis nobis Pater misit.*" [2] This restoration was the result of His whole life, but more especially of the death which He underwent for us: " *Peccatum suum proprium non habens, passus est ille pro nobis,*" [3] and not for us generally but for our sins.

> " Post omnes iniurias et contumelias passus quoque et crucifixus, ut nos pati et mori exemplo suo doceret; ut nulla sit homini excusatio pro se non patienti, cum passus sit ille pro nobis; et, cum ille passus sit *pro alienis peccatis,* multo magis pro peccatis suis pati unumquemque debere." [4]

Cyprian reminds us of the first verses of *Isaias* liii., but only to show that the coming of the Lord was to be in meekness, and that He was to be led to death as a sheep; Cyprian does not otherwise determine the meaning of the passage. [5] He elsewhere also quotes the Johannine text: " *Ipse est deprecatio pro peccatis nostris* " (1 *John* ii. 2), but he only applies this to Christ's heavenly intercession on our behalf.[6]

Yet Cyprian is not unaware that Christ's death was a Sacrifice which our High Priest offered to

---

[1] *Testimon.* ii. 10 and 27 ; i. p. 74 and 94.
[2] *Ad Demetr.* 16 ; i. p. 362.
[3] *Ep.* lviii. 6 ; ii. p. 662. *Cp. ibid.* 3, p. 659.
[4] *Ad Fortunat.* 5 ; i. p. 326.
[5] *Test.* ii. 13 and 15 ; i. p. 77 and 80.
[6] *Ep.* lv. 18 ; ii. p. 637. *Cp. De Domin. orat.* 3 ; i. p. 268.

His Father; a perfect Sacrifice pre-figured in the victims of the Old Law and commemorated in the unbloody sacrifice of the New. In the same epistle a short sentence even contains an elementary statement of *satisfacient* substitution : *Nos omnes portabat Christus qui et peccata nostra portabat*,[1] which is elsewhere more clearly expressed :

"Non aspernatur Dei Filius carnem hominis induere et, cum peccator ipse non esset, *aliena peccata portare* ; immortalitate interim posita, fieri se mortalem patitur, ut innocens pro nocentium, salute perimatur."[2]

St. Cyprian has much more to say concerning the effects of our Saviour's death. He frequently states that we are redeemed by the blood of Christ.[3] By being redeemed we were quickened ; this is a common saying of St Cyprian's : "*Vero de agno, per quem redempti ac vivificati sumus.*"[4] "*Offerre nos Patri, cui nos sua sanctificatione restituit, æternitatem nobis immortalitatemque largiri, ad quam nos sanguinis sui vivificatione reparavit.*"[5] This quickening pre-supposes that our sins have been wiped out : "*Delicta . . . ante contracta . . . Christi sanguine et sanctificatione purgantur,*"[6] and that our death has been destroyed : "*Eleemosyna a morte liberat, et non utique ab illa morte quam semel Christi sanguis exstinxit, et a*

---

[1] *Ep.* lxiii. 13; ii. p. 711. *Cp.* passim, 4, 14 and 17, pp. 703-714.

[2] *De bono pat.* 6, i. p. 401. *Cp. De lapsis*, 17 : "Veniam . . . solus potest ille largiri, qui peccata nostra portavit, qui pro nobis doluit, quem Deus tradidit pro peccatis nostris."

[3] *De dom. orat.* 30; i. p. 289. *Cp. De op. et eleem.* 2 and 17; i. pp. 274 and 287. *Ep.* lv. 19; ii. p. 637.

[4] *Ad Fort.* 3; i. p. 318 and 6, p. 327. *Cp. De bono pat.* 8, p. 403, and *Ep.* lxiii. 2; ii. p. 702.

[5] *De op. et eleem.* 26; i. p. 394.

[6] *Ibid.* 2, p. 374.

R

qua nos aqua salutaris baptismi et Redemptoris nostri gratia liberavit." [1]

Cyprian explains no further what he means by this death; but the context seems to show that he is alluding to everlasting death, which he elsewhere describes as the "second death," making a distinction which was afterwards to become classical.[2] At any rate being delivered from death and sin we become sons of God.[3] This Divine sonship we owe also to our Saviour's Passion: "*Filius Dei passus est, ut nos filios Dei faceret.*" [4]

To conclude we quote a few texts in which all these ideas are clumped together, and which consequently seem to express most fully St. Cyprian's thought:

"Venia confitenti datur et ad immortalitatem sub ipsa morte transitur. Hanc gratiam Christus impertit, hoc munus misericordiæ suæ tribuit subigendo mortem trophæo crucis, redimendo credentem pretio sui sanguinis, reconciliando hominem Deo Patri, . . . vivificando mortalem regeneratione cœlesti." [5]

Another passage to the same effect is the following:—

"Quod conservandis et vivificandis nobis Pater Filium misit ut reparare nos posset, quodque Filius missus esse et hominis filius vocari voluit ut nos Dei filios faceret: humiliavit se ut populum qui prius iacebat erigeret, vulneratus est ut vulnera nostra curaret, mori sustinuit ut immortalitatem mortalibus exhiberet." [6]

We are elsewhere bidden to listen to a soliloquy of the devil, who is rejoicing that he secured his sovereignty over men so much more easily than the Redeemer.

[1] *Ep.* lv. 22 ; ii. p. 639.
[2] *De mortal.* 14 ; i. p. 306. " Mori timeat qui non Christi cruce et passione censetur, qui *ad secundam mortem* de hac morte transibit."
[3] *De dominica oratione,* 11 ; i. p. 274.
[4] *Epist.* lviii. 6 ; ii. p. 662.
[5] *Ad Demetrianum,* 26 ; i. p. 370.
[6] *De op. et eleem.* i. p. 373.

"Ego pro istis nec alapas accepi, nec flagella sustinui, nec crucem pertuli, nec sanguinem fudi, nec familiam meam pretio passionis et cruoris redemi, sed nec regnum illis cœleste promitto, nec ad paradisum restituta immortalitate revoco." [1]

Thus we see that Cyprian connects with Christ's death, both our future immortality, which is the greatest benefit of Salvation—the reader will note how our author here comes into contact with the Greek theologians—and the forgiveness of sins and our reconciliation with God, which are the necessary conditions of immortality. In other words, though Cyprian's explanations are scarcely deeper than Tertullian's, he is, even more than the latter, a partisan of realism.

Among those who laid the foundations of Latin theology must be reckoned the author of the *Tractatus Origenis*. M. Tixeront sums up as follows this writer's soteriological doctrine [2]: Christ was the Second Adam. In Him the likeness of God, which had been lost by sin, was restored. The *recapitulation* idea is in the writer's mind though he does not expressly formulate it. By the Second Adam we were saved. The *Tractatus* represents the Atonement under two forms —as a redemption properly so-called, Christ's blood being the price with which He buys us "*prœmio sui sanguinis nos a mortuis liberavit*," and as a Sacrifice and expiation which Christ, as at once a Priest and a Victim, by taking on Him our sins, has offered for us.

"Sacerdos, inquam, hic noster . . . semetipsum in sacrificio dedit." "Hic suspensus est Dominus, ut peccata nostra . . . in ligno crucis per eumdem hominem affixa punirentur."

We can see that, with all their slight differences of

---

[1] *De op. et eleem.* 22, p. 390.

[2] TIXERONT, *op. cit.* p. 360 *f.* Cp. *Tractatus Orig.* ed. BATIFFOL (Paris, 1900), xviii. p. 197 ; xix. p. 206; ii. p. 15.

expression, these writers hold like views, and that, so far, the prevailing tone of the theology on the Atonement is undoubtedly "realistic." Though their theology has no great depth, their faith teaches them that there is no Salvation without the death of the cross.

III

This we cannot say for certain other writers who contributed much to Latin literature towards the end of the third, and beginning of the fourth, century.

Sabatier states that "the majority of the Fathers lay more stress, in Christ's work, on the doctrine He taught and the example He left, than on His sufferings and death."[1] To prove his statement he adduces the following passage from Lactantius :—

" God, having decided to deliver man, sent into the world a Master of virtue, who by His precepts taught men to be innocent, and by His actions opened to them the way of righteousness, in which, by following their Master's footsteps, they might reach life everlasting. Hence He became incarnate and clothed Himself with flesh that He might supply man, whom He had come to instruct, with both encouragement and example. After having been a model of righteousness in all the duties of life, it only remained for Him to teach them that endurance of pain and that scorn for death in which perfect virtue consists. For this cause He delivered Himself to a wicked nation, though by His prophetic spirit He could have escaped their plots or by His power of miracles could have brought them to naught. He therefore suffered torments, being scourged and crowned with thorns ; nor did He hesitate to suffer death that man might no longer

[1] A. SABATIER, op. cit. p. 44 f.

stand in fear of it." Lactantius gives a like explanation of Christ's choice of a cross as the instrument of His death. He chose to die a slave's death that His example might appeal to all (*ne quis esset omnino, qui cum non posset imitari.*) [1]

In other passages Lactantius fails to complete the thought here expressed. The general cause of the Incarnation he considers to have been the lessons of teaching and example. Christ was the Mediator between God and man, becoming a man that He might serve men as a model, and remaining God that His precepts might come with a Divine authority.[2] Christ's Priesthood was that of a preacher.[3] *Isaias* liii. is merely a prophecy of Christ's Passion and of the blindness of men and the crime of the Jews.[4] What cleanses men from their sins is the doctrine of Christ : "*Peccatorum labibus et vitiorum maculis inquinatos doctrina eius purificatura esset eruditione iustitiæ.*" [5]

Among the works of Lactantius is a treatise on *The Anger of God,* in which he vigorously defends this Divine attribute against the Stoic conception of a God devoid of all feeling. He tempers this Divine anger by God's mercy ; did God attend to His Justice alone, not one man would be left alive ; but as a matter of fact God only awaits man's repentance.[6] Only once, and then in very general words, does Lactantius compare Christ to the Paschal Lamb, because He bestows Salvation on all those who on

---

[1] LACTANT. *Inst. div.* iv. 26.—*P.L.* vi. ; col. 528-529.
[2] *Ibid.* 25 ; col. 524. Cp. *Epitome* l. ; *ibid.* col. 1057.
[3] *Ibid.* iv. 13 ; col. 490. Cp. 11-12 ; col. 478-480.
[4] *Ibid.* 16 and 18 ; col. 498 and 506-507.
[5] *Ibid.* 26 ; col. 526.
[6] *De ira Dei,* 20-21.—*P.L.* vii ; col. 138-140.

their foreheads bear the mark of His blood—*i.e.* the sign of the cross. In the same passage he seems to state that Christ's death despoiled Hell[1]; but generally speaking, Lactantius never rises above a kind of philosophic moralism.

In this he was following his own master Arnobius. This writer, to justify Christ's death to the pagans, had merely observed that it was undeserved,[2] that the only object of the Incarnation was to make God to be seen and to be of easy access to man; Christ's death, though it did not involve His Godhead, is nevertheless a mystery on account of the examples of virtue it contains.[3] Arnobius also criticises the pagan sacrafices, but in words which would be equally effective against the Mosaic offerings, and without ever alluding to Christ's sacrifice.[4]

Were such cases as these at all numerous, M. Sabatier would be quite right in discerning a latent " rationalism " under the specious " supernatural metaphysics " of the Fathers.[5] But the apologetic works of such recently-converted rhetors can scarcely be taken as representative of the innermost Christian thought at the time. However much a few individual Latins may have been disposed to this sort of philosophism, the real Latin tradition was on the side of that realism which in its earliest form was represented by Tertullian and St. Cyprian, and the subsequent developments of which we shall now consider.

[1] *Inst. div.* iv. 26; col. 530-531. *Cp. ibid.* iv. 12; col. 481.
[2] Arnob. *Adv. Gentes*, I. 40-41. *P.L.* v.; col. 769-770.
[3] *Ibid.* 60-64; col. 800-805.
[4] *Ibid.* vii., *passim.*
[5] Sabatier, *op. cit.* p. 45, note 1.

CHAPTER XIV

ST. HILARY—ST. AMBROSE

In spite of the poorness of their formulæ and the shallowness of their ideas, we have seen that the earliest Latin writers are distinctly on the side of realism. This is all we could expect from a theology which was then only beginning and whose main efforts were demanded in other quarters—viz. in apologetics and in the practical care of souls. Moreover we can easily make up for what is absent among the earliest of our writers by referring to the great Doctors of the fourth century. In spite of the influence which Greek theology had on them, these Latin Fathers carefully put into the background the speculations which the Greeks preferred, and of set purpose centred their attention on the Saviour's atoning death, so much so that from the very beginning we find among all the Latins that very idea which Greek thought only succeeded in reaching after many and prolonged efforts.

I

Ritschl writes : " The Latin Nicene Fathers, Hilary and Ambrose, continue to describe the doctrine [of the Atonement] after the manner of Athanasius." [1] This is true more especially of St. Hilary, for certain of his texts do remind us of the speculative views of

[1] Ritschl, *op. cit.* i. p. 15.

the Greeks. For instance, he describes the economy of Salvation as follows :—

" Sin and death, like a dreadful plague, had stricken mankind. Only God could give a remedy and send the Physician whom we needed. Mankind was longing for the Saviour, because the Law and the Prophets were no longer of any avail. What was needed was that the Son of God should come Himself, and by putting on our flesh cure it of its ills " :

" Nonnisi ex assumptione carnis nostræ hi morbi nostri corporis auferendi et ex assumptione carnis salus nostra omnis in Deo est." [1]

Elsewhere he comes to a like conclusion :

" Non ille eguit homo effici . . . ; sed nos eguimus ut Deus caro fieret et habitaret in nobis, id est assumptione carnis unius interna universæ carnis incoleret." [2]

In Christ's person the whole of the human race was mysteriously comprised and thereby sanctified :

" Humani generis causa Dei Filius natus ex virgine est . . . ut homo factus naturam in se carnis acciperet, perque huius admixtionis societatem sanctificatum in eo universi generis humani corpus existeret." [3] " Naturam in se universæ carnis 'assumpsit, per quam effectus vera vitis genus in se universæ propaginis tenet." [4]

The following text makes still more curious reading. This is Hilary's commentary on the Gospel sentence, *Non potest civitas abscondi* (MATT. v. 14) :—

" Civitatem carnem quam assumpserat nuncupat ; quia, ut civitas ex varietate ac multitudine consistit habitantium, ita in eo per naturam suscepti corporis *quædam universi generis humani congre-*

---

[1] HILAR. *In Ps.* xiv. 8-1. —*P.L.* ix. ; col. 296-297.
[2] *De Trinitate*, ii. 25.—*P.L.* x. ; col. 67.
[3] *Ibid.* ii. 24 ; col. 66.
[4] *In Psalm* li. 16.—*P.L.* ix. ; col. 317.

gatio continetur. ¦Atque ita et ille ex nostra in se congregatione
fit civitas, et nos per consortium carnis suæ sumus civitatis
habitatio." [1]

This is, of course, a mystical way of stating that
Christ was the perfect representative of mankind
and that, by the nature we share in common, we
are intimately united with Him. The Greek ¦Fathers
had said, and Aquinas was to repeat after them,
that Christ is the head of a body of which we are the
members. Here we find the same idea, only expressed
under a less correct metaphor.

But though our salvation required the Incarnation,
St. Hilary maintains that it was actually accomplished
only on the cross ; such had been God's plan even
from the beginning.[2] This is why St. Hilary constantly represents the cross as the great mystery of
Salvation (*sacramentum ineundæ crucis*)),[3] without,
however, denying to Christ's other actions their real
virtue : "*Nobis et passus et mortuus est et resurrexit . . .
qui cum esset Deus, omnia ad salutis nostræ incrementa
susceperit*," [4] and he sums up his teaching in a somewhat ambiguous phrase : "*Nascitur itaque Deus as-
sumptioni nostræ, patitur vero innocentiæ, postremo
moritur ultioni.*" [5]

In all this Hilary sees God's goodness, who carried
His mercy so far as to will to redeem us, and to secure
this object sacrificed His only Son.

---

[1] *In Matth.* iv. 12. *Ibid.* col. 935.

[2] " Numquid possibile erat non pati Christum ? Atquin iam a
constitutione mundi sacramentum hoc in eo erat salutis nostræ
ostensum." *In Matth.* xxxi. 7. *P.L.* ix. 1068. *Cp. Ps.* liv. 13.
Ibid. ; col. 354.

[3] *In Matth.* xvii. 9 ; col. 1017 ; xxviii. 2 ; col. 1064 ; xxxiii. 5 ;
col. 1074. *De Trin.* x. 10 *f.* *P.L.* x. 350 *f.*

[4] *Ps.* lxvii. 21. *P.L.* ix. 458.
De Trin. ix. 7. *P.L.* x. 286.

"Proprio Filio suo non pepercit . . . non utique pro adoptandis adoptato, neque pro creatis creaturæ; sed pro alienis suo, pro nuncupandis proprio. Quære virtutem dicti ut magnitudinem charitatis intelligas." [1]

He also perceives in this the Goodness of the Son, who, through obedience and love, accepted his mission (*per dilectionem efficiendi mandati*).[2] He yearned for His Passion and went so far as to beseech His Father that nothing might prevent the prophecies from being fulfilled.[3]

His Passion was all the more free from the fact that Christ by His nature was incapable of suffering. Everyone knows that St. Hilary has been suspected of Docetism.[4] According to him Christ's body was a heavenly one, sharing all the heavenly privileges; it was by an act of will and love that He subjected Himself to our infirmities, to His Passion and to death. He stood in no need of food; when He wept it was not through human emotion; when He was troubled in the Garden it was not through fear of His Passion, but through His foreseeing the flight of His disciples. In the sweat of blood, which Hilary unwillingly allows to have happened, he prefers to see the power of God rather than a sign of the Man's weakness.[5]

He says much more in a like strain, and without

---

[1] *De Trin.* vi. 45. *P.L.* x. 194. *Cp. Ps.* cxviii. 2. *P.L.* ix. 543. *Cp. Ps.* lxvii. 22 ; col. 459.

[2] *De Trin.* ix. 55 ; col. 326. *Cp.* x. 11-12 ; col. 351 *f.*

[3] *Ps.* cxxxix. 12. *P.L.* ix. ; col. 821. *Cp. Ps.* lxviii. 17 ; col. 480.

[4] *Cp.* Döerholt. *Op. cit.* pp. 92-96 and Bardenhewer, ii. pp. 281-282.

[5] *Cp. Ps.* cxli. 8 ; col. 836. *In Matth.* xxxi. 4-5 ; col. 1067-1068. *De Trin.* x. 37. *P.L.* x. ; col. 373, *ibid.* 40 ; col. 375 & 42 ; col. 377.

difficulty we may find such formulæ as the following, which show that Christ's sufferings were apparent only: —" *Putatur dolere, quia patitur.*" [1] " *Et pro nobis dolet, non et doloris nostri dolet sensu. Fallitur humanæ æstimationis opinio, putans hunc dolere quod patitur.*" [2] He had already said that the Saviour had been harmlessly struck by the Passion, as air, or water, or fire is harmlessly divided by the arrow. [3]

The explanation of this singular, and in many respects unfortunate, language has already been given by others. St. Hilary prefers to rest his attention on the eternal person of the Word which is in Christ. It was from this Person that all Christ's actions proceeded and yet it was not touched by Christ's sufferings ; these are the two truths which St. Hilary wished to defend against the Arians, and hence the oddness of his statements. He had no intention of denying that our Saviour suffered in His human nature, but he wished to make it clear that this suffering did not wound or otherwise affect His Divine nature. [4]

At any rate his words prove that, as yet, the theological vocabulary was unsettled. We shall have occasion to see that, on the question with which we are concerned, St. Hilary's exegesis will occasionally be somewhat spoilt by his unsatisfactory use of words,

---

[1] *Ps.* cxxxviii. 3.   *P.L.* ix. ; col. 794.

[2] *De Trin.* x. 47.   *P.L.* x. ; col. 381.

[3] *Ibid.* x. 23 ;   col. 361-362.   " Sensit impetum passionis, non tamen dolorem passionis, . . . ut telum aliquod aut aquam perforans, aut ignem compungens, aut aera vulnerans."

[4] " Unigenito Deo, quamvis infirmitas nostra suscepta sit, tamen divinitatis suæ non est abolita natura . . . : universa quæ mortis nostræ sunt ita pertulit, *ut in eum inciderent hæc potius quam inessent,* dum infirmitas nostra magis est quam naturalis in Deo est." *Ps.* liv. 6.   *P.L.* ix. ; col. 359.

though we shall not fail, in spite of this, to find that he largely shared the traditional views. Indeed the fact that he shared them at all is in itself sufficiently remarkable.

St. Hilary applies *Isaias* liii. and the vigorous statement of St. Paul's, " He was made sin for us," to the Incarnation alone.[1] In another passage he appears to consider that the Passion had only the value of an example: Christ crucified our infirmities, meaning that they died with Him in His Passion, that we may be strong in the day of battle.[2]

But we must not imagine that this exhausts St. Hilary's thought. In particular he is quite clear about the penal character of Christ's death, and in fact, as Ritschl acknowledges, he was the real founder of the Latin theology: " *Quamquam passio illa non fuerit condicionis et generis, tamen suscepta voluntarie est, officio quidem ipsa satisfactura pœnali, non tamen pœnœ sensu lœsura patientem.*"[3]

The meaning of the text is clear, but Dr. Schwane's translation gives neither its meaning nor its scope: " *It was necessary to give, instead of our chastisement, a voluntary satisfaction* without the Sufferer being diminished by experiencing this punishment." Dr. Schwane continues: " The dogma of Christ's *satisfacient* substitution here finds its first explanation and it is expressed more clearly than it had been by any other Father."[4] The historian's observation

---

[1] *De Trin.* x. 47.—*P.L.* x ; col. 381.

[2] " Ideo peccata nostra portat et pro nobis dolet : quia fidei in nobis calore fervente, cum adversus diabolum sit decertandum, omnes infirmitatum nostrarum dolores cum corpore eius et passione moriuntur." *In Matth.* xxxii. 10. *P.L.* ix. ; col. 1069.

[3] *Ps.* liii. 12, *ibid.* col. 344.

[4] SCHWANE, *Hist. of Dogma* (*French trans.* by DEGERT), ii. p. 413.

is even worse than his translation. As a matter of fact this text simply expresses one of St. Hilary's pet ideas: The Passion in itself was a penalty and it fulfils the duty of a penalty, but the Divine sufferer did not feel the pain. We elsewhere find the same idea in different words:

> "In corpus Domini irruens passio nec non fuit passio, nec tamen naturam passionis exseruit: dum et pœnali ministerio desævit, et virtus corporis sine sensu pœnæ vim pœnæ in se desævientis excepit." [1]

Hence the text in question in no way refers to any satisfaction rendered by Christ, still less does it deal with a satisfaction exacted by God's Justice. It is therefore inaccurate to state that we here find any explanation of the dogma.

Not only was death a penalty, but in the case of Christ it was undeserved; being guiltless He did not deserve death, and paid the penalty of sins which He did not commit.

> "Quæ non rapuerat tunc repetebatur exsolvere. Cum enim debitor mortis peccatique non esset, tamquam peccati et mortis debitor tenebatur. Pœnas scilicet insipientiæ et delictorum, quas non rapuerat, repetebatur exsolvere." [2]

Hence the sins with which Christ was burdened were our own: "*Percussus est Dominus peccata nostra suscipiens et pro nobis dolens.*" He was struck by God that we might receive life by His death.

> "Non pepercerat primo illi de terræ limo Adamo . . . ut naturam corporis eius Adam e cœlis secundus assumens, parique morte percussus, eam rursus in vitam æternam iam sine pœnæ æternitate revocaret." [3]

St. Hilary also looks on Christ's death as a sacrifice which takes away our curse and works our salvation.

[1] *De Trin.* x. 23. *P.L.* x. 362. [2] *Ps.* lxviii. 7-8. *P.L.* ix. 474.
[3] *Ibid.* 23; col. 484.

" Maledictorum se optulit morti ut maledictum legis dissolveret, *hostiam se ipse Deo Patri voluntarie offerendo.* Deo Patri, legis sacrificia respuenti, hostiam placentem suscepti corporis offerendo . . . omnem humani generis salutem oblatione sanctæ huius et perfectæ hostiæ redempturus." [1]

In the above text Hilary speaks of ¦redemption, he returns again to this point. Redemption is the most general result of Christ's Sacrifice :

" *Redemit nos cum se pro peccatis nostris dedit* ; redemit nos per sanguinem suum, per passionem suam, per mortem suam, per resurrectionem suam. Hæc magna vitæ nostræ pretia sunt." [2]

Another result of the Sacrifice was the destruction of the decree of death pronounced against us :

" Delens per mortem sententiam mortis . . . ; cruci se figi permittens, ut, maledicto crucis, oblitterata terrenæ damnationis maledicta figeret omnia." [3]

Above all, our Saviour's death was the expiation of our sins :

" Sciens vetera delicta sua et antiquæ impietatis crimina Deo propitianda esse per Christum. Ipse enim secundum Apostolum nostra placatio est." [4]

And lastly in consequence of this it reconciles us with God.

" Est Unigenitus Dei Filius . . . redemptio nostra, pax nostra *in cuius sanguine reconciliati Deo sumus.* Hic est qui venit tollere peccata mundi, qui cruci chirographum legis affigens edictum damnationis veteris delevit. . . . Ipse pro peccatis nostris et propitiatio, et redemptio, et deprecatio est iniquitatum nostrarum, quia ipse earum propitiatio sit, non recordans." [5]

---

[1] *Ps.* liii. 13. *P.L.* ix. 345.

[2] *Ps.* cxxxv. 15. *Ibid.* col. 776. *Cp. in Matth.* xx. 12 ; *ibid.* col. 1033 ; xxxii. 6 ; col. 1072.

[3] *De Trin.* i. 13. *P.L.* x. 35. *Cp. ibid.* ix. 10, col. 289, and *Ps.* lxvii. 23. *P.L.* ix. 459.

[4] *Ps.* lxiv. 4. *P.L.* ix. 415.

[5] *Ps.* cxxix. 9, *ibid.* 723.

In another passage Hilary describes at length the relations of God with us : " In the beginning the whole of Creation was agreeable to God, and more especially man, because he was made to God's image. But God's judgments change according to man's conduct ; thus when man had sinned, He even repented of having created him. But now that we have emerged from sin He restores us His love." This change we owe to Christ's mediation : " *Reconciliati enim sumus per corpus et sanguinem Christi ex inimicis in filios Deo.*" [1]

The final result of all this is to restore us to life everlasting :

" Nos ad divinitatis suæ naturam trahens . . . cuius morti consepeliremur in Baptismo, ut in æternitatis vitam rediremus . . . et morientes vitiis immortalitati renasceremur : *ipso pro nobis ex immortalitate moriente, ut ad immortalitatem una cum eo excitaremur ex morte.*" [2]

From all this we see that, whatever influence Greek thought may have had on him, Hilary nevertheless expressed with considerable vigour and precision the results of Christ's death. His ideas are of course lacking in system, and are sometimes shrouded in a peculiar mystical garb ; but though he never succeeded in evolving a synthesis, he did not fail to state again all the divers elements of the traditional realism.

II

St. Ambrose's teaching is at once clearer and fuller. According to this Doctor the only object of the Incarnation was to redeem us : " *Quæ erat causa Incarnationis, nisi ut caro quæ peccaverat per se redimeretur ?* " [3]

---

[1] *Ps.* cxlix. 3, col. 886.   [2] *De Trin.* i. 13.   P.L. x. 34-35.
[3] AMBROS. *De Sacr. Inc.* vi. 56.   *P.L.* xvi. 832.

This is why Christ, in order to redeem the whole of man, had to assume our whole nature.[1] Every one of Christ's actions helps to save us :

" Ipse est Christus qui natus est ex virgine ; ipse est qui mirabilia fecit in populo ; ipse qui mortuus est pro peccatis nostris et resurrexit a mortuis. Unum horum si retraxeris, retraxisti salutem tuam." [2]

It was St. Ambrose who said that the baby-cries of Christ wiped away our sins.[3] The Passion however remains the main, and indeed the only, means of Salvation : " *Quamvis enim simili modo assumptionis et passionis sint admiranda mysteria, plenitudo tamen fidei in sacramento est passionis.*" [4]

Ambrose describes at length the qualities and fruits of this Passion. He considers the Saviour's death as a Sacrifice [5] foreshadowed in that of Abel [6] and in all the offerings of the Olden Law [7]; as the sole and lasting Sacrifice [8] by which we are delivered from sin :

" Per crucem dominici corporis absoluti. . . . Illum oportebat pro omnibus mori, ut in eius cruce fieret remissio peccatorum et sanguis ipsius mundi inquinamenta lavaret. . . . Venit ut in sanguine suo omnium peccata dilueret." [9]

---

[1] AMBROS. *De Sacram. Inc.* vii. 67 *f*; col. 835.

[2] *In Luc.* vi. 101.—*P.L.* xv. col. 1695.

[3] *Ibid.* ii. 41, col. 1568.

[4] *De Spiritu Sancto,* lib. iii., xvii. 126.—*P.L.* xvi. ; col. 806.

[5] *Ps.* xxxviii. 25.—*P.L.* xiv.; col. 1051. *Cp. Ps.* xxix. 12; col. 1061.

[6] *De Sacram. Inc.* i. 4.—*P.L.* xvi. ; col. 819.

[7] " Nunc in hœdi typo, nunc in ovis, nunc in vituli offerebatur. Hœdi, quod sacrificium pro delictis sit ; ovis, quod voluntaria hostia ; vituli, quod immaculata sit victima." *De Spiritu Sancto,* i. 4 ; *ibid.* col. 705.

[8] *Luc.* x. 8.—*P.L.* xv. ; col. 1806.

[9] *Ps.* xxxix. 2, 14 and 17.—*P.L.* xiv. ; col. 1059-1063. And elsewhere: " Peccatum omnium factus peccata generis abluebat humani." *De Sacr. Inc.* v. 39.—*P.L.* xvi. ; col. 828. *Cp. Ep.* lxv. 10 ; *ibid.* col. 1224.

In another passage Ambrose states that Christ nailed our sins to His cross: "*Christi caro damnavit peccatum, quod nascendo non sensit, quod moriendo crucifixit.*"[1] He took away the decree of death which was against us: "*Qui delicta donavit et chirographum tulit; qui chirographum tulit affixit illud cruci.*"[2] He destroyed death itself: "*Mortem enim mors facta est susceptio mortis in Christo.*"[3] He it is that by His Resurrection ensures to us life everlasting: "*Carnem susceperat ut morte sua omnibus resurrectionem acquireret.*"[4] Finally He raises us to a heavenly nature like unto His own: "*Ad vulnera nostra descendit ut, usu quodam et copia sui, naturæ compotes nos faciat esse cœlestis.*"[5]

All these benefits which we owe to Christ's death show its worth. St. Ambrose also allows to it a penal character which enables us to understand it still better. The word satisfaction is not unknown to him and he uses it to describe our acts of penance, but on one occasion he makes use of it in connection with Christ's death:

"Ideo suscepit Iesus carnem, ut maledictum carnis peccatricis aboleret; et factus est pro nobis maledictum, ut benedictio absorberet maledictum. Suscepit enim et mortem ut impleretur sententia, *satisfieret iudicato*: Maledictum carnis peccatricis usque ad mortem."[6]

---

[1] *De Pœn.* lib. i., iii. 13, *ibid.* col. 470. *Cp. Ep.* lxiii. 112, *ibid.* col. 1219. "Peccata nostra suæ affixit cruci."

[2] *De Pœn.* lib. iii., ii. 13., *ibid.* col. 592. *Cp. Ep.* lxxiii. 11, col. 1253.

[3] *De Fide.* lib. iii., xi. 84. *P.L.* xvi. 607. *Cp. in Luc.* viii. 26. *P.L.* xv. 1773.

[4] *Ep.* vii. 12. *P.L.* xvi. 908. *Cp. Ep.* iv. 5; *ibid.* col. 890.

[5] *In Luc.* v. 46. *P.L.* xv. 1648. *Cp. De Sacr. Inc.* iv. 23. *P.L.* xvi. 825.

[6] *De fuga sœculi,* vii. 44. *P.L.* xiv. 589.

S

Evidently he is not speaking here of Satisfaction in the modern theological meaning of the term, but of a satisfaction given to the law of death which had been pronounced of old against the sinner. His idea is consequently not far removed from that of Athanasius.

St. Ambrose merely tells us that Christ died for our sins :

" Pro nobis, non pro se dolebat; et infirmatus est non propter sua, sed propter nostra peccata, ut suo nos livore sanaret."[1] " Pro me doluit, qui pro se nihil habuit ut doleret . . . Doles, Domine, non tua, sed mea vulnera ; non tuam mortem, sed nostram infirmitatem.   Infirmatus es, sed propter peccata nostra."[2]

In another passage, drawing his inspiration from St. Paul, he repeats that Christ was made sin and a curse for our sakes : " *Peccatum es, O homo ; ideo peccatum fecit Christum suum omnipotens Pater. Hominem fecit qui peccata nostra portaret.*"[3] This does not, however, mean that He really became sin, but only that He took on Him our sins.

" Peccatum non fecit, sed peccatum factus est.   Ergo in peccatum conversus est Dominus?   Non ita ; sed quia peccata nostra suscepit, peccatum dictus est.   Nam et maledictum dictus est Dominus, quia nostrum suscepit ipse maledictum."[4]

St. Ambrose likewise takes *Romans* viii. 3 as a reference to the expiation for sin :

" Damnavit peccatum, ut peccata nostra in sua carne crucifigeret ; factus pro nobis ipse peccatum, ut nos essemus in ipso iustitia Dei.

---

[1] *Ps.* lxi. 6 ; *ibid.* col. 1168.

[2] *In Luc.* x. 56 *f.*   *P.L.* xv. 1818.

[3] *In Ps.* 118, xviii. 42.   *P.L.* xv. 1467.   *Cp. de Sacr. Inc.* v. 39. *P.L.* xvi. ; 828, and *ibid.* vii. 76 ; col. 837.

[4] *De Sacr. Inc.* vi. 60, col. 833.   This is the text as we said above which surprised Harnack. We may mention that we were not able to find it in the place to which he referred us.   *Exp. in Ps.* 119, x. 14.   *Cp. De fide.* lib. ii., xi. 93 *f*; *ibid.* col. 580.   *Ps.* xl. 35.   *P.L.* xiv. 1084.

Ergo pietatis est susceptio peccatorum ista, non criminis. Per hoc peccatum nos Deus æternus absolvit, qui Filio suo proprio non pepercit et peccatum eum fecit esse pro nobis."[1]

He also adds that our Saviour condemned sin by His example, teaching our sinful flesh to loathe for the future the vices in which it used to indulge. All these texts go to prove that Christ substituted Himself for us; but in yet another passage Ambrose casts this idea into a quasi-legal form: "*Hominis causam locumque susceperat*,"[2] and then, giving the rein to that taste for allegory which he had acquired from the Greeks, our Doctor proceeds to press the comparison down to the smallest details:

"Ex terra virgine Adam, Christus ex virgine: ille ad imaginem Dei factus; hic imago Dei. . . . Mors per arborem, vita per crucem. . . . In deserto Adam, in deserto Christus: sciebat enim ubi posset invenire damnatum, quem ad paradisum resoluto errore revocaret. Sed quoniam sæcularibus indutus exuviis redire non potest, nec paradisi incola potest esse nisi nudus a culpa, exuit veterem hominem, novum induit, ut, quia solvi non queunt divina decreta, *persona magis quam sententia mutaretur*."[3]

The principle last expressed—viz. the unalterableness of the Divine decrees—might have yielded a rich crop of consequences. Ambrose, however, merely makes this incidental allusion to it. But he again in another place states the substitutionary character of Christ's death: "*Contraximus chirographum culpæ, pœnam sanguinis debebamus: venit Dominus Iesus, suum pro nobis obtulit*."[4] From this Ambrose infers that, like good servants, we should give all to Him who paid so dearly for us.

[1] *Ps.* xxxvii. 5, 6; *ibid.* col. 1011 *f.*

[2] *De interpel. Iob et David*, x. 27.—*P.L.* xiv.; col. 848.

[3] *In Luc.* iv. 7.—*P.L.* xv.; col. 1614. *Cp. Ps.* xxxv. 3.—*P.L.* xiv.; col. 954.

[4] *De Virg.* xix. 126.—*P.L.* xvi.; col. 299-300. *Cp. Epist.* xli. 7; *ibid.* col. 1115 and *in Luc.* vi. 26.—*P.L.* xv.; col. 1675.

We have seen how Ambrose, after having described the salutary effects of Christ's Passion, emphasises its penal side. He only just missed co-ordinating the two ideas, for the principle of their conjunction was, as we have seen, not altogether unknown to him.

But we must proceed. Ambrose did not confine himself to seeking the causes of Salvation, he also sought to determine its conditions, and in this lies the most original element of his doctrine.

He first of all points out that Christ alone redeemed us :

"Solus ex omnibus in sua carne peccata nostra suscepit, solus Dei agnus peccatum totius mundi abstulit; solus chirographum decreti sanguinis sui effusione delevit." [1]

In fact He alone could redeem us, so much so, that from the point of view of the Redemption itself we may say that the coming and the death of Christ were necessary. This is clearly stated by St. Ambrose. What general could God send us to wage war against the devil ? An angel ? But they, too, fell. A Seraph ? But when one came to the earth it was to cleanse the lips of a single prophet. Hence He had to seek even higher for the Divine leader who alone is above the world.[2] Christ's Person and death were especially needed for the forgiveness of sin :

"Solus Dominus Iesus tali dignus electus est morte, qua tolleret peccatum mundi." [3] "Quæ maior misericordia, quam quod pro nostris flagitiis se præbuit immolandum ut sanguine suo mundum lavaret *cuius peccatum nullo alio modo potuisset aboleri.*" [4]

One reason for this is, that to deliver others, a man must be without sin :

[1] *Ps.* xl. i.   *P.L.* xiv. 1069.   *Cp. Ep.* xlix. 5.   *P.L.* xvi. 1155.
[2] *In Luc.* iv. 9.   *P.L.* xv. ; 1615.
[3] *Apologia proph. David,* v. 22.   *P.L.* xiv. 860.
[4] *Ps.* xlvii. 17 ; *ibid.* col. 1152.   *Cp. Ps.* xliii. 11 ; col. 1094.

"Quot vitia, tot retia ; quot peccata, tot laquei. . . . Omnes retibus tenebamur ; nullus alium eruere poterat, cum seipsum non posset exuere. *Talis ergo necessarius fuit, quem vincula generationis humanæ delictis obnoxia non tenerent, non cepisset avaritia, non ligasset dolus. Is solus erat Iesus.*" [1]

Another reason was that, as is evident, no mere man could suffice to clear the world :

"Quoniam nullus hominum tantus esse potuit, qui totius peccata tolleret mundi . . . (*quis enim tantus homo in quo omnium peccata morerentur*), idcirco non unus e plebe, non unus e numero, sed Filius Dei a Deo Patre electus est, qui, cum supra omnes esset, pro omnibus se posset offerre ; quem mori oportuit, ut, cum esset fortior morte, alios liberaret." [2]

Here is a last passage in which St. Ambrose exposes a similar idea with all the vigour and exactness that could be claimed :

"Ipse est solus qui redimet hominem. . . . Sed *quare hic solus redimet ?* Quia nemo potest eum æquare pietate, ut pro servulis suis animam suam ponat ; nemo integritate : omnes enim sub peccato. Solus Redemptor eligitur, qui peccato veteri obnoxius esse non possit."

St. Ambrose goes on to probe yet more deeply this Redemption. Though Christ stood in no need of it, it was more than was needed for the whole world :

"Cum reconciliaverit Deo mundum, utique ipse reconciliatione non eguit. Pro quo enim peccato suo propitiaret Deum, qui nulla peccata cognovit ? . . . Nec pretium redemptionis animæ suæ dat, *cuius sanguinis pretium poterat abundare ad universa mundi totius redimenda peccata.* Recte ergo alios liberat, qui pro se nihil debeat."

Henceforward it would be superfluous for us to make expiation : "*Quia propitiatio omnium Christus est et ipse est universorum redemptio.*" And the reason

---

[1] *Ps.* 118, vi. 22.   *P.L.* xv. 1275.
[2] *In Luc.* vi. 109.   *P.L.* xv. ; 1698.

of this is the following, by which St. Ambrose explains yet more fully his idea :—

" Cuius enim hominis sanguis iam idoneus est ad redemptionem sui, cum pro redemptione omnium suum sanguinem Christus effuderit ? Est ergo cuiusquam sanguis qui Christi possit sanguini comparari ? Aut quis tam potens homo qui pro se propitiationem suam dare possit supra eam propitiationem, quam in se optulit Christus, qui solus Deo mundum reconciliavit per suum sanguinem ? Quæ maior hostia ? quod præstantius sacrificium ? qui melior advocatus . . . ? *Non quæritur ergo propitiatio et redemptio singulorum, quia omnium pretium sanguis est Christi . . . qui solus Patrem reconciliavit.*"

Hence man stands in no further need of expiating his sins: " *Ergo homo non dabit iam propitiationem suam nec redemptionem ; quia semel ablutus est a peccato per sanguinem Christi.*" [1] But he must continue to obey the commandments of God and if he should happen to commit sins after Christ's expiation has been applied to him in baptism, he must wipe them out by works of penance.[2]

We have just been told that Christ's death was necessary for our Salvation, but this necessity was merely relative or hypothetical, and in no way prevents Christ's death from being entirely free :

" Manifestum est et Christum potuisse non mori : sed noluisse ut nobis mors illa prodesset." [3] " Potuit Christus non mori si voluisset : sed neque refugiendum mortem putavit, neque melius nos quam moriendo servasset." [4]

Hence our redemption in some sense demanded the Incarnation, and inversely our redemption is the best proof of the Incarnation :

[1] *Ps.* xlviii. 13-15. *P.L.* xiv. ; col. 1160-1161.

[2] *In Luc.* vii. 156. *P.L.* xv. ; col. 1740. *Cp. De lapsu Virg.* viii. 37.—*P.L.* xvi. 378. *De Pœn.* lib. ii. c. v. 36, *ibid.* ; col. 506, and *Ep.* ii. 29 ; *ibid.* col. 887.

[3] *In Luc.* iii. 48. *P.L.* xv. 1611.

[4] *De excessu Sat.* ii. 46. *P.L.* xvi. 1327.

" Nullum [cruce] maius divinæ personæ est testimonium : nihil est quod magis esse ultra humana videatur, quam toto unum se optulisse pro mundo. Hoc vel solo plene Deus declaratur." [1]

Here we find, half-a-century earlier, all the ideas, and almost the same expressions, as in St. Cyril of Alexandria.

Thus when we probe St. Ambrose's thought to the bottom we find that Christ's death redeems and purifies us, not merely because it is a sacrifice and an expiation and a penal substitution, but mainly because of the transcendant quality of the Sufferer. We must admit that the doctrine of St. Ambrose is lacking in uniformity, and that he has not reached a synthesis, but at least he has put the various details of the Atonement in a very clear light.

III

These same details will be explained yet better in two commentaries on St. Paul which belong to a slightly later period. Already, at the beginning of the fourth century, the epistles of St. Paul had been studied by Marius Victorinus, who embodied his work in commentaries which, for the feebleness of their dogmatic side, put us in mind of the theology of Lactantius, though in Victorinus we do find some slight echo of the traditional beliefs concerning the Atonement.[2]

But a commentary of far greater importance than this obscure work is that which has come down to us under the ægis of St. Ambrose. Its unknown

---

[1] *In Luc.* v. 102. *P.L.* xv. 1663. *Cp. Ep.* vii. 8. *P.L.* xvi. 907.

[2] *Cp.* MAR. VICTORIN. *In Gal.* i. 5. *P.L.* viii. ; col. 1148. *Cp. In Philipp. ibid.* col. 1209, and *Eph.* i. ; col. 1243, 1253-5, 1258.

author was a methodical and exact student, and if in his work we find little that is new, we do find in it much that is well, even though briefly, put.

Ambrosiaster repeats St. Paul's sayings that Christ died for us and for our sins, nor does he fail to lay stress on the proof that this furnishes of His love for us.[1] His death was a sacrifice in an odour of sweetness to God. But this doctrine of St. Paul immediately suggests a difficulty to the writer. Did Christ's executioners then commit no sin? He answers this by saying that the whole value of Christ's Sacrifice, in God's eyes, was in the love and obedience which Christ manifested by it:

" Christus Deo se dicitur optulisse, dum occidi se passus est, in Dei patris sui voluntate perdurans. . . . Immeritus qui occiditur placet Deo, non quia occiditur, sed quia usque ad mortem iustitiam conservavit."

This further leads the writer to explain how Christ delivered Himself, and yet at the same time was delivered by His Father:

" Deus illum tradidisse dicitur, dum illi occidi permisit. Dum enim dissimulat, tradit; si enim noluisset permittere, non fuisset occisus. . . . Quod autem Christus ipse se optulit aut Deus illum tradidit unum est ; quia amborum una voluntas est." [2]

Our commentator also follows St. Paul in declaring that Christ was made sin and a curse ; that He was made sin, in Levitical language, simply means that He was made the victim of our sins:

" Homo factus est Christus causa peccati . . .; propter quod autem omnis caro sub peccato est, factus caro factus est etiam peccatum. *Et quoniam oblatus est pro peccatis, non immerito peccatum factus legitur* : quia et hostia, in lege, quæ pro peccatis offerebatur, peccatum nuncupabatur." [3]

---

[1] Ps. AMBROS. *Rom.* v. 6-10.—*P.L.* xvii. ; col. 90-91.
[2] *Eph.* v. 2 ; col. 394.   [3] *2 Cor.* v. 22 ; col. 298.

We may likewise explain how Christ was made a curse: "*Propterea pro maledictis oblatus, factus est maledictum.*" The writer is careful to point out that St. Paul does not say that Christ was "cursed," which would necessitate a personal expiation, but that He was "a curse," by which he describes a merely outward and legal penalty.[1]

Ambrosiaster has much to say concerning the happy results of Christ's death. By it we were redeemed and are delivered from our sins.[2] He also casually states that Christ alone could redeem us: "*Tam caro empti sumus, ut a nullo redimi potuissemus nisi a Christo qui omnium dives est.*"[3] And he even essays to explain how He did so:

"Sanguis Domini sanguinem nostrum redemit, id est totum hominem salvum fecit. Caro enim Salvatoris pro salute corporis, sanguis vere pro anima nostra effusus est."[4]

By our Saviour's death we were delivered from death. The writer returns to this point frequently,[5] and explains it by telling us that there are two kinds of death, that of the body and that of the soul, or the "second death." The former concerns all men, the latter only strikes the wicked. Nevertheless, the souls, even of the just, were, before Christ's coming, compelled to go to hell.[6] Christ's work consisted in delivering these souls and in preserving us from that death: "*Quia omnes necesse est mori causa Adæ, pro omnibus mortuus est Christus ut eos a secunda morte*

---

[1] *Gal.* iii. 13; col. 354 *f.*

[2] *Eph.* i. 7; col. 374. *Cp. Col.* i. 14; col. 422.

[3] 1 *Cor.* vii. 23; col. 221.

[4] 1 *Cor.* xi. 26; col. 243.

[5] *Cp. Gal.* iii. 13; col. 355. *Rom.* iii. 25; col. 80 and iv. 25; col. 88. *Col.* i. 22; col. 425. 2 *Tim.* i. 9; col. 486.

[6] *Rom.* v. 12; col. 92. *Cp.* col. 95.

liberaret." [1] He elsewhere expresses the same idea even more clearly : " *Nostri causa occidi se passus est, ut nos, data venia, a secunda morte erueret, id est a pœna inferni.*" [2] Once delivered from death Christ calls us to life everlasting.[3]

In a word the whole plan prepared by God's goodness for the Salvation of man depends on the coming and Passion of Christ :

"Sciens Deus propositum benignitatis suæ quo censuit peccatoribus subvenire, tam iis qui sunt apud superos quam iis qui in infero tenebantur, utrosque diutissime exspectavit, evacuans sententiam qua iustum videtur omnes damnari. . . . *In Christo proposuit Deus, id est disposuit propitium se futurum humano generi*, si credant . . . Ideo in sanguine ipsius, quia morte eius liberati sumus : ut et manifestaret illum mortuum et mortem passione eius damnaret." [4]

We have only spoken of Ambrosiaster's better side ; we must now add that he credits the devil with far too much—of this we shall speak later— and that his taste for distinctions leads him to some unfortunate subtleties. Thus he distinguishes between Justification and the forgiveness of sins [5]; whilst he sometimes ascribes to the Incarnation the work of our reconciliation and to Christ's death that of our redemption.[6] But these slight blemishes must not be allowed to discredit the value of his work ; evidently they did not injure it in the eyes of the ancients, for, during the whole of the Middle Ages,

[1] 2 *Cor.* v. 15 ; col. 296. *Cp. Col.* i. 20 ; col. 425.

[2] *Rom.* iv. 25 ; col. 88. *Cp.* vii. 4 ; col. 107.

[3] " Mori se passus est, ut illum morti erutum paradiso redderet immortalem." 1 *Tim.* i. 15 ; col. 161. *Cp. Eph.* ii. 17 ; col. 380.

[4] *Rom.* iii. 25-26 ; col. 80.

[5] *Rom.* iv. 25 ; col. 88.

[6] 1 *Tim.* ii. 5-7 ; col. 467.

theologians made the fullest use of both the doctrines and the formulæ of the pseudo-Ambrose.

Side by side with Ambrosiaster we find another Latin expositor of the works of St. Paul, who in the past has been confounded with the genuine St. Jerome. His real identity has, however, long since been established, and he is now known to be none other than the monk Pelagius, against whom St. Augustine contends. His mistaken opinions concerning grace and original sin do not, however, prevent this writer from expressing the traditional views regarding Christ's work with a precision scarcely short of that of Ambrosiaster.

Christ did not deserve to die, being innocent; His death was a proof of His love and a necessary means of our Salvation :

"Ut quid indebite pro nobis mortuus est, nisi ut manifestaret suam charitatem, . . . cum ille pro nobis impiis nec vitam suam præposuerit, *ne necessariam nobis denegaret mortem ?*" [1]

His death was necessary because on it God had made our forgiveness to depend : " *Quem proposuit Deus propitiatorem . . . ut propitietur eis, qui credunt se eius sanguine liberandos. . . . Propterea passus est Christus ut propositum Dei sedaret quo tandem punire decreverat peccatores.*" [2] For some expiation of our sins was necessary, and Christ alone could furnish it : " *Solus inventus est qui ut immaculata hostia pro omnibus qui erant in peccatis mortui offerretur.*" [3] This was the reason why He was made to be sin —*i.e.* a sacrifice for sin [4]; a spontaneous Sacrifice which pleased God on account of the love which

[1] Ps. Hieronym. *Rom.* v.—*P. L.* xxx. ; col. 667.

[2] *Ibid.* iii. 25 ; col. 661.

[3] 2 *Cor.* v. 15 ; col. 785.

[4] *Rom.* viii. ; col. 680. Cp. 2 *Cor.* v. 21 ; col. 786.

it revealed : " *Voluntarie ipse se tradidit, non ab alio invitus traditus est. . . . Suavissimus Deo odor est caritas.*"[1]

The first result of this Sacrifice was to destroy sin and cleanse our souls,[2] the next was to deliver us from death : " *Mortuus est pro nobis ut nos non moreremur*"[3]; from the context we perceive that the author is here speaking of the everlasting death of the soul.

So far we have met only questions and answers similar to those in Ambrosiaster; but Pelagius goes further, and declares that, if we have been delivered, this is because in God's sight there is a certain equivalence between Christ's undeserved death and the death we had so richly deserved : " *Nos redemit sanguine suo de morte. . . . Omnes rei eramus mortis ; cui se ille indebite tradidit, ut nos suo sanguine redimeret.*"[4] And again : " *Indebito maledicto eius nostrum debitum compensatum est.*"[5]

We thus find in both these pseudonymous writers an endeavour to determine the precise character of the traditional data ; in other words, these two writers were both of them theologians, even in the narrowest sense of the word.

Hence it is perfectly true that the Western Patristic theology, on the subject of the Atonement, is wholly "realistic." But we should like it to be noticed that not one of the Western ideas is new, and that we had already found every single one of them—though sometimes more crudely expressed—in the theology of the East. This fact, which is of great value to us, is, nevertheless, of a character to greatly embarrass certain historians of dogma.

---

[1] *Eph.* v. 2 ; col. 835.

[2] *Rom.* iv. 25 ; col. 665. Cp. *Col.* i. 14 ; col. 854, etc.

[3] 1 *Thess.* v. 10 ; col. 869. Cp. *Rom.* viii. ; col. 681, v. col. 668.

[4] *Ibid.* iii. ; col. 661.   [5] *Gal.* iii. ; col. 812-813.

CHAPTER XV

THE SUM OF THE LATIN THEOLOGY

ST. JEROME—ST. AUGUSTINE

NOTHING is more misleading than to clump together in the same chapter, as if their testimony were of exactly the same weight, two Fathers who, by their character and their work, differed so much as St. Jerome and St. Augustine. St. Augustine's great culture and his world-wide influence—to use Harnack's expression—give his doctrines a value which is certainly not matched by those of the exegetical hermit of Bethlehem. But apart from the fact that these two Fathers lived at the same time and consequently must be taken together, it will be interesting to see how the bent of their respective minds led them to give in their work each a different place to the same doctrine.

I

St. Jerome had little concern for speculation. His one wish was to arrive at the true sense of the Scriptures; for the dogmatic meaning of the texts he cared but little; his Commentaries are admittedly the weakest part of his work. Hence we must not expect to find in him anything new concerning the Atonement, or be surprised if he turns out to be rather behind his time.

St. Jerome when he meets a classical passage on

the Atonement allows it to pass unperceived; even when a text detains him, his explanation of it is usually very general and indefinite. Thus Christ is a Lamb because His blood redeems us, and the commentator proceeds to press the metaphor : not only did this Lamb die for us, but it clothed us with its wool against the cold of infidelity.[1] Elsewhere St. Jerome tells us that Christ's death was a Sacrifice ; he does not dwell on this aspect of it, but immediately goes on to seek its moral applications ; we must sacrifice ourselves for our neighbours as He sacrificed Himself for us.[2] In another place, wishing to explain the object of Christ's Sacrifice, this is what he says :

"Dedit se Filius ut iniustitiam quæ erat in nobis iustitia ipse subverteret. Tradidit se sapientia, ut insipientiam expugnaret. Sanctitas et fortitudo se optulit, ut spurcitiam infirmitatemque deleret."

It would be difficult to find anything less definite than the above ; but in close proximity to this passage we find another which admirably describes the agreement between the Father's Will and the Son's concerning the work of our Atonement :

"Neque Filius se dedit pro peccatis nostris absque voluntate Patris, neque Pater tradidit Filium sine Filii voluntate : sed hæc est voluntas Filii voluntatem Patris implere."[3]

St. Jerome does not explain how or why Christ

[1] HIERONYM. *In Isaiam.* lib. xiv.—*P.L.* xxiv.; col. 509 : "Non solum sanguine suo nos redemit, sed et lanis operuit, ut algentes infidelitate sua veste calefaceret."

[2] *In Eph.* lib. iii. (v. 2).—*P.L.* xxvi.; col. 519 : "Quo modo enim ille se tradidit pro nobis, sic et iste pro quibus potest libentur occumbens imitabitur eum qui oblationem et hostiam in odorem suavitatis se tradidit et fiet ipse oblatio et hostia Dei in odorem suavitatis."

[3] *Gal.* i. 4 ; *ibid.* col. 314. *Cp. Gal.* ii. 20 ; col. 346. *In Matth.* lib. iii. xvi. 23. ; *ibid.* col. 120.

became sin and a curse ; he only sees in this a sign of God's wisdom :

"Nullum debet movere quod Christus pro nobis maledictum factus sit, quia et Deus ipse, cum nesciret Christus peccatum, pro nobis peccatum fecit, et Salvator de plenitudine Patris exinanivit se, . . . ut quod stultum erat Dei sapientius fieret hominibus."

He is, however, happier in what he says subsequently when He tells us that Christ's death is our life :

"Iniuria Domini nostra gloria est. Ille mortuus est ut nos viveremus. Ille descendit ad inferos ut nos ascenderemus ad coelum. Ille factus stultitia ut nos sapientia fieremus. . . . Ille pependit in ligno ut peccatum quod commiseramus in ligno, ligno deleret appensus." [1]

Hence our Saviour's office was to reconcile us to God : "*Omnes post offensam Patri nostro reconciliandi sumus ; non per merita nostra, sed per gratiam Salvatoris.*" [2] So true is it that Christ is our reconciliation that, save through His precious blood, no one can draw nigh to God :

"Cum in eo sint omnia, procul tamen esse ab impiis dicitur. . . . Et diligentius intuendum quod absque cruore Domini Iesu nemo appropinquet Deo, quia ipse est pax nostra." [3]

Lastly, in explaining *Isaias* liii., St. Jerome openly acknowledges the penal character of Christ's death. Christ suffered really and not merely in appearance. He bore on the cross the weight of our sins : "*Pendebat in cruce et factus pro nobis maledictum peccata nostra portabat.*" Hence He suffered for our sins that by His wounds He might heal us. He suffered in our stead the penalty of our misdeeds : "*Quod

[1] *Gal.* iii. 13 ; *ibid.* col. 363. *Cp. ibid.* col. 360.
[2] *In. Ep. ad Titum.* ii. 11 ; *ibid.* col. 586.
[3] *Eph.* ii. 14 ; *ibid.* col. 473.

enim nos pro nostris debebamus sceleribus sustinere, ille pro nobis passus est." [1] Yet, a little farther on, his expressions again become weak:

". . . ut quod propter imbecillitatem virium ferre non poteramus pro nobis ille portaret." "Peccata portavit quasi medicus languorem ægroti." [2]

In other words, though St. Jerome re-echoes the traditional sayings, his teaching lacks both firmness and precision. His belief in the Atonement cannot be called into question, but his theology is too poor and indefinite. Does this prove that a man may be conspicuously successful in exegesis and yet be a second-rate theologian? At any rate St. Jerome has earned sufficient glory in his own field not to covet the more modest renown of the theologian.

II

Of a very different calibre was the mind of St. Augustine, who revelled in speculative matters, and whose opinions on every question of this nature show the high-water mark of Patristic thought. Not indeed that he, any more than the other Fathers, ever wrote a special treatise on the Atonement; but he so often deals with it in his many works that by collecting and comparing the fragments we shall find ourselves in possession of the most complete and perfect exposal of the Redemption ever given by a Latin Father.

According to St. Augustine, the Incarnation of the Son of God depended entirely on sin: "*Si homo non perisset, Filius hominis non venisset.*" [3] But the

[1] *In Isaiam* liii.—*P.L.* xxiv. 506 *f.*

[2] *Ibid.* col. 508 and 512.

[3] AUGUSTIN. *Serm.* clxxiv. 2.—*P.L.* xxxviii. col. 940. *Cp. Serm.* clxxv. 1; col. 945.

existence of sin did not make the Incarnation necessary; God had plenty other means of reconciling us, though none more fitting the Incarnation:

"Non alium possibilem modum Deo defuisse, cuius potestate cuncta æqualiter subiacent; sed sanandæ nostræ miseriæ convenientiorem modum alium non fuisse, nec esse oportuisse." [1]

St. Augustine elsewhere expresses the same idea in a different form:

"Non poterat aliter sapientia Dei homines liberare, nisi susciperet hominem? . . . Poterat omnino; sed, si aliter faceret, similiter vestræ stultitiæ displiceret." [2]

In this M. Sabatier sees a proof of the "inconsistency of Christian thought." [3] But this is only because he fails to note the distinction between relative and absolute necessity. At no time was it believed that the Incarnation was absolutely necessary for our Salvation—it was considered as necessary only consequently on the plan of Salvation freely chosen by God. In this there was no inconsistency and no wavering of opinion, the distinction between the two kinds of necessity being known even to St. Athanasius. Hence God's free decree is always understood in such sentences as: "*Non liberaretur humanum genus, nisi Sermo Dei dignaretur esse humanus*" [4]; and in all the other formulæ which speak of Christ's Incarnation and death as necessary.

Having made this remark we may now proceed to consider St. Augustine's view concerning the Atonement. We have been told that he "conceives of the work of the Mediator under two aspects: the

[1] *De Trinit.* lib. xiii. c. x. 13.—*P.L.* xlii.; col. 1024. *Cp. ibid.* xvi. 21; col. 1030.

[2] *De Agon. Christ.* xi. 12.—*P.L.* xl. col. 297.

[3] Sabatier, *op. cit.* p. 52.

[4] *Sermo.* clxxiv. 1.—*P.L.* xxxviii. 940.

T

Mediator had as man to appease God and as God to convert man's heart. The two missions are profoundly different ; the former is the work of the Man-God, the latter that of the God-man." [1]

The work of expiation and reconciliation which is the main cause of our salvation, and forms the objective Atonement, is by St. Augustine clearly made to depend on Christ's death. As Harnack says: "He conceived of the Man Jesus as the Mediator, as the Victim and Priest by whom we are redeemed and reconciled with God. His death, as the Church teaches, is the sure foundation of our faith in the Redemption." [2] Augustine waxes angry with those carnal-minded Christians who fear to think of the mystery of the cross, and who perceive in it merely an example of virtue :

" Animalis homo . . . non percipit quæ sunt spiritus Dei, id est quid gratiæ credentibus crux conferat Christi; et putat hoc illa cruce actum esse tantummodo ut nobis usque ad mortem pro veritate certantibus imitandum præberetur exemplum." [3]

He himself is far from being of the number of the " carnal minded," and he repeats what St. Paul says —viz. that " Christ crucified has been made by God, wisdom, righteousness, justification, and redemption." In the many passages in which he refers to this idea we find, as it were, a twofold current ; like his predecessors he ascribes to Christ's death both a salutary and a penal character.

He looks on Christ's death as a sacrifice prefigured in the Old Testament offering: *Antiqui, quando adhuc sacrificium verum quod fideles norunt, in figuris prænuntiabatur, celebrabant figuras futuræ*

[1] E. Portalié in *Dict. de Théol. cath.* art. *Augustin.* col. 2368.

[2] Harnack-Choisy. *Précis*, p. 270. *Cp.* p. 287.

[3] *In Ioan.* tr. xcviii. 3.—*P.L.* xxxv. ; col. 1881-2.

rei.[1] The sacrifice which was thus foreshadowed is now continued in the sacrifice of the Mass :

"Huius sacrificii caro et sanguis, ante adventum Christi, per victimas promittebatur; in passione Christi, per ipsam veritatem reddebatur; post ascensum Christi, per sacramentum memoriæ celebratur."[2]

Its merit arises from the fact that Christ offers Himself freely[3] in such wise that He is at once the Priest and the Victim. With the coming of this Sacrifice all others were brought to naught :

"Ipse offerens, ipse et oblatio. . . . Huius sacrificii multiplicia variaque signa erant sacrificia prisca sanctorum, cum hoc unum per multa figuraretur, tamquam verbis multis res una diceretur. Huic summo veroque sacrificio cuncta sacrificia falsa cesserunt."[4]

His Sacrifice was likewise an expiation of our sins. It is thus that Augustine understands St Paul's "*peccatum fecit,*" and he adds that the result of this "sin" was to destroy our sin :

"Peccatum oblatum est et deletum est peccatum. Fusus est sanguis Redemptoris et deleta est cautio debitoris. Ipse est sanguis qui pro multis effusus est in remissionem peccatorum."[5] "Morte sua quippe uno verissimo sacrificio pro nobis oblato quid-quid culparum erat . . . purgavit, abolevit, exstinxit."[6]

But our sins are wiped out because we have been reconciled with God : "*Idem ipse unus verusque*

[1] *Ps.* xxxix. 12. *P.L.* xxxvi. ; col. 441. *Cp. Ps.* lxxiv. 12 ; col. 955 and *Ps.* xxi. ii. 27-28 ; col. 178.

[2] *Contra Faustum,* xx. 21.—*P.L.* xlii. ; col. 385.

[3] *Cp. Ps.* xxi. ii. 23.—*P.L.* xxxvi. ; col. 176. *Serm.* clii. 9.— *P.L.* xxxviii.; col. 824 and *De Trin.* lib. iv. c. xiii. 16.—*P.L.* xlii. ; col. 898.

[4] *De Civ Dei.* x. 20. *P.L.* xli. 298.

[5] *Sermo.* cxxxiv. iv. 5. *P.L.* xxxviii. 745. *Cp. Serm.* clii. 10-11 ; *ibid.* col. 824 *f* and *Serm.* civ. 8 ; col. 845.

[6] *De Trin.* lib. iv. c. xiii. 17. *P.L.* xlii. 899. *Cp. Ep. Ioan.* i. 5. *P.L.* xxxv. 1982. *Cp. ibid.* col. 2033.

mediator, per sacrificium pacis reconcilians nos Deo." [1]
Farther on Augustine expounds the well-known text
of St. Paul: "If when we were enemies we were
reconciled to God by the death of his Son" (*Rom.*
v. 10), a text which allows of his explaining himself
in greater detail.

"What does this mean, that we are reconciled
by the death of His Son? Was it that the Father,
being vexed with us, was so pleased with His Son's
death that He took us again into His friendship?
Was it that the Son was already so kindly disposed
towards us as to be willing to die for us whilst the
Father was so angry that He could not be otherwise
appeased than by the death of His Son? But, if so,
why then does the Apostle say: 'If God be for us,
who is against us?' (*Rom.* viii. 31). He who spared
not His own Son but delivered Him for us, how
could He but give us every good thing with Him?
Had the Father not wished us well, would He have
delivered His Son for us? Is there not an apparent
contradiction between the two texts? In the first
we are told of the Son who died for us and by His
death reconciled us to the Father; according to the
second it seems as if the Father was the first to love
us, for He it was that spared not His Son for us
but delivered Him unto death for our sake.

"But we know that God loved us, not only before
His Son died for us but even before He created the
world, as the Apostle bears witness when he says:
He hath chosen us before the foundation of the
world (*Eph.* i. 4). Again, the Son was not delivered
against His will, as by a pitiless Father, for the
Apostle says of Him: He loved me and delivered
Himself for me (*Gal.* ii. 20). Hence everything

[1] *De Trin.* lib. iv. c. xiv. 19. *P.L.* xlii. 901.

was done agreeably in all, to the Father and to the Son and to the Holy Ghost who proceeds from both one and the other. But we were justified by the blood of Christ and reconciled to God by His death. How this was done I will now try to explain." [1]

We see here how St. Augustine already gives a simple answer to a question which even now worries certain theologians. As to the explanation to which he refers in concluding, it is based on the theory of our deliverance from the captivity of the devil, of which we shall speak elsewhere. We must, however, point out that this deliverance is by St. Augustine subordinated to the forgiveness of sins and to our reconciliation with God,[2] hence his solution of the question is not vitiated by what is really an erroneous explanation of one of its consequences.

St. Augustine in another passage speaks of this propitiation through Christ's blood and he states— without, however, explaining how—that the death of the Guiltless cleansed and redeemed the guilty :

"Apud te propitiatio est. Et quæ est ista propitiatio nisi sacrificium ? Et quod est sacrificium nisi quod pro nobis oblatum est ? *Sanguis innocens fusus delevit omnia peccata nocentium* : pretium tantum datum redemit omnes captivos." [3]

In yet another place Augustine explains what he means by " propitiation ": " *Non dabit Deo propitiationem : id est placationem qua flectat Deum pro peccatis.*" [4] We may finish the proof ourselves. Christ on the cross became a propitiation for us, therefore

---

[1] *De Trin.* lib. xiii. c. x. 14 and xi. 15 ; col. 1025.

[2] " Si ergo commissio peccatorum per iram Dei iustam hominem subdidit diabolo, profecto remissio peccatorum per reconciliationem Dei benignam eruit a diabolo." *Ibid.* xvi. 21 ; col. 1030.

[3] *Ps.* cxxix. 3. *P.L.* xxxvii. ; col. 1697-1698.

[4] *Ps.* xlviii. 9. *P.L.* xxxvi. 549.

He averted God's anger from us. St. Augustine, however, does not explore the mystery any further, but he tells us elsewhere that Christ alone was able to thus obtain for us mercy :

" Per quam unam victimam fieret remissio peccatorum." [1]
" Omnis humana natura iustificari et redimi ab ira Dei iustissima, hoc est a vindicta, nullo modo potest nisi per fidem et sacramentum sanguinis Christi." [2]

This shows us the greatness, and the immense moment of the Sacrifice, without, however, our being able to discern why it was so sovereignly efficacious.

III

Besides the forgiveness of sins and reconciliation with God, another result of Christ's death will show us another of its characters. St. Augustine never wearies of repeating that Christ's death delivers us from death. Under this word several ideas are denoted.

The most evident passage would at first sight seem to be the following one, from his great work on the Trinity, in which he expounds a principle almost mathematical in its rigour :—

" Merito quippe mors peccatoris veniens ex damnationis necessitate, soluta est per mortem iusti venientem ex misericordiæ voluntate, dum simplum eius congruit duplo nostro."

St. Augustine immediately goes on to explain that this " double death " is that of the soul and that of the body, both of which arise through sin. For this death our Saviour brought a single remedy, in His death which is at once a mystery and an example :

[1] *Contra Faust.* xxii. 17. *P.L.* xlii. 409.
[2] *De natura et gratia,* lib. i. 2. *P.L.* xliv. 249. *Cp. De Genesi,* lib. x. c. xiv. 25. *P.L.* xxxiv. 419.

"Huic duplæ morti nostræ Salvator noster impendit simplicem suam, et ad faciendam utramque ressuscitationem nostram, in sacramento et exemplo præposuit et proposuit unam suam."

In other words a mystery to the inner man and an example to the outward man (*interioris hominis sacramentum, exterioris exemplum*); the mystery being in that the "old man" which is in us was crucified with Christ on the cross, thus exciting us to penance and wholesome mortification by which the death of sin within us is destroyed; whilst the example consists in that Christ teaches us not to fear persecutions and death; thus by His single death the Saviour cured our twofold death.[1]

Augustine also ascribes a like result to the Resurrection, and here it is easy to see that what he ascribes to the Saviour's death is a merely moral effect on our double death.

But St. Augustine does not confine himself to considering the moral effects of Christ's death; in other places he represents death as a mighty power from which Christ redeems us, and which He breaks and slays by His own death. "*Mortuus est potestate ; et hoc est pretium nostrum quo nos a morte redimeret.*"[2] This same idea suggests to our author some striking antitheses:

"Ipsa morte liberavit nos a morte: morte occisus mortem occidit. . . . Ergo mortem suscepit et mortem suspendit in cruce; et de ipsa morte liberantur mortales. . . . In morte Christi mors mortua est, quia vita mortua occidit mortem, plenitudo vitæ deglutivit mortem."[3]

We have already met similar expressions among the earlier Latin Fathers and still more frequently

[1] *De Trin.* lib. iv. c. ii. 4 and iii. 5-6.—*P.L.* xlii. ; col. 889-892.
[2] *De natura et gratia*, xxiv. 26.—*P.L.* xliv. ; col. 260.
[3] *In Ioan.* xii. 10 and 11.—*P.L.* xxxv. ; col. 1489-1490.

among the Greeks. Nor does St. Augustine conceal that he is here speaking of the " second death," of that everlasting death which is the award of sin : " *Propter illum mortuus est, ut ille non in sempiternum moreretur.*" [1] The reason that we are thus delivered is that Christ suffered an undeserved bodily death ; by this He delivered us from the everlasting death which we deserved :

" Tantum beneficii collatum est hominibus, ut a Dei filio . . . mors temporalis indebita redderetur, qua eos a sempiterna morte debita liberaret." [2]

It is true that St. Augustine lays down this principle when speaking of our deliverance from the power of Satan, and it is not impossible that in his mind the two points of view were somewhat confused. But, without now entering into a question which we shall deal with afterwards, we may say that it is certain that Augustine acknowledges no personal rights to Satan and that in other words he only considers him as the executor of the decrees of God's Justice. There are, moreover, in the principle here laid down by St. Augustine, wider issues than the particular case he contemplates. We shall see this by examining with the help of his other writings the kind of penal substitution which he ascribes to our Saviour's death.

His doctrine rests on two fundamental principles, that death is the penalty of sin and that Christ who was innocent did not merit this penalty. Hence it is to Christ that St. Augustine applies the well-known verse of the psalm (lxviii. 5) :

---

[1] *Ps.* xlviii. 8.—*P.L.* xxxvi. ; col. 549. *Cp. Serm.* cccxliv. 4.— *P.L.* xxxix. ; col. 1515.

[2] *De Trin.* lib. xiii. c. xvi. 21.—*P.L.* xlii. 1030.

"Non rapui et exsolvebam; non peccavi et pœnas dabam. . . .
Delicta nulla Christus habuit: fuit delictorum susceptor, sed non
commissor." [1]

Our Saviour's innocence turns His death into a
Sacrifice of expiation:

"Nos enim ad mortem per peccatum venimus; ille, per iustitiam.
Et ideo cum sit mors nostra pœna peccati, mors illius facta est
hostia pro peccato." [2]

It was on this account that His death delivered us
from the death which we had so richly merited. St.
Augustine frequently connects Christ's undeserved
death with our deliverance: "*Quam propterea Dominus indebitam reddidit, ut nobis debita non noceret.*" [3]
He even states that, save by this substitution, there
was no means of saving us: "*Ille nisi indebitum
solveret, nunquam nos a debito liberaret.*" [4]

St. Augustine also tells us plainly that it was the
penalty of our sins that Christ suffered:

"Pro nobis mortem, *hoc est peccati pœnam sine peccato subire
dignatus est.* . . . Solus pro nobis suscepit sine malis meritis pœnam
ut nos per illum sine bonis meritis consequeremur gratiam. Quia,
sicut nobis non debebatur aliquid boni, ita nec illi aliquid mali.
Commendans ergo dilectionem suam in eos quibus erat daturus
indebitam vitam, pati pro eis voluit indebitam mortem." [5]

He explains likewise St. Paul's text: "He was
made a curse for us" (*Gal.* iii. 13):

[1] *Ps.* lxviii. 9-10.—*P.L.* xxxvi. 848 *f.*   Cp. *Ps.* xliv. 7; *ibid.* col.
498.

[2] *De Trin.* lib. iv. c. xii. 15.—*P.L.* xlii. 898.

[3] *Ibid.* c. xiii. 17; col. 899.   Cp. *In Ioan.* tr. lxxix. 2.—*P.L.*
xxxv.; col. 1838-9.

[4] *Serm.* clv. 7.—*P.L.* xxxviii.; col. 845.   Cp. *Serm.* cxci. 1; col.
1010.

[5] *Cont. duas epist. Pelag.* lib. iv. c. iv. 6.—*P.L.* xliv.; col. 613.
Cp. *Ps.* xxxi. 18.—*P.L.* xxxvi.; col. 270.

" Filius Dei semper vivus in sua iustitia, mortuus autem propter delicta nostra, in carne suscepta ex pœna nostra. Sic et semper benedictus in sua iustitia, maledictus autem propter delicta nostra, in morte suscepta ex pœna nostra. . . . Si confiteris mortuum, *confitere suscepisse pœnam peccati nostri sine peccato nostro.* Iam vero ubi audis pœnam peccati . . . crede *per divinæ sententiæ iustitiam* ex maledictione venisse." [1]

Unfortunately St. Augustine has nothing more to say concerning the nature of this sentence of Divine Justice; our author seems scarcely to have adverted to this idea, which could have been worked out so admirably.

In his exposition of the Epistle to the Galatians Augustine mentions and refutes a curious interpretation of some timorous Christians, who, to save Christ from the legal curse, did not scruple, in spite of the evident meaning of the text, to apply the curse to Judas. St. Augustine's own view is that the curse signifies that Christ bore the penalty of our sins :

" Ex parte quippe mortali pependit in ligno. Mortalitas autem unde sit notum est credentibus : ex pœna quippe est et maledictione primi hominis, *quam Dominus suscepit et peccata nostra pertulit in corpore suo super lignum.*" [2]

An opinion which he expresses again more briefly as follows :—" *Non enim ulla ipse delicta habuit, sed nostra portavit*" [3]; in other words, Christ substituted Himself for us : " *Delicta nostra sua delicta fecit, ut iustitiam suam nostram iustitiam faceret.*" [4] Lastly, in a text which reads almost like one from the Schoolmen, he declares that Christ's death destroyed both the fault and its penalty : " *Suscepit Christus sine reatu*

---

[1] *Contra Faust.* xiv. 6-7. *P.L.* xlii. 298.
[2] *Exp. in Gal.* 22. *P.L.* xxxv. 2120.
[3] *Tract. adv. Iudæos,* v. 6. *P.L.* xlii. 54.
[4] *Ps.* xxi. ii. 3. *P.L.* xxxvi. 172.

supplicium nostrum, ut inde solveret reatum nostrum et finiret etiam supplicium nostrum." [1]

We thus find that St. Augustine ascribes to our Saviour's death a salutary value and also a penal value. If we look closely we find too that the former value is made dependent on the latter ; though St. Augustine does not indeed teach this formally, nevertheless that this was his belief is evident from his successive references to the matter. If Christ by His death wipes away our sins and reconciles us to God, this is because His undeserved death is the payment of our debt. Here we have the idea of vicarious Satisfaction, but, like the other Fathers, St. Augustine does no more than affirm it without condescending to investigate its reasons.

IV

But St. Augustine did not forget to bestow due attention on the moral work of the Redeemer : " Without fear of being contradicted we may say that none of the Fathers laid so much stress on the moral side of the Incarnation. In fact this is what gives his doctrine its personal stamp." [2]

Protestant critics are not only too glad to acknowledge this, but are even inclined to consider this side of his doctrine to the exclusion of the highly dogmatic utterances which we have just passed in review. The true historian will, however, give due prominence to both one and the other side of the great Doctor's teaching.

The Incarnation is the great testimony of God's love for us, for God, by means of it, dispels our dark-

[1] *Contra Faust.* xiv. 4. *P.L.* xlii. 297.
[2] E. PORTALIÉ. *Op. cit.* col. 2372.

ness and calls us to life Divine : "*Factus particeps mortalitatis nostrœ, fecit nos participes divinitatis suœ.*"[1] This is the well-known theme of the Greek Fathers, and to it Augustine frequently returns.[2]

But he lays still more stress on the humility of God incarnate. This idea is considered by Harnack as the centre of Augustine's Christology,[3] and by M. Portalié as "one of his profoundest conceptions." "In God's plans humility was the deepest lesson to be learnt from the Incarnation. Everywhere, even in the most theoretical of his works, Augustine combines the two-fold object of the mystery: an expiation to the Father in heaven, and a rehabilitation of humanity by the unspeakable condescension of God-made-man."[4]

We fell through pride ; God recalls us by the example of His humility :

"Christus homine indutus, per quem vivendi exemplum nobis daretur, hoc est via certa qua perveniremus ad Deum. *Non enim redire potuimus nisi humilitate,* qui superbia lapsi sumus. Huius igitur humilitatis exemplum, id est viæ qua redeundum fuit, ipse Reparator noster in se ipso demonstrare dignatus est."[5]

St. Augustine does indeed state, and states it too with deep feeling, that the Incarnation is the highest testimony we have of God's love :

"Quæ maior causa est adventus Domini, nisi ut ostenderet Deus dilectionem suam in nobis? . . . Si amare pigebat, saltem nunc redamare non pigeat."

But he immediately mentions also His humility :

[1] *De Trin.* lib. iv. i. 2-3 and ii. 4.—*P.L.* xlii. ; col. 888-889· *Cp.* lib. xiii. c. ix. 12 ; col. 1023-4.

[2] *Serm.* cxxi. 5.—*P.L.* xxxviii. ; col. 680. *Cp. Serm.* cxix. 5 ; *ibid.* col. 675. *Serm.* cxciv. 3 ; col. 1016. *Serm.* clxxxvii. 4 ; col. 1002. *Serm.* cxcii. 1 ; col. 1012.

[3] HARNACK, *Dogmengeschichte*, iii. pp. 122-124.

[4] E. PORTALIÉ, *op. cit.* col. 2372.

[5] *De fide et symbolo,* iv. 6.—*P.L.* xl. ; col. 185.

" Dominus Iesus Christus, Deus homo, et divinæ in nos dilectionis indicium est et humanæ apud nos humilitatis exemplum." [1]

In a word, humility is the greatest mystery of the Saviour :

" Humilitatem qua natus est Deus . . . et perductus ad mortem summum esse medicamentum quo superbiæ nostræ sanaretur tumor, *et altum sacramentum quo peccati vinculum solveretur.*" [2]

Lastly, in a short formula, we find described both the expiatory value of Christ's death and the moral value of the Incarnation, a formula which is really the synthesis of St. Augustine's teaching : " *Iniquorum et superborum una mundatio est sanguis iusti et humilitas Dei.*" [3]

At the present day such pious moral considerations are left to ascetic theology, dogmatic theology confining itself to the speculative side. But such considerations still form a part of Catholic doctrine, and Protestants are wrong in making this separation a pretext for incriminating the dryness of our dogmatism. This division, which arose through the progress of the sacred sciences, was unknown to the Fathers, and its absence resulted in their doctrine being much more living, though less didactic. We have here two different methods, but no real opposition, for surely no Catholic theologian ever manifested any desire of forfeiting the legacy left by St. Augustine.

We shall bring our study of St. Augustine to a conclusion by taking the *Enchiridion* which contains the summary of his teaching.[4]

---

[1] *De catech. rudibus,* iv. 7-8. *P.L.* xl. 314-6. Other texts are quoted by PORTALIÉ, *loc. cit.*

[2] *De Trin.* lib. viii. c. v. 7. *P.L.* xlii. 952.

[3] *Ibid.* lib. iv. c. ii. 4 ; col. 889.

[4] *Enchiridion,* 27-70 *P.L.* xl. 245-265.

Mankind having fallen through sin was going from bad to worse, and was now the merest *massa damnata.* God, who might justly have left men to their own devices, remembered His mercy (c. xxvii.).

Hence He willed to redeem men ; but as they were under the Divine anger a mediator was required who might reconcile us and appease God's anger by His sacrifice :

" In hac ira cum essent homines, necessarius erat mediator, hoc est reconciliator, *qui hanc iram sacrificii singularis . . . oblatione placaret."* [1]

This Mediator was Christ, who offered Himself as the Sacrifice for our reconciliation:

" Christum pro nobis peccatum fecit Deus, cui reconciliandi sumus, *hoc est sacrificium pro peccatis, per quod reconciliari valeremus.* Ipse ergo peccatum ut nos iustitia " (c. xli.). [2]

Thereby He destroyed original sin, and at the same time all other sins which have been committed since :

" . . . ut unus peccatum tolleret mundi sicut unus peccatum misit in mundum . . . nisi quod ille unus unum peccatum misit in mundum : iste vero unus non solum illud unum, sed cuncta simul abstulit quæ addita invenit." [3]

By His Sacrifice the room left in heaven by the angels' downfall has been filled, and men have been freed from corruption and restored to life everlasting (c. lxii.). Nevertheless, satisfaction is required of each one individually for the sins committed after baptism (c. lxx.).

Finally M. Portalié agrees with Harnack in considering the following text as the most perfect expression of the Augustinian system :—" *Neque per*

---

[1] *Enchiridion,* 33 ; col. 248-249.
[2] *Ibid.* 41 ; col. 253.
[3] *Ibid.* 48-50 ; col. 255-256.

ipsum liberaremur unum mediatorem Dei et hominum Iesum Christum, nisi esset et Deus. Cum genus humanum peccata longe separaverunt a Deo, per mediatorem qui solus sine peccato natus est, vixit, occisus est, reconciliari nos oportebat Deo usque ad carnis resurrectionem in vitam æternam [this is the primary object of the Incarnation—viz. restoration, and reconciliation with God]: *ut humana superbia per humilitatem Dei argueretur ac sanaretur et demonstraretur homini quam longe a Deo recesserat* [this is the secondary object of the Incarnation, the moral work of the Humble Christ, an important, but all the same a secondary, work]; *et Unigenito suscipiente formam servi, quæ nihil ante meruerat, fons gratiæ panderetur* [this indicates the result of the work of redemption, which was not merely forgiveness and deliverance, but also justification]; *et carnis etiam resurrectio redemptis promissa in ipso Redemptore præmonstraretur* [this being the function of the Resurrection]; *et per eamdem naturam quam se decepisse lætabatur, diabolus vinceretur.*" [1]

[1] *Enchiridion,* 108 ; col. 282-3. Cp. PORTALIÉ, *op. cit.* col. 2373-4, and HARNACK, iii. p. 190, note 2.

CHAPTER XVI

ST. AUGUSTINE'S LEGATEES—ST. LEO, ST. GREGORY THE GREAT

THOUGH the mediæval theology, and indeed all Christian thought, is in a large measure dependent on St. Augustine, his direct heirs were the last of the Latin Fathers, who most faithfully of all reflect or repeat his teaching. It will be ages before we again meet a creative mind among the theologians of the West, but St. Augustine succeeded in summing up so well the previous work of both East and West, he held so high a rank because of the breadth and depth of his knowledge, that he was willingly accepted as the master of the following generations. On most questions even the best minds were content to bow to his authority. On the matter of the Atonement, indeed, we shall find St. Leo reverting to the speculation of the Greeks, but his foreign importation found no market, and his successors among Western theologians again returned to the "realist" views, couching them in the formulæ bequeathed to them by St. Augustine. We shall find no new conceptions, but we shall see the ideas prevalent of old, again and again reproduced and emphasised.

I

We shall first cast a glance at the contemporaries and immediate disciples of St. Augustine.

John Cassian tells us that it was not in man's

power to redeem mankind from sin because no one
was without sin :

"Non est humanæ opis redimere populum a captivitate peccati.[1] . . . Quia nullus solvere vinctos possit, nisi immunis a
vinculis; nullus eximere peccatores, nisi peccato carens." [2]

St. Prosper of Aquitaine has it that Christ's death
was the remedy of original sin : " *Contra vulnus
originalis peccati, verum et potens ac singulare remedium est mors Filii Dei Domini nostri Iesu Christi.*" [3]
His death was a Sacrifice which reconciles us to God.

"Se hostiam Deo verus Agnus optulerat. . . . Nemo hominum,
ante reconciliationem quæ per Christi sanguinem facta est, non aut
peccator aut impius fuit." [4]

St. Peter Chrysologus adds that this death delivers
us from ours [5] in such wise that it is not the guilty
but his guilt that perishes : " *ut non reus pereat sed
reatus.*" [6]

These divers doctrinal elements are found again
in the homilies of St. Maximus, Bishop of Tours.
Christ's death was a Sacrifice in which our Saviour
was at once the Priest and the Victim.[7] One died
that all might be saved,[8] and He who died was the
only one who could appease God's anger and redeem
us : " *Cuius solius sanguine placandus erat Deus et
universa redimenda mortalitas.*" [9] His death re-

---

[1] Ioan. Cass. *De Inc. Christi*, iv. 12.—*P.L.* l. ; col. 93.

[2] *Ibid.* v. 15 ; col. 136.

[3] Prosper. Aquit. *Resp. ad cap. object. vincent.* I.—*P.L.* li. ;
col. 177.

[4] *De vocatione omnium gentium*, ii. 16 ; *ibid.* col. 703.

[5] Petr. Chrysol. *Serm.* cli.—*P.L.* lii. ; col. 603.

[6] *Ibid. Serm.* cx. ; col. 503.

[7] Maxim. Taur. *Serm.* xxx.—*P.L.* lvii. 595.

[8] *Hom.* lii. ; col. 348.

[9] *Serm.* lviii. ; col. 650.

U

deems us, cleanses us and delivers us from everlasting death.[1]

In St. Paulinus of Nola likewise we read that Christ's death was a perfect sacrifice, and that on this account it reconciles us with God.[2] The Saviour fastened to His cross both our sin and our curse, making Himself to be sin and a curse for our sakes.[3] But Salvation also consists in a restoration of our nature. Sin had so deeply wounded it that every remedy was powerless; as only the potter can make his vessel anew so was it necessary for God to come to us:

"Ita Dominus omnium, qui omnes fecerat, dignatus est ad nostra descendere nosque suscipere in corpore suo, ut reficeret eadem arte et potestate qua fecerat."[4]

A few pages farther the same author explains that Christ in taking our flesh destroyed the matter of sin which had been in it ever since Adam; and that He united all things, not only by destroying the sin which was fixed as a wall between us and God, nor merely by uniting in a single faith both Jew and Gentile, but by establishing harmony in our nature itself:

". . . ut in unoquoque nostrum qui crederemus, natura sibi nostra congrueret et discordia quæ prius versabatur in nobis . . . pace fidei solveretur."[5]

Does not this read like a stray fragment of the "physical" Atonement of the Greek Fathers? It is

[1] *Hom.* xlviii.; col. 337. *Cp. Hom.* lxxxiii.; col. 438, and *Sermo.* xl.; col. 616.

[2] PAULIN. NOL. *Ep.* xi. 8.—*P.L.* lxi.; col. 196. *Cp. Epist.* xx. 3; col. 245. *Epist.* xii. 2; col. 201.

[3] *Epist.* xxiii. 14-15; col. 265-266.

[4] *Epist.* xii. 3. *Ibid.* col. 201.

[5] *Ibid.* 6; col. 203.

in fact highly probable that the Pelagian controversy, which led to a deeper pondering on the mystery of our downfall, also led Christian thought to seek for this corruption an inner, quasi-organic remedy. Hence theologians would lay stress on the union of our nature with God in Christ, and thus emphasise the great efficaciousness of the Incarnation ; thus the study of original sin again brought into the field the mystic conception of the Easterns. We should, no doubt, look for the principle of this recrudescence of the speculative view in the works of St. Augustine, whom as a rule St. Paulinus faithfully echoes ; at any rate, what is merely hinted at by St. Paulinus is formally taught by the greatest of St. Augustine's earlier disciples, Pope St. Leo the Great.

II

St. Leo frequently describes the ravages of sin in our nature, and sums them all up in our captivity under Satan. The devil gloried in the success which had attended his efforts to entice men to ruin and so spoil the plans of God. Surely God was bound to take revenge on Satan, and this being necessary, was not our redemption also something necessary ? St. Leo occasionally uses words which would seem to favour this view :

"Opus fuit . . . ut incommutabilis Deus, cuius voluntas non potest benignitate privari, primam pietatis suæ dispositionem sacramento occultiore compleret." [1]

But elsewhere he clearly states that our Salvation was an entirely gratuitous work of God's goodness:

[1] Leo Magnus. *Serm.* xxii. 1. *P.L.* liv. 194. This is textually repeated in *Ep.* xxviii. 3, col. 765.

" *Causa reparationis nostræ non est nisi misericordia Dei.*" [1] In any case, had it not been for Adam's fall the Incarnation could not have taken place, though the occurrence of the former event has made the latter to some extent necessary :

"Sed quia invidia diaboli mors introivit in orbem terrarum, aliter solvi captivitas humana non potuit, nisi causam nostram ille susciperet, qui et verus homo fieret et solus peccati contagium non haberet." [2] " Post illam humanæ prævaricationis primam et universalem ruinam . . . nemo tetram diaboli dominationem, nemo vincula diræ captivitatis evaderet; nec cuiquam aut reconciliatio ad veniam aut reditus pateret ad vitam, nisi *coæternus et coæqualis Patri Deo Filius Dei etiam hominis filius esse dignaretur.*" [3]

By this St. Leo means that the Redeemer must unite in Himself both natures : " *Hoc fides catholica tradit, hoc exigit ut in Redemptore nostro duas noverimus convenisse naturas.*" [4] This is what he means when he constantly repeats that had the Son of God not become man we should never have been delivered from death, from damnation, and from sin.[5] This very union of the two natures has its reason ; we must transform our own natures. Nor must we only consider the moral teaching of the Redemption : " *Adicienda erat veritas redemptionis moralibus institutis et corruptam ab initio originem novis renasci oportebat exordiis.*" [6] It was necessary to alter our condition, an alteration which we ourselves could not bring about : " *Letali vulnere tabefacta natura nullum*

---

[1] *Serm.* xii. 1 ; *ibid.* col. 169. *Cp. Serm.* lxvi. 1 ; col. 365. " Miserendi nostri causam Deus *nisi in sua bonitate* non habuit."

[2] *Serm.* lxxvii. 2 ; *ibid.* col. 412.

[3] *Serm.* lii. 1 ; col. 314.

[4] *Serm.* liv. 1-2 ; col. 319.

[5] *Epist.* xxviii. 2 ; col. 759. *Ep.* xxxi. 2 ; col. 792. *Ep.* lix. 4 ; col. 870. *Ep.* clxv. 9 ; col. 1169. *Epist.* clxxi. 2 ; col. 1215.

[6] *Serm.* xxiii. 3; col. 201.

*remedium reperiret, quia condicionem suam suis viribus
mutare non posset."* [1] This is why our Saviour, in
order to achieve this reformation, had to be both God
and man :

"Nisi esset Deus verus non afferret remedium; nisi homo
verus, non præberet exemplum." [2] "Nisi Verbum Dei caro fieret
et habitaret in nobis, nisi in communionem creaturæ Creator ipse
descenderet, *et vetustatem humanam ad novum principium sua nativitate
revocaret,* regnaret mors ab Adam usque in finem, et super omnes
homines condemnatio insolubilis permaneret." [3]

Hence the work of our Salvation comprised a
negative side consisting in the healing of our corrupt
nature, and a more positive side involving our recon-
struction on a new plan. The ultimate result of the
latter is to make us to be born again to God, to the
extent of sharing in the Divine nature.[4] Hence it
was the Incarnation which laid the basis of the restoration of our nature which was completed by the
whole life and work of the Redeemer.

"Nihil enim non ad nostram salutem aut egit aut pertulit, ut
virtus quæ inerat capiti inesset etiam et corpori." [5]

All the actions of the Incarnate Word were at
once mysteries and examples.[6] Among all of them
none was of more moment than the Passion ; by itself
it was our Salvation : *" Passio Christi salutis nostræ
continet sacramentum."* [7] It was even indispensable :
" *Nullum salvaret illæsus, qui pro omnium salute erat*

[1] *Serm.* xxiv. 2 ; col. 205.   *Cp. Serm.* lvi. 1 ; col. 326.
[2] *Serm.* xxi. 2 ; col. 192.   *Cp. Serm.* xxxviii. 2 ; col. 261.
[3] *Serm.* xxv. 5 ; col. 211.
[4] *Serm.* xxii. 5 ; col. 198.   *Cp. Serm.* xxv. 5 ; col. 211.
[5] *Serm.* lxvi. 4 ; col. 367.
[6] *Serm.* xxv. 6 ; col. 212.   *Cp. Serm.* xxxviii. 1 ; col. 257 and xxxix.
3 ; col. 264.
[7] *Serm.* lv. 1, col. 323.   *Cp. Serm.* lvii. 1 ; col. 329.

moriturus."[1]   This was why Christ willingly underwent death.

St. Leo perceives a twofold meaning in the Passion
as in the Saviour's other works; it was at one and
the same time a mystery and an example.   "[*In cruce*]
Salvator noster et sacramentum condidit et exemplum."[2]
But he does not clearly indicate what this mystery or
sacrament implies.   His leading idea is that of our
deliverance from the bondage of Satan, of which we
shall speak hereafter; on every other matter St. Leo
cultivates a certain indefiniteness and does little more
than repeat occasionally the sayings handed down by
his predecessors.

He does however consider our Saviour's death as
a Sacrifice.[3]   In fact it was the one sole Sacrifice
towards which all the ancient sacrifices pointed.
One of its results was to deliver us from everlasting
death: "*Æternæ mortis vincula temporali sunt
Domini morte disrupta,*"[5] and another still more
momentous result was to reconcile us with God:
"*Offerenda erat pro reconciliandis hostia.*"[6] "*Se novum
et verum reconciliationis sacrificium offerens Patri.*"[7]

We were reconciled and our sins were wiped out
because our guiltless Saviour assumed and repaired
the faults of our guilty nature:

---

[1] *Serm.* lix. 1; col. 338.   *Cp. Serm.* lxiii. 4 ; col. 355 ; *Serm.* lii. 4 ;
col. 315.

[2] *Serm.* lxiii. 4 ; col. 355.   *Cp. Serm.* lxvii. 5 ; col. 371.   *Serm.*
lxxii. 1 ; col. 390.

[3] *Serm.* v. 3 ; col. 154.   *Cp. Serm.* lv. 3 ; col. 324, and *Serm.* lx. 2 ;
col. 344.

[4] *Serm.* lxviii. 3 ; col. 374.   *Cp. Serm.* lix. 7 ; col. 341.

[5] *Serm.* lxx. 1 ; col. 380.   *Cp. Serm.* xxi. 2 ; col. 191 and *Serm.*
lix. 8 ; col. 342.

[6] *Serm.* xxiii. 3 ; col. 201.

[7] *Serm.* lix. 5 ; col. 340.   *Cp. Serm.* lxvi. 1 ; col. 365.

" Nostræ diluebantur maculæ, nostræ expiabantur offensæ: quia natura, quæ in nobis rea semper fuerat atque captiva, in illo innocens patiebatur et libera." [1]

Or, to put the matter in a nutshell, he took our place "*ut per eum ageretur omnium causa, in quo solo erat omnium natura sine culpa.*" [2] Had He not consented to do so, our Salvation could never have been wrought.

" Quæ reconciliatio esse posset, quo modo humano generi repropitiaretur Deus, nisi omnium causam mediator susciperet ? " [3]

The best summary of St. Leo's doctrine will be found in a passage where, addressing the Docetæ, he reminds these heretics that Christ's sacrifice alone could redeem and reconcile us. The death of God's saints and martyrs is indeed a precious example of virtue, but the Saviour's death alone is an expiation for the world, because by means of it our debt was paid, and because in Him we all died and rose again." [4]

" Dicant quo sacrificio reconciliati, quo sanguine sint redempti. Quis est qui tradidit semetipsum oblationem et hostiam Deo in odorem suavitatis? Aut quod unquam sacrificium sacratius fuit quam quod verus Pontifex altari crucis per immolationem suæ carnis imposuit? Quamvis enim in conspectu Domini multorum sanctorum pretiosa mors fuerit, nullius tamen insontis occisio propitiatio fuit mundi. Acceperunt iusti, non dederunt coronas, et de fidelium fortitudine exempla nata sunt patientiæ, non dona iustitiæ. Singulares quippe in singulis mortes fuerunt, nec alterius quisquam debitum suo fine persolvit, *cum unus solus Dominus noster Iesus exstiterit, in quo omnes crucifixi, mortui, sepulti, etiam sint suscitati.*"

Thus was St. Leo led by the part he took in the Christological controversy, and in consequence of the Pelagian quarrel which had drawn attention to our

---

[1] *Serm.* lvi. 3 ; col. 328.
[2] *Serm.* lix. 1 ; col. 338.
[3] *Epist.* clxv. 4 ; col. 1162. *Cp. Serm.* lxxvii. 2 ; col. 412.
[4] *Serm.* liv. 3 ; col. 359-360.

inner corruption, to conceive of our Salvation as being mainly a rehabilitation of our nature and thus to revert to the older Greek speculation. Though he was not unmindful of the worth of the cross, he spoke relatively seldom of it; only the outlines of realism were known to St. Leo. In this there is nothing to surprise us if only we bear in mind that his principal concern was the mystery of the Incarnation; but all the same, though his doctrine may pass muster, it is weak when compared to that of his predecessors and successors within the Latin Church.

III

In the fifth century the Augustinian realism found a far more faithful and fuller expositor in St. Fulgentius. He, also, has it that the object of the Incarnation was to restore our nature: "*Ad hoc Christus voluit creari ut per eum posset homo, qui vetustate perierat, innovari.*"[1] Neither man nor angel was able to undertake such a work,[2] God only could accomplish it, and even God was compelled to assume the whole of our nature in order to transform it wholly.[3]

But Fulgentius lays especial stress on Christ's work of expiation, and considers that, for this too, the Incarnation was needed:

"Nullatenus humana natura ad auferendum peccatum mundi sufficiens atque idonea fieret nisi in unionem Verbi Dei transiret."[4]

"Talis est remissio peccatorum ut pro ipsa fieret homo Unigenitus Dei, pro ipsa etiam sanguis eius fuisset effusus."[5]

---

[1] FULGENT. *Resp. contr. Arian.* Obj. iii. *P.L.* lxv. 209. *Cp. Ep.* xvii. c. vi. 11 ; *ibid.* col. 457.

[2] *Ad Trasimund,* ii. 2 ; col. 246.

[3] *Ibid.* i. 10 ; col. 233, and i. 13 ; col. 237 *f.*

[4] *Epist.* xvii. c. iv. 9 ; col. 457.

[5] *De remiss. pecc.* i. 4 ; col. 530. *Cp.* 5 ; col. 531.

The Word-made-Flesh accordingly offered Himself in Sacrifice for us and for our sins.[1] The result of this Sacrifice, of which Christ was at once the Priest and the Victim, was the forgiveness of our sins[2] and consequently our reconciliation with God :

"Ipse igitur in se uno totum exhibuit quod esse necessarium ad redemptionis nostræ sciebat effectum, idem scilicet sacerdos et sacrificium . . . : sacerdos per quem reconciliati; sacrificium quo reconciliati."[3]

Another result of this sacrifice was our deliverance from death both of the soul and of the body :

"Mors Filii Dei, quam sola carne suscepit, utramque in nobis mortem, animæ scilicet carnisque destruxit. . . . *Excepto enim illo, quis est homo qui morte destruxerit mortem.*"[4]

One reason of these happy results is that Christ stands for the whole of human nature : "*Christus pro nobis factus hostia . . . : in quo ipsa natura nostri generis vera est hostia salutaris.*"[5] He consequently took on Him all our sins : "*Quoniam peccata non habuit propria, portare dignatus est aliena,*"[6] and underwent their penalty : "*Habens ex nobis usque ad mortem iniquitatis nostræ pœnam.*"[7]

Fulgentius does not seem, however, to have retained the quasi-legal principle, according to which our Saviour's undeserved death is the equivalent of

[1] *Ad Tras.* i. 12 ; col. 236. *Cp. Ep.* xvii. c. xiii. 27 ; col. 468. *De fide.* xxvi. 67 ; col. 701.

[2] *De fide.* xix. 60 ; col. 699.

[3] *De fide.* 22 ; col. 682. *Cp. De Inc.* 14 ; col. 581. "Talis erat iste pontifex, ut ad reconciliationem humani generis, semetipsum pro nobis offerret."

[4] *Epist.* xvii. c. viii. 16 ; col. 460.

[5] *Ep.* xiv. 37 ; col. 425.

[6] *Ad Tras.* iii. 29 ; col. 293. *Cp. De verit. prædest.* lib. i. c. ii. 5 col. 605.

[7] *De fide.* 12 ; col. 677.

the death we deserved. But Cæsarius of Arles, one of his contemporaries, expresses it as follows in the very terms of St. Augustine :—" *Qualitates captivitatis reparavit munus redemptionis ; id est pro debita morte offerret indebitam.*" [1]

Another reason of our Salvation is, according to St. Fulgentius, the quality of the Redeemer. For us to be reconciled He had to be both God and man :

" Quia per peccatum homo fuit separatus a Deo, inter Deum irascentem hominemque peccantem talis utique mediatoris debuit intervenire persona, quæ ad propitiandum Deum homini totum verumque in se Deum de Deo natum haberet, et ad reconciliandum hominem Deo totum verumque in se de homine natum hominem contineret." [2]

This was why His blood was necessary and sufficient for the remission of sins :

" Est omnibus hominibus necessarius sanguis Christi, qui in remissionem fusus est peccatorum et solus potest delere omne peccatum." [3]

The reader will have seen that St. Leo and St. Fulgentius both consider the Atonement from the same point of view. Neither the one nor the other deals with the question for its own sake but only as an adjunct to the question of the Incarnation, and in order to find in the former an argument for the latter and a new proof of the existence of two natures in the person of our Saviour. But whereas St. Leo, in the matter of Salvation, is more attentive to the inward restoration of our nature, St. Fulgentius considers rather the Saviour's work of mediation and expiation. Our Saviour wipes out our sins with His

---

[1] Cæsar. Arelat. *Hom.* v., *de Paschate.* *P.L.* lxvii. 1052.

[2] Fulgent. *Ad Tras.* i. 15. *Loc. cit.* col. 238.

[3] *De verit. prædest.* lib. iii. xxii. 36 ; col. 669.

blood and reconciles us to God—a work which could be performed by none other than by God united to human flesh. Like Cyril of Alexandria, Fulgentius bases his teaching concerning Christ's person on the requirements of Christ's work. Nevertheless his Christological doctrine serves to illustrate the work of the Atonement and brings out more fully both its grandeur and its conditions. This is the reason why, whereas St. Leo's doctrine usually remains in the regions of mere speculation, that of Fulgentius furnishes a new testimony to the prevalence of realism.

IV

The last of the Latin Fathers was St. Gregory the Great. Like St. John Damascene in the East, this great Pope is remarkable more for the good use which he made of the teaching of his predecessors than for having produced anything particularly new. Nevertheless, on the matter of the Atonement we shall find that he not only summed up most happily the traditional sayings, but that he also made clear several individual points, and here and there attempted a synthesis in which we have a foretaste of the theology of the Middle Ages.

According to St. Gregory the Incarnation would not have occurred had it not been for sin.[1] But sin having entered the world the Incarnation became in some sense necessary. God alone could restore human nature (*per Creatorem necesse est ut creatura liberetur*). The Prophets were only forerunners of the great Physician of our ills.[2] But the Redeemer

---

[1] GREGOR. MAGN. *Moral.* lib. iii. c. xiv. 26.—*P.L.* lxxv. ; col. 612.

[2] *Ibid.* lib. xviii. c. xliv.-xlv. 72-73.—*P.L.* lxxvi. ; col. 80-81.

had also to be a man (*hoc procul dubio fieri debuit quod redemit*).[1]

But we must be careful not to understand all this as implying any absolute necessity; everything in fine depended on God's free and merciful love for man. It was through His mercy alone that God willed to redeem man and yet not the angels. The latter, being pure, spirits might have easily resisted temptation; but man was more feeble and his very weakness claimed God's pity.[2] Christ became incarnate through love,[3] but He was also sent by His Father through love of us that He might die for the world's Salvation without, however, ever being deprived of His Father's affections:

" Pater Filium misit, qui hunc pro redemptione generis humani incarnari constituit. Quem videlicet in mundum venire ad passionem voluit, sed tamen amavit Filium, quem ad passionem misit." [4]

This text shows us that the object of the Incarnation was to redeem us and to redeem us by the Passion. This does not mean that Gregory is unaware of the other benefits conferred by the Incarnation, for he writes elsewhere:

" Ad hoc apparuit Deus in carne, ut humanam vitam admonendo excitaret, exempla praebendo accenderet, moriendo redimeret, resurgendo repararet." [5]

But the Passion remains the greatest work of our Salvation. Its most comprehensive result was to deliver us from everlasting death. Following in the

---

[1] *Moral.* lib. iv. c. vii. 12.   *P.L.* lxxv. ; col. 643.

[2] *Moral.* lib. ix. c. l. 76 ; *ibid.* 900-901.

[3] *In Euang. Hom.* xxxviii. 9.   *P.L.* lxxvi. 1287.   " Per caritatem venit ad homines."

[4] *Ibid. Hom.* xxvi. 2.   *P.L.* lxxvi. 1198.

[5] *Moral.* lib. xxi. c. vi. 11 ; *ibid.* col. 196.   Cp. *Regul. past,* lib. i. 3. *P.L.* lxxvii. 16.

footsteps of St. Augustine, St. Gregory points out
that on account of our sins we had been condemned
to a twofold death : to real death, which is the death
of the soul ; and to bodily death, which is the shadow
of the former.   Christ by His mere bodily death
delivered us from both :

" Ad nos quippe venit qui in morte spiritus carnisque tenebamur ;
unam ad nos suam mortem detulit et duas nostras quas reperit
solvit." [1]   " Nos, quia et a Deo mente recessimus et carne ad
pulverem redimus, pœna duplæ mortis adstringimur.   Sed venit ad
nos qui pro nobis sola carne moreretur . . . et nos ab utraque
liberaret." [2]

The reason of all this is that our Lord did not
deserve to die : " *Ille pro humano genere qui morti
nihil debebat occubuit.*" [3]   Hence He bore the penalty
of our sins : " *Pœnam culpœ nostrœ sine culpa suscepit.*" [4]   And the undeserved death of the Guiltless
compensates for the penalty deserved by the guilty
according to the legal principle laid down by St.
Augustine and textually repeated by Gregory :
" *Dominus pro nobis mortem solvit indebitam, ut nobis
mors debita non noceret.*" [5]   This same principle is
elsewhere expressed by our Doctor in a more personal
form :

" Expediebat ut peccatorum mortem iuste morientium solveret
mors iusti iniuste morientis." [6]   " Eos ille a debitis suis eripuit, qui
pro nobis sine debito mortis debitum solvit, ut nos ideo sub iure
hostis debita nostra non teneant, quia pro nobis mediator . . .

---

[1] *Moral.* lib. iv. c. xvi. 30-31.—*P.L.* lxxv. 653.

[2] *Moral.* lib. ix. xxvii. 41 ; *ibid.* col. 881.   *Cp. Moral.* lib. xiv.
c. liv. 67 ; *ibid.* col. 1074.   " Sua passione nos a perpetua morte
liberavit."

[3] *In Euang. hom.* xxv. 9.—*P.L.* lxxvi. ; col. 1195.

[4] *Moral.* lib. xiii. c. xxx. 34.—*P.L.* lxxv. ; col. 1032.   *Cp. In
Ezech. hom.* iv. 20.—*P.L.* lxxvi. ; col. 984.

[5] *Moral.* lib. xvii. c. xxx. 47.—*P.L.* lxxvi. ; col. 33.

[6] *Moral.* lib. xxxiii. c. xv. 31 ; *ibid.* col. 692-3.

gratuito reddidit quod non debebat. Qui enim pro nobis mortem carnis indebitam reddidit nos a debita animæ morte liberavit." [1]

In a word our Saviour paid the penalty of the human race: "*Priusquam Redemptor noster morte sua humani generis pœnam solveret.*" [2]

In these words we see expressed with the utmost clearness the doctrine of penal satisfaction. This doctrine suggests to Gregory the classical difficulty: How can God, who is just, punish the guiltless? To this our Doctor replies by exposing the plan of Salvation and the salutary results of Christ's death:

"Sed si ipse indebitam non susciperet, nunquam nos a debita morte liberaret. Pater ergo cum iustus sit, iustum puniens, omnia iuste disponit; quia per hoc cuncta iustificat quod eum qui sine peccato est pro peccatoribus damnat. . . . Qui iuxta semetipsum frustra afflictus est, iuxta vero nostra acta non frustra. . . . In se quidem admissa non habuit, sed cruore proprio reatus nostri maculam tersit." [3]

St. Gregory also speaks in another passage of our reconciliation, and tells us that it involves two things —the changing of our hearts by penance and the appeasing of God's wrath, both of which were effected by the Passion:

"Videat [vir sanctus] quam perverse homo deliquerit, videat quam districte conditor contra hominem irascatur et mediatorem Dei et hominis Deum et hominem requirat. . . . Redemptor quippe humani generis, mediator per carnem factus, quia iustus in hominibus solus apparuit et tamen ad pœnam culpæ etiam sine culpa pervenit, *et hominem arguit ne delinqueret et Deo obstitit ne feriret*: exempla innocentiæ præbuit, pœnam malitiæ suscepit. Patiendo ergo utrumque arguit, qui et culpam hominis corripuit et iram iudicis moriendo temperavit: atque in utrisque manum posuit, qui et exempla hominibus quæ imitarentur præbuit, et Deo in se opera quibus erga homines placaretur ostendit." [4]

---

[1] *In Euang. hom.* xxxix. 0; *ibid.* col. 1299.
[2] *Moral.* lib. iv. c. xxix. 56.—*P.L.* lxxv.; col. 666.
[3] *Moral.* lib. iii. c. xiv. 27; *ibid.* col. 613.
[4] *Moral.* lib. ix. c. xxxviii. 61.—*P.L.* lxxv; col. 893-894.

From this we see that if the Saviour's death reconciles us and wipes out our sins this is not merely because it had the value of an example—a view which Harnack seemingly ascribes to St. Gregory[1]—but because it is a real expiation. Both the objective and the subjective Atonement hold a place in St. Gregory's mind.

St. Gregory also states that there was no one else who could thus expiate the sins of others: "*Nullus quippe ante hunc exstitit qui sic alienis reatibus intercederet ut proprios non haberet.*" Which is merely another way of stating that none save the God-Man could be our Redeemer. In another passage Gregory dwells at length on the same idea, and comes to the conclusion that it was necessary for the Word of God to take flesh, both in order to give us an example and in order to become a Mediator who, on account of His innocence, would be listened to by God:

" Nullus erat qui apud Deum pro peccatoribus loquens a peccato liber appareret. . . . Proinde venit ad nos Unigenitus Patris, assumpsit ex nobis naturam, non perpetrans culpam. Sine peccato quippe esse debuit, qui pro peccatoribus intervenire potuisset."[2]

It is true that the word "intervention" or "intercession" here used is ambiguous, but we find in yet another place a similar synthesis woven round the idea of sacrifice, one which sums up the providential plan of Salvation, and may perhaps be considered as the most complete exposition of the Atonement to be found in ancient Latin theology.

---

[1] *Dogmengeschichte*, iii. p. 243.

[2] *Moral.* lib. xxiv. c. ii. 2-4.—*P.L.* lxxvi. ; col. 287-289.　*Cp. ibid.* iii. 5-6 ; col. 290.　" Quia nullus erat cuius meritis nobis Dominus propitiari debuisset, Unigenitus Patris, formam infirmitatis nostræ suscipiens, solus iustus apparuit, ut pro peccatoribus intercederet."

For our sins to be wiped out a sacrifice was needed, the sacrifice of an innocent victim : " *Delenda erat culpa, sed nisi per sacrificium deleri non poterat.*" Now, what sacrifice could possibly suffice to cleanse men ? The blood of beings without reason evidently fell short of what was required ; a reasonable victim was needed : " *Requirendus erat homo qui pro hominibus offerri debuisset, ut pro rationali peccante, rationalis hostia mactaretur.*" But on the other hand, all men being sinners, none was able to cleanse us : " *Inquinata quippe inquinatos mundare non potuisset.*" Hence the Son of God Himself became man :

"Sumpta est ab illo natura, non culpa. Fecit pro nobis sacrificium, corpus suum exhibuit pro peccatoribus victimam sine peccato, quæ et humanitate mori et iustitia mundare potuisset."[1]

This conspectus may justly be described as the finest, the broadest, and at the same time the most accurate, we have met so far, but it is unfortunately lacking in solidity. The idea of sacrifice, which is the centre of the synthesis, is itself not duly established ; it is posited but not explained or justified. We had occasion to show that Origen hit upon a similar combination of ideas, and that his synthesis was open to precisely the same objections. That two Fathers, one of whom lived at the dawn and the other at the decline of the Patristic era, should have so far agreed in their net results, shows that, though realism never died out in the Church, it made very little progress in the direction of more accurate theological expression.

We have finished our survey of the Latin Fathers, and our readers will have been able to verify the truth of the statement we made in beginning—viz.

[1] *Moral.* lib. xvii. c. xxx. 46. *P.L.* lxxvi. 32-33.

that the Latin Fathers brought no new elements into the field. They tell us that Christ died for us and for our sins, that His death blots out our sins, reconciles us with God and destroys our death. To explain the salutary efficaciousness of His death they use the figures of ransom and sacrifice; they point out that the debt of the guilty was paid by the Innocent. Examining the conditions of the work of redemption they come to the conclusion that it could be accomplished by none save by Christ. Not one of these ideas is wanting in the Greek theology. As we said, the only real difference is in this, that the more positive mind of the Latins disapproved of those mystical speculations which sometimes led astray the subtler understandings of the Greeks, and that among the Latins, Christ's death being always considered as the great event of Salvation, we find a more uniform tradition. If we add that the Latin language helped the Western Fathers by furnishing them with precise expressions approximating the exact formulæ of legal definitions, we shall have described all that there is in their theology. Among the Greeks there was more motion and variety, among the Latins there was more regularity, but the general trend was the same on both hands.

To conclude, neither the Greek nor the Latin Fathers ever dealt directly with the problem of the Atonement. They merely spoke of it incidentally when commenting on the Scriptures, or when dealing with doctrinal truths allied to it. Hence the Fathers give us no real synopsis of the doctrine, but, on the other hand, they do give us a multitude of fragmentary views and texts concerning details of the doctrine, and by carefully piecing these together we can form

x

them into a real theology. The foundation of all
is the truth of faith, so profoundly embedded in the
Christian consciousness, that Salvation came through
the Cross of the Son of God. They all consider
Christ's death as being more than a mere example ;
it has a value outside of us and in the Divine plans ;
it has a real though mysterious efficaciousness and
a value which is at once objective and final. This
supernatural efficaciousness is seen in its twofold
action : Christ's death, firstly, appeases God's anger,
and, secondly, it is a penalty—the penalty of our sins
voluntarily undergone by our Saviour in our stead.
These two ideas of expiatory sacrifice and of penal
substitution seem to sum up all the many straggling
sayings of the Fathers on the subject. The Fathers
of the Church, whether in the East or the West,
did not enter more deeply into the meaning of these
ideas. They had much to say of substitution and
of sacrifice, they affirmed the fact and described its
effects, but they never sought its inmost reason or
its ultimate cause. This was to be the work of the
Middle Ages.

Such is our impression of the doctrine of the Atonement during the Patristic period. It was then that
the outlines of the realist view were laid down and
the first theological explications suggested, which
though they scarcely trenched on the real mystery
nevertheless made a beginning of the fuller explanation to be realised in later times. Harnack admits
that early Latin theology contained all the elements
of the realism of the Redemption, and even the germ
of that doctrine of Satisfaction which was afterwards
to prevail in the Schools. For our part we have
found these same ideas even among the Greeks.
Hence we may say that Realism was the prevalent,

if not the only, doctrine of the whole of tradition. Those only can affect to deny this who seek to mould history according to their own ideas, and who above all wish to make it appear that the Church has erred. The facts which we have passed in review show us that there was no contradiction between the dogmatic traditions of East and West. History informs us that there were some slight differences of view which, however, are not sufficient to constitute a divergency, and still less a contradiction, and that the two great centres of Christian thought were content with a like faith and a like theology expressed in but slightly different language.

END OF VOLUME I.

THE RIVERSIDE PRESS LIMITED, EDINBURGH.

ImTheStory.com

Personalized Classic Books in many genre's

Unique gift for kids, partners, friends, colleagues

Customize:

- Character Names

- Upload your own front/back cover images (optional)

- Inscribe a personal message/dedication on the
  inside page (optional)

Customize many titles Including
- Alice in Wonderland
- Romeo and Juliet
- The Wizard of Oz
- A Christmas Carol
- Dracula
- Dr. Jekyll & Mr. Hyde
- And more...

CPSIA information can be obtained at www.ICGtesting.com
Printed in the USA
LVOW101157111212

310969LV00032B/1685/P